HOW DEEP IS THE WOUND?

A GUIDE TO INVESTIGATING, UNDERSTANDING, AND RESOLVING YOUR EMOTIONAL PAIN

ANTONIETA CONTRERAS

SENTIMENT PUBLISHING

Copyright © 2025 by Antonieta Contreras

All rights reserved.

No portion of this book may be reproduced in any form without written permission from the publisher or author, except as permitted by U.S. copyright law.

General Disclaimer

This publication is designed to provide accurate and authoritative information regarding the subject matter covered. It is sold with the understanding that neither the author nor the publisher is engaged in rendering legal, investment, accounting, or other professional services. While the publisher and author have used their best efforts to prepare this book, they make no representations or warranties with respect to the accuracy or completeness of the contents and specifically disclaim any implied warranties of merchantability or fitness for a particular purpose. Sales representatives or written sales materials may not create or extend any warranty. The advice and strategies contained herein may not be suitable for your situation. You should consult a professional when appropriate. Neither the publisher nor the author shall be liable for any loss of profit or any other commercial damages, including but not limited to special, incidental, consequential, personal, or other damages.

Medical/Psychological Disclaimer

This book is for educational purposes only and does not constitute medical, psychological, or therapeutic advice. The information provided should not replace professional mental health care. Always consult qualified healthcare providers for medical or psychological concerns. If you're experiencing thoughts of self-harm, contact emergency services immediately.

The author and publisher disclaim any liability for any adverse effects arising from the use or application of the information contained in this book. Individual results may vary, and any testimonials or examples should not be construed as guarantees of specific outcomes.

By reading (or listening to) this book, you accept its limits and agree to use the information at your own risk.

Editor: Fern Diaz

Book cover by Alex Stikeleather

Photo of the author by Jos Diaz-Contreras

Illustrations by the author

First edition, August 2025

Sentiment Publishing

Contents

Dedication	1
Acknowledgements	2
PREFACE	4
INTRODUCTION THE MOST IMPORTANT PART OF HEALING IS FINDING OUT WHAT IS ACTUALLY WRONG	7
1. WOUNDS HOW TO UNDERSTAND WHAT IS HAPPENING WHEN YOU ARE IN EMOTIONAL PAIN (AND WHEN YOU RESOLVE IT)	15

    Get to Know the Basics of your Inner World

    Learn to See Emotional Pain as a Spectrum, from "Hurt" to "Traumatized"

    Feel the Effect of Becoming your Own Ally

2. EMOTIONS HOW TO UNCOVER THE TRUTH ABOUT WHY FEELINGS HURT SO MUCH	61

    Kick Off With a Step-by-Step Guide to Deconstructing Your Emotions

    Find Out How Emotions Work for and Against You

    Discover Where All That Emotional Pain Comes From

    Change Your Emotions (Yes, It's Possible)

3. TRAUMA — 111
HOW TO ACHIEVE A FULLER UNDERSTANDING OF THE RELATIONSHIP BETWEEN FEAR AND EMOTIONAL INJURIES
- Turbocharge Your Trauma Education
- See What Happens When Dread Takes Over
- Leave the Past Where it Belongs

4. DISCONNECTION — 153
HOW TO RECOGNIZE THE IMPACT OF CRITICISM, BETRAYAL, REJECTION, AND NEGLECT
- Make Sense of Heartbreak, Insecurities, and Other Ego Threats
- Identify Wounds that Cause Numbness or Neediness
- Examine Growing Brains and Their Fractures
- Transition From Silent to Whole

5. UNLOVE — 215
HOW TO RECOGNIZE THE IMPACTS OF HEARTBREAK, MANIPULATION, AND ABUSE
- See How Abuse Shows Up and Shapes Us
- Uncover the Effect of Mind Games and Other Narcissistic Impulses
- Confront the Price of Closeness and Bonding
- Choose Yourself and Participate in Healthier Love

6. THE DEEPEST WOUNDS — 263
HOW TO UNDERSTAND THE IMPACT OF UNAVOIDABLE CIRCUMSTANCES
- Recognize the Realities of Trauma Beyond the Event
- Become an Expert in Trauma Responses (Beyond Fight or Flight)
- Detect the Varied Impact of a Traumatic Childhood
- Heal From Trauma Using Your Own Wisdom

EPILOGUE — 306
WHERE MY JOURNEY MEETS YOURS

Exercises List — 310

Questions List — 314

TO MY SON

for your wisdom, your courage, and your immense goodness

you inspire me every day to be better, to try harder, to reach deeper

you teach me that humaneness is its own form of wisdom and that love blooms effortlessly in a clear heart.

TO MY DAUGHTER

for your gentle fortitude and luminous spirit

you constantly remind me that wonder lives in the smallest moments and that life is more than the sum of those moments

you fill up my days with laughter and dreams and make my world fulfilling.

AND TO YOU

for motivating me every day to continue writing and learning

you remind me that understanding begins with listening

and that healing happens when we dare to be seen.

Acknowledgements

THANKS TO THOSE WHO HELPED ME LEARN BY ASKING QUESTIONS

To my followers on Quora, Medium, Psychology Today, and my blog: Your continuous support and encouragement have shaped not just my writing, but also my understanding of what it means to contribute meaningfully to conversations about mental health. You've become a vital presence in my life as both a writer and someone committed to offering insights that might ease your journey.

But my gratitude extends far beyond those who follow and comment. I want to thank the millions of individuals who courageously ask questions and seek answers about mental health. Your willingness to be vulnerable, to admit uncertainty, and to actively pursue understanding is both admirable and inspiring. Through your questions, comments, and shared experiences, you've created a living library of human wisdom that no academic text could capture. You've taught me that real knowledge emerges not from having all the answers, but from being brave enough to ask the questions.

ACKNOWLEDGEMENTS

THANKS TO THOSE WHO TRUSTED ME WITH THEIR HEALING

To the remarkable individuals who have invited me to witness their healing journeys: Walking alongside you as you navigate the path from pain to growth has been one of my life's greatest privileges. This book exists because of what you've taught me. Watching you transform suffering into wisdom, fear into courage, and wounds into sources of strength has been the most profound education I could receive. Your trust in sharing your struggles and victories has shaped every insight in these pages. You are the true authors of the wisdom I've attempted to convey.

THANKS TO MY EDITOR

I am deeply grateful to Fern, the incredible editor of both this book and my previous one. She is beyond brilliant, always supportive, and endlessly inspiring. Fern encouraged me to write my first English article, and look where we are now! Her editing skills have been invaluable—she served as both a gentle guide and a keen strategist, dissecting chapters, challenging concepts, and motivating me to always go farther.

PREFACE

Hold on—are you the same Antonieta Contreras who answers questions about trauma online?

The question caught me off guard at a cocktail party at my alma mater. I had arrived late, randomly selected a table, and was just settling in when a fellow attendee's eyes lit up with recognition. I blushed and admitted that yes, I was that person.

Before long, she—an author herself—slid her chair closer. *"So... when are you going to write a book with all those great answers?"* That question lodged itself in my mind—and here we are.

Over the years, I've worn many hats: therapist, teacher, clinical supervisor, and, perhaps unexpectedly, online trauma educator. Those 2,000-plus Q&A posts have reached over 40 million people, revealing something I couldn't ignore: we're collectively hungry for clarity about trauma and emotional pain, yet we're often drowning in misinformation.

In our eagerness to validate suffering, we've begun labeling every hurt as "trauma." That troubles me. I see daily how many people are convinced they're permanently damaged by experiences that, while painful, represent the normal texture of human life. On top of that, we've created a culture where questioning someone's self-diagnosis feels taboo or invalidating, even when that label might be keeping them trapped in a story that isn't serving them at all. It can actually work against their mental health.

The brain doesn't distinguish between real and imagined threats. When we repeatedly frame past experiences as traumatic—even those we'd previously integrated and moved beyond—we literally rewire our nervous system toward hypervigilance. I've watched people transform neutral childhood memories into sources of profound distress simply by viewing them through today's popular trauma lens. They begin to see themselves as victims or survivors of experiences that were simply... life. What exactly did they survive? Did they survive their parents' imperfect attempts at love? A childhood that, like most childhoods, contained both joy and disappointment? Mom's intention to anxiously parent them? Having parents that struggled to feed and help them learn?

Neuroscientist Iain McGilchrist brilliantly describes how our left brain craves categories and diagnoses while our right brain perceives context and wholeness. Modern mental health culture has become dangerously left-brain dominant, obsessing over *"what happened to you"* while ignoring *"who you are"* and *"what you're capable of becoming."* Even artificial intelligence systems now amplify these distortions, trained on popular but fundamentally flawed "average" understandings of human resilience (AI systems learn from the masses, not from nuanced clinical understanding).

This book emerged from curating the most intriguing (and most read) questions from my online work—those that reveal the crucial difference between genuine traumatization and life's inevitable bruises. My commitment as a therapist has been to explore approaches that actually reduce suffering and unleash human potential.

I believe healing ripples outward in ways we can barely imagine. When one person finds clarity about their own emotional landscape, it touches their family, their community, and their corner of the world.

Each chapter in this book represents not just answers to compelling questions but a step toward reclaiming our birthright of wholeness and recognizing that while emotional pain is universal, it isn't always traumatic.

My deepest hope? That these pages assist you in distinguishing between wounds that require active healing and those that merely require gentle resolution. I hope you learn to ask yourself the essential question, *"How deep is the wound?"*—not through the lens of trending psychological labels, but through an honest assessment of its actual impact on your capacity to live, love, and grow.

Ultimately, I hope you rediscover your remarkable capacity for transformation, which exists far beyond any diagnosis or category that others might assign to pain that was never meant to define you.

With gratitude,

ANTONIETA

INTRODUCTION

THE MOST IMPORTANT PART OF HEALING IS FINDING OUT WHAT IS ACTUALLY WRONG

"Trauma is the painful failure to adapt; emotional wounds are adaptation in progress."

What if everything you've been told about trauma is keeping you trapped in pain?

As a therapist, my measure of success is whether my work helps people ease their suffering, rewrite their stories, and rediscover joy. From my perspective, healing isn't just individual; it ripples outward, touching families, communities, and generations. Your healing matters.

I write this book believing that truly understanding your wounds is the first step to transforming pain into strength and reclaiming the life you deserve.

Why now? Not too long ago, I stood in clinic corridors and auditoriums explaining to mental health professionals what "trauma" meant—for most, the clinical use of the term and the neurobiology of survival were eye-openers. Today, you can walk past any playground and overhear kindergarteners discussing their "trauma" and nervous systems, while adults toss around "gaslighting" as casually as they talk about the weather. We've swung from unawareness to oversaturation. Words like "trauma," "fight-or-flight," "dysregulation," "narcissistic abuse," and many others are now used so often and casually that they've begun to lose their real meaning.

This trend deeply troubles me. The overuse and misuse of mental health language are reducing the rich complexity of human suffering and making a single label—"trauma"—its main box, pathologizing ordinary experiences while dismissing serious clinical disorders. How can you truly understand your wounds if you lack the vocabulary to convey your own experience—if you use the same word for your amputation that someone else uses for their bruise?

This book offers an approach that has been missing. It offers the tools and understanding you need to assess the actual depth of your wounds—and I'm going to show you how to get closer to a better way of functioning in the world.

The Lost Art of Adaptation

When I was growing up, resilience wasn't a common term, not even for psychologists. The word I remember being used to describe someone who was good at dealing with tough situations was "adaptable." Being adaptable meant being "well adjusted" to life's challenges, even when they were unfair or painful. It wasn't heroic or a sign of victimhood; it was simply a quality some naturally had or could learn—one that helped people live more fully by finding ways to grow through whatever came their way.

But that word has faded—adaptable. I haven't heard it used in years. Maybe it sounds too Darwinian, or it doesn't fit our current trauma-focused narrative. Yet the capacity for adaptation never actually disappeared—it's wired into our biology, whether we acknowledge it or not.

Resilience entered mainstream discourse around the same time people became widely aware of trauma. It's hard to picture resilience now without its engineering origin— *"metal that springs back after stress."* The term gained popularity in psychology in the 1970s, when researchers noticed that some children thrived despite poverty, illness, or parents struggling with mental health. The researchers suggested resilient people had the capacity to bounce back from hardship almost effortlessly. Decades later, we know resilience is not only innate. It's more like a system feature that can be strengthened with practice—it isn't necessarily automatic but shaped by experience, support, and conscious effort.

What has been learned is that **adaptability is proactive**—it tweaks your approach to fit the environment, while **resilience is reactive**—it kicks in when things go wrong. Evolution favored both, yet they operate on different principles. This shift has fundamentally changed how we approach emotional pain: we've narrowed our choices to two—either endure the suffering or bounce back to who we were before. But there's a third way: adapting. In this book, I'll show you how adaptation offers something neither resilience nor endurance can—the ability to grow through pain rather than merely despite it, turning hardship into wisdom and strength.

When Everything Became Trauma

Back in the '80s, when greater academic understanding of trauma and PTSD gave the concepts more cultural presence, extreme experiences were the focal point—veterans and survivors of violence or abuse. Then researchers noticed that the fight-or-flight response driving trauma also occurs with everyday stress. Since stress is inherently subjective—what overwhelms one person might barely register for another—this opened the door to viewing trauma as equally subjective. For many people struggling with unvalidated pain, the trauma label finally offered recognition that their suffering was real and deserved attention. The line between what constitutes trauma versus normal stress became blurred.

Fast-forward to today, and almost every hurt is labeled trauma and every struggle a threat. We can classify heartbreak, neglect, embarrassment, and even a bad dream under that category. As critic Chris Black quips on his podcast *How Long Gone*, *"We all think about our problems too much, because now that's rewarded in society."* This shift isn't entirely surprising. In a culture that historically dismissed emotional pain as weakness or self-indulgence, the trauma framework finally gave people permission to acknowledge their suffering as legitimate. Yet in our rush to validate pain, we may have overcorrected—expanding trauma to include experiences that, while genuinely difficult, don't require trauma-level interventions or lenses.

This has serious clinical implications. Imagine visiting a doctor because your leg hurts. You mention you had a fracture years ago, and the doctor decides to treat that decades-old break by putting on a cast or suggesting surgery. That would cause pain, not healing.

Now imagine going to therapy and reporting your past difficult experiences and having your story interpreted as trauma. Clinicians may start revisiting old scars as if they're open injuries, treating what might be normal struggles as lifelong diagnoses. This isn't healing—it's reinjuring.

I'm all for talking openly about our emotional struggles—it's necessary. But when we label everything painful as a matter of survival and judge ourselves and others as broken and damaged, we shift into a mental state that ignores our natural tendency to adapt. We're equipped to learn and grow, not just to live scanning for predators.

A Different Path Forward

I wrote this book to help you sort through this confusion and find out *How Deep is the Wound?* The idea is to help you find the answer, keeping in mind that many of your pains are signs of how your system has learned to adapt or has been trying to.

Use these mantras, and when you repeat them, let them come alive in your body:

- *"Not every struggle is trauma."*

- *"My reactions make sense."*

- *"My emotional pain has meaning."*

Most of what feels overwhelming is your mind learning, reorganizing, and protecting you. Yes, the path to growth includes scratches, pain, distress, and setbacks—but which wound is which? How deep are they? And how do you resolve them?

I know it can feel scary to see yourself in a different light—especially if the trauma lens has offered a comforting "answer" for why you act the way you act. Yet I've seen firsthand how freeing it is when people shift their approach and begin to see themselves more clearly—not just their pain or actions, but the whole person underneath it.

Not all pain is equal. Trauma is a seismic shock to your nervous system that can turn your life upside down and distort your reality in ways that keep you scanning for the next threat. Emotional wounding, though, is managed by a different system—one designed to get your attention about situations you need to learn from.

Conflating adaptation with survival risks misdiagnosing everyday pain as catastrophe. A child with strict parents learns to navigate unpredictability—that's adaptation. Labeling it "complex trauma" might overwrite their natural strengths with a story of fragility.

This book is my way of sitting with you, sharing what I've learned, and helping you understand the type of wounds—from regular pain to severe trauma—you have so you can find the right way to resolve them.

Understanding Your Emotional System

Picture this: Imagine a child attempting to capture their mother's attention. They might start by gently pulling her arm or saying *"Mom."* If she doesn't respond, the child escalates their attempts by calling out *"MOM!"* and then *"MOOOOOM!!!"* If she's still unresponsive, they may scream or throw a tantrum, often forgetting what they originally needed in the first place.

That's how our emotions work. When they first arise, they're like that gentle tug—a quiet signal trying to get our attention. But if we ignore them, dismiss them, or push them away, they escalate. What started as a manageable feeling becomes increasingly intense, demanding, and disruptive. Eventually, the emotion becomes so loud and overwhelming that you lose sight of its original message—what it was trying to tell you about your needs, boundaries, or safety. This escalation is one key reason emotions can feel so overwhelming and painful. By the time you're forced to pay attention, you're dealing with the emotional equivalent of a full tantrum rather than the gentle tug that could have been easily addressed. Through these pages, you'll discover how your emotional system works—with patterns, healing mechanisms, and signals about what it needs. You'll learn how to listen to your emotions before they escalate.

Your pain isn't as permanent as it feels, and your potential for transformation is greater than you've been told. For starters, you need to tell bruises from cuts, deep wounds from scars, and active injuries from bad memories. Most importantly, you need to reconnect with your innate capacity to heal. Old scars don't need reopening; they need understanding. Open wounds need care, not endless rumination. Your emotional system isn't fragile—it's adaptive by design. Healing isn't about erasing pain but restoring flexibility.

How to Use This Book

Everything in mental health exists on a spectrum—from mild to severe, with endless variations in between. When you encounter new psychological concepts, this book explains why we should resist the urge to apply them to everything and everyone. Your struggles are unique to you, even if they fall somewhere on the same spectrum as others. Throughout this book, I'll explain both ends of the spectrum for most of the important issues that can hurt us and cover as many variations as possible.

While I've written this book to be accessible and practical, it's built on extensive peer-reviewed research detailed in my clinical work *Traumatization and Its Aftermath* (Routledge, 2023). Readers who want to explore the scientific foundation further can find the complete bibliography and citations at https://www.antonietacontreras.com/bibliography

To make the reading easier, I use *italics for examples, thoughts, metaphors, or self-talk;* **bold for key concepts;** and "quotation marks" around specific terms. Words matter when we're talking about pain, so here's how I'll use these important ones:

Emotional pain: Sharp, immediate hurt from specific experiences—heartbreak, loss, rejection. Your psyche's version of physical pain that signals something needs attention.

Struggles: Daily human friction. The challenges and conflicts that come with existing in a complex world. Normal growing pains.

Wounds: Deeper impacts that linger after the initial hurt. Difficult experiences that change how you move through the world, usually with stories about what happened and what it means about you.

Injuries: A deeper type of wound. I'm choosing to separate wounds from injuries, with wounds being more connected to adaptation and injuries more connected to survival.

Trauma: An active injury. Consequences of threatening experiences that overwhelm your nervous system's ability to process what happened, leaving you operating in survival mode long after danger has passed.

Suffering: The whole human experience of dealing with pain—both inevitable hurt from being alive and optional layers we add through confusion, avoidance, shame, and stories that perpetuate pain.

Resolution: The process of working through emotional pain until it no longer controls your daily life by integrating experiences in ways that restore your sense of choice and agency.

Healing: The restoration of function and wholeness. While complete healing may not always be possible, meaningful recovery often involves rebuilding multiple areas—regulation, clear thinking, sense of self, and capacity for connection.

Understanding the nature and depth of your wound is the first step toward choosing the right path forward. Read with curiosity, not urgency. Let the questions guide you to answers your psyche is ready to hear.

Your Journey Through Six Chapters

Chapter One redefines emotional pain itself. You'll learn to distinguish between struggles, emotional pain, wounds, and trauma—discovering why accurate assessment determines your healing path and why most of what overwhelms you actually proves your system works correctly.

Chapter Two reveals the emotional architecture nobody taught you. You'll understand how emotional patterns develop over time, why some people seem drawn to emotional pain, and how to recognize when your emotional system needs recalibration versus complete repair.

Chapter Three cuts through trauma mythology to show what trauma actually is neurobiologically. If you've wondered whether your experiences "count" as trauma, this grounds you in science instead of anxiety, helping you distinguish genuine trauma from other forms of emotional injuries.

Chapter Four maps disconnection wounds—what happens when we lose belonging, safety, or worth through betrayal, neglect, abandonment, or emotional invisibility. You'll get practical tools for healing these relational injuries and learn the crucial difference between addressing neglect and processing trauma.

Chapter Five explores relationship injuries—narcissistic abuse, manipulation dynamics, trauma bonding, and attachment wounds that create confusion in human connection. You'll gain clear frameworks for recognizing exploitative people and understanding why we get trapped in harmful relationships, plus hope for building secure connections.

Chapter Six addresses complex questions from actual trauma recovery—why healing feels scary, what post-traumatic growth really looks like, what constitutes actual "childhood trauma" and how traumatic experiences in childhood affect adult life, and realistic guidance for the non-linear journey from survival to thriving.

The last section of each chapter focuses on healing.

Each chapter includes practical exercises and assessments designed not to fix you but to create space for insight, feeling, and conscious choice about how you want to respond to your experiences. These aren't quick fixes—they're invitations to remember capacities you've always had but may have forgotten how to access, integrating approaches from several healing modalities. Some exercises will apply to your situation, and some won't. Once you find an exercise, practice, or quiz that fits your needs, follow it consistently. Incorporate these exercises into your daily routine. Resolution and healing are achieved through sustained effort and dedication. **Reprogramming the brain requires repetition and discipline.**

You deserve to understand your wounds. You deserve to reclaim your story. Most importantly, you deserve to be the ultimate authority on your own experience—to decide for yourself how deep your wounds go and what kind of attention they need. Let's begin this journey of understanding and empowerment together.

Chapter One

WOUNDS

HOW TO UNDERSTAND WHAT IS HAPPENING WHEN YOU ARE IN EMOTIONAL PAIN (AND WHEN YOU RESOLVE IT)

"The same experience can become either wisdom or burden, depending on the story we tell ourselves about what it means."

What if everything you've been told about emotional healing is only half the story?

Let's explore together how that could be true.

For decades, the dominant narrative blamed people for their own suffering. If someone struggled emotionally, they were labeled "neurotic," "paranoid," or "hysterical"—terms that had no scientific foundation but plenty of power to shame. Emotional pain was dismissed as "self-sabotaging" or "resistance," as if struggling meant the person was choosing to suffer.

But today, we've swung to the other extreme. Almost every painful experience gets labeled as trauma, and we've started seeing ourselves primarily as victims—of our circumstances or of others' actions. Social media has contributed to turning victimhood into a trend, with industries profiting from the notion that we are all broken. The "trauma culture" we live in has moved from *"everything is your fault"* to *"nothing is your fault,"* risking the loss of our power to influence our own emotional responses, our sense of agency, and, ultimately, our healing.

We also live in a sea of labels—"narcissist," "sociopath," "victim," "survivor"—assigned to people we don't even know, often without understanding their circumstances or the complexity of their experiences. We have a tendency to pathologize and judge (demonize?) others without giving it much thought, without understanding the meaning of what we say, or considering the consequences our words can have on the sense of self of those we label. Let's imagine we could break free from this narrative and choose a path that leads to a deeper understanding of ourselves. How would it feel to see ourselves through a lens that embraces complexity rather than demanding simple explanations? What if we could hold space for the reality that we are neither completely broken nor perfectly whole, but beautifully, messily human?

The truth is, emotional struggles are far more within your control than you've been led to believe. There's a way to rethink emotional suffering beyond limiting categories—a way to truly understand what's happening beneath the surface and reclaim your power to heal.

Breaking free from the current unhealthy narrative starts with recognizing what you can actually control. Instead of focusing entirely on the event/person/actions that caused you distress, you can shift your attention to how to process and integrate it—how you relate to your pain and whether you allow it to define you. For example, someone treated you disrespectfully and hurt your feelings. You experience a series of sensations and emotions that go from a boiling feeling to deflation. Your system clearly indicates that it needs attention; however, I bet most of us would instead ruminate for hours about the person who disrespected us, their words, their actions, the injustice, and the unfairness... until we feel lost, wishing to disappear or get even. While doing that, the system runs wild on stress hormones that flood the body with toxic chemicals, creating inflammation, disrupting sleep, weakening the immune system, and leaving us physically and emotionally depleted—essentially making us sick from the inside out.

Too often, we leave our emotional responses unresolved, unknowingly reinforcing our suffering. Instead, I suggest you shift from seeing yourself as a victim of trauma to actively addressing your pain. The key lies in understanding that while emotional pain is real and demands your attention, how you work with it determines whether your response becomes adaptive or gets trapped in patterns that perpetuate misery.

Picture yourself slamming on your brakes as you see something darting in front of you. Your heart pounds as your muscles tense and your breath turns shallow. Seconds later, you realize it was just a dog—unharmed. Although the immediate danger passes quickly, the rush of fear and adrenaline lingers not because you want it, but because that's how your system is designed to respond. However, it's also designed to bounce back, especially if helped by reassuring thoughts like, *"Wow, that was close—but nothing bad happened," "I'm glad I'm a careful driver,"* or *"Next time I'll stay alert on this road."* This scenario represents an **adaptive emotional response**—your nervous system activates appropriately to protect you, processes the experience completely, learns from it, and returns to baseline functioning. This adaptive response leaves you more prepared, not damaged.

Now imagine that, instead of these balanced thoughts, you start replaying anxious ideas, such as *"That dog could have died because of me," "I'll never tell anyone," "What if next time I'm not so lucky?"* or *"I should never drive this road again."* The result of feeding those thoughts is that whenever you drive down similar roads, you might feel uncomfortable, tense, ashamed, or overly cautious—even when no real danger exists. This lingering unease, though it doesn't dominate your life, can still influence your confidence and decisions.

That is how an **emotional wound** forms. An emotional wound is a lasting sensitivity that develops when distressing experiences remain unprocessed due to distorted interpretations, which leave emotions unmetabolized and create reactive patterns long after the situation has ended. Unlike an adaptive response that helps our system return to baseline, an emotional wound keeps you partially unresolved and reactive to reminders of the original experience. Not trauma, but lasting emotional pain, over-cautiousness, and some negative schema development.

Finally, imagine that the intense fear persists without relief, cycling for months. Thoughts such as *"Roads are never safe,"* *"Something terrible will definitely happen if I drive,"* or *"I'm dangerous behind the wheel"* now fuel your fear. These thoughts fundamentally alter how you feel each day, how you see yourself and others, and how you engage with life. Hypervigilance and anticipating danger become your norm. Nightmares about driving are constant, etc. This final scenario represents **trauma—a lasting emotional injury that stays active, fundamentally reshaping your world every day.**

In this chapter, we'll look at what emotional suffering really is—from daily stress to deep trauma—and how it's not just what happens to you, but how you make sense of it, that shapes both your conflicts and your chances to overcome them. Before you can recover your life, you must first understand what you're actually struggling with. The depth of your wound determines the path to your recovery.

Get to Know the Basics of your Inner World

"Pain is meant to be a temporary response tied to a specific occurrence, asking to be resolved as it happens."

These are great times. We have reached a level of comfort and progress in technology and science that sci-fi literature didn't anticipate. And yet, we keep suffering as if we didn't know much about ourselves. Well, there is something we could do: accept that **pain is an inevitable part of the human experience.** You can't escape it, no matter how much you wish otherwise. But understanding pain—its role, its purpose, and how it interacts with your life—can fundamentally change how you tolerate, deal with, and resolve it.

Fortunately, a fundamental truth is coming to light: **you have far more power over your emotional well-being than you may have considered.** This power doesn't lie in controlling what happens to you—that's often impossible—but in recognizing the brain characteristics that your mind can use in your service, rather than the other way around.

To grasp this concept, start with a simple yet profound distinction: What's the difference between your brain and your mind? Understanding this will help explain why you have more influence over your emotional responses than you might have thought.

Is there a real difference between the brain and the mind?

If I had to answer this question in a single line, I'd say the brain is our biological processor—the physical organ made of tissue, cells, and chemicals—while the mind operates more like an electrical system that creates our conscious awareness with the ability to direct our responses.

Try to visualize the brain as the physical structure we can touch—an intricate network of neurons and tissue housed within our skull. But the mind? That's where a fascinating phenomenon happens. **The mind is the dynamic electrical activity constantly firing through those neurons**, creating everything from our deepest emotions to our most fleeting thoughts. And here's what's remarkable: this electrical activity creates our consciousness—our ability to observe our own thoughts, direct our attention, and choose how we respond.

BRAIN
Biological

Neurons
Cells
Tissue
Neurotransmitters

MIND
Electrical

Thoughts
Neural Networks
Electrical Signals
Patterns of Activity

Brain vs Mind

While the brain is the physical tissue we can examine and measure, the mind emerges from the electrical activity flowing through it. That activity is called "action potentials"—invisible pulses of energy that travel from one neuron to another, connecting different parts of our brain. These electrical patterns create the programs that drive our mental processes, influencing everything from our smallest impulses to our biggest decisions, in ways science is still working to explain.

I like thinking of the brain and the mind like a lamp and the light it produces. *The brain is the lamp—a physical structure with circuits and components that process energy. The mind is the light that the lamp emanates—an intangible result of the lamp's functioning.* Our brain absorbs signals from our senses, our life experiences, and even subtler environmental influences—social cues, cultural patterns, or intuitive responses to situations we've encountered before—even when they're out of our awareness. The mind then takes these inputs and weaves them together into thoughts, memories, predictions, emotions, and experiences.

Obviously, the brain doesn't work in isolation—it relies on constant interaction with the environment to gather the rich mix of elements that shape our inner experiences. Beyond the traditional five senses, science now includes balance (vestibular sense), body position (proprioception), and internal bodily states (interoception). Some researchers even point to "neuroception"—an unconscious process that scans for safety or threat in our surroundings—as an additional sense.

But here's what makes this process powerful (and magical): these multiple layers of sensory input don't just passively flow into our consciousness. Perception isn't just a passive reception of external information; it's an active process that results from the brain's interpretation and filtering of those signals based on our past, emotions, and expectations. This implies that the lens we use to view the world profoundly shapes our subjective experience of it. A constant dance between the information coming in and the meaning we make of it creates what we call **"reality"**—which explains why two people can experience the exact same event yet walk away with completely different stories about what happened.

Once we understand how much perception shapes our emotional responses, it becomes clear how crucial it is to take charge of it. Developing healthy ways of perceiving ourselves and our surroundings can be one of the most transformative areas for personal growth and resilience.

For example, imagine receiving a text message that simply reads, "Can we talk?" If your initial interpretation is rooted in fear, you might feel anxious or defensive, preparing for bad news. But if you actively consider other possibilities—like a friend wanting to share good news—your emotional state remains calmer and more open. This small shift in how you engage your mind shows how you can alter your perception, emotions, and ultimately your response, illustrating just how powerful your interpretations can be. If you find yourself anticipating the worst outcome, take a moment to consider, *"What evidence do I actually have for this prediction?" "What are some alternative scenarios that could unfold?"* Instead of rushing to conclusions, approach situations with genuine curiosity. Replace *"I know exactly what this means,"* with *"I wonder what's really going on here,"* while keeping connected to the present and to the reactions of your body.

Supportive environments and relationships can enhance our capacity for positive perception, while chronic stress or hostile environments can narrow our perceptual range and bias us toward threat detection. This is why understanding that the mind is shaped by what we encounter matters—but more importantly, understanding that we can actively direct how we process those encounters.

Our mind holds the remarkable power of guiding and instructing our brain on how to respond. While the brain houses the machinery (neurons, synapses, neurotransmitters), the mind—encompassing our thoughts, feelings, interpretations, decisions, and intentions—can guide how the machinery operates in a given moment. Traditionally, our cultural understanding positioned the mind as something we experience rather than something we can train—a witness to life's events rather than a tool for intentional living. Only recently have we come to understand that we have the ability to actively take ownership and command.

Picture your brain as an orchestra filled with instruments—neurons, circuits, and all the physical components. Your emotions and instincts function similarly to the spontaneous sounds that each instrument naturally produces when allowed to play independently. But your mind? Your mind is the conductor. It can guide the tempo, adjust the volume, and coordinate the instruments to create harmony instead of chaos.

This illustrates how something intangible (the mind/conductor) can direct what emerges from the tangible (the brain/orchestra), ultimately shaping our experience. By choosing hopeful thoughts, reframing negative situations, or practicing self-compassion, we're giving the brain new directions—helping it respond calmly instead of panicking. This doesn't mean we can magically delete all our troubles, but it does mean we have remarkable power to shape how we handle them.

Within the "trauma culture" framework, we have come to believe that the nervous system is the director of the orchestra and that we are at the mercy of the tune it wants to play, but under closer look, we can see that our brain and nervous system "take over" and default to survival responses **only when the mind has essentially given up**—when our thoughts tell us we can't cope, that we are powerless, or that there is no hope. When the mind withdraws its guidance, the brain falls back on its most primitive protective mechanisms, those that, as we'll see later in detail, can end up hurting us at different levels of depth.

Understanding the brain-mind distinction is fundamental to everything that follows in this book. The mind encompasses our beliefs, experiences, and the meaning we assign to them. This broader view helps explain why two people with similar circumstances can have vastly different experiences. It also illustrates the necessity of both our brain and mind working together in a coordinated manner: the brain, which has automatic responses, efficiency, anticipatory mechanisms, and complex sensory processing; and the mind, which possesses the capacity for conscious direction, meaning-making, and choice.

The remarkable power of the mind to guide and instruct our brain on how to respond is where your agency resides, and this is where healing commences.

> **Sensory Visualization: The Luminous Orb Practice.** Let me show you what I mean with a short exercise. You may have done the one imagining squeezing a lime in your mouth and feeling the sensations. Remember how you salivate almost automatically? This one requires a little more of your imagination and your concentration.
>
> Please pause for a moment and close your eyes.

> Breathe deeply, and while exhaling, imagine you're holding a warm, glowing orb of light in your hands. It's soft, pulsing faintly. As you focus, it shifts color based on your breathing—deep blue when you inhale, warm gold when you exhale. See it in your mind while you feel its gentle heat spread up your arms. Notice how your shoulders relax or your chest feels lighter.
>
> Stay there for a minute or two.
>
> With practice, you'll see your mind's ability to shape sensation and calm your body with nothing but intention.

My therapist told me I lack mental space. What are they talking about?

We can consider mental space to be the "internal stage" where our thoughts, memories, images, and feelings play out. It isn't a literal location in the brain but rather emerges from how the brain's networks work together. Just like a theater stage provides the place where a play happens, this internal space is where different mental processes—perception, imagination, emotional feedback—unfold and interact.

This metaphor gives us a way to talk about the subjective sense of having "room" to think, visualize, or recall events. We can feel our mental space expand when we're calm and contract when stress overwhelms us—even though no physical space actually exists.

We need this internal space to resolve our emotional wounds and trauma. Changing the meaning of our emotional experiences requires giving our thoughts, feelings, and memories room to interact and reorganize until new understanding emerges. Mental health is directly connected to integration, and we can't integrate when we lack space to process multiple elements simultaneously. For example, when we feel both anger towards someone who has hurt us and love for that same person, we need to bring both emotions into one space before we can find the specific meaning that can help them integrate.

The illustration below visualizes this concept. Notice in the first diagram that the available space is very limited, making the problem feel overwhelming and impossible to tackle. In the second diagram, the problem itself is exactly the same, but there is much more mental space to examine it from different angles. Without mental space, we feel overwhelmed. With expanded space, we can hold multiple problems or emotions simultaneously—even intense, conflicting ones—and manage them more effectively.

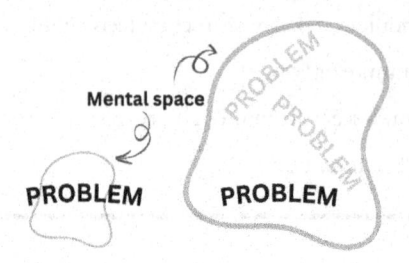

How can we create mental space? First, identify the signs of a lack of mental space, such as circling thoughts, mental fogginess, or feeling overloaded or disoriented by feelings and thoughts. Then you can begin expanding your mental space through practices that create distance between you and your thoughts—such as visualization or meditation that clears and calms your thinking brain.

When we have enough mental space, we can reframe our emotional experiences, gradually transforming how we understand and integrate them—from unbearable to manageable to resolved.

> **Mental Spaciousness: The Expanding Room Technique.** Let's try a short exercise to create some mental space.
>
> Begin by noticing if you're feeling crowded by thoughts or emotions—perhaps your mind feels cluttered with worries, overwhelmed by competing demands, or compressed by intense feelings that seem to take up all available mental space. Simply acknowledge, *"I need a bit more space to handle these feelings."*
>
> Close your eyes and imagine your mind as an open room. Focus on it, and as you go, make it bright, spacious, and calm.
>
> Continue expanding this space—slowly add more size, more light, more quiet, and more spaciousness until it feels vast and peaceful.
>
> After several minutes, it'll feel large enough. Then, place whatever is troubling you—that anxious or negative thought—somewhere within this room.
>
> Notice you can see it clearly, yet there's space around it.

> Play with it, move it around, and notice what else is there. Finally, imagine the issue crumbling or fading into the room's spaciousness.

WHAT DOES IT MEAN TO BE MENTALLY ILL? DOES HAVING A DIAGNOSIS LIKE PTSD COUNT AS BEING "INSANE"?

Have you noticed how much progress we have made in reducing mental health stigma? We are experiencing greater openness and understanding of our struggles by creating environments where people feel safe to share their experiences—like their diagnosis, their conflicts, and their discomforts. While the outcome is largely positive, it has also created some confusion. Sometimes the line gets blurred between normal emotional responses to life challenges and clinical mental health conditions. This distinction is important—not to minimize anyone's suffering, but to ensure people receive support and treatment appropriate to their specific situations and needs—to their wound's right depth.

You may not know this, but historically, mental illness was defined differently than today because psychiatry used to emphasize severe conditions like psychosis or madness. For centuries, mental illness meant visible "insanity" or significant disconnect from reality, leading to stigmatization, confinement, or exclusion from society.

Only in the past several decades—particularly since the mid-20th century—has the definition of mental health changed significantly, broadening the interpretation of what constitutes mental illness. Psychiatry and psychology have increasingly shifted toward a spectrum view, stating that mental health exists along a continuum rather than in discrete categories of "healthy" versus "disordered." This broader perspective includes many conditions where people function normally in daily life while experiencing emotional, cognitive, or behavioral disturbances.

Are you aware of how many diagnoses exist today? There are around 300-450 diagnostic categories! And it has become all too common to use the names of diagnoses to label people based on only a few characteristics or behaviors. People often say, *"I'm depressed,"* after experiencing just a couple of days of low mood, or they might exclaim, *"They are so bipolar!"* when observing mood swings between excitement and gloominess. I don't think there's anyone who hasn't suspected one of their family members, coworkers, or friends of being "narcissistic" or "OCD" only based on a broad and superficial concept of what those labels really mean.

Conditions such as depression, anxiety, PTSD, and ADHD are considered mental illnesses, even when individuals maintain their full connection to reality and are functional members of society. Although this perspective claims to be more compassionate, it poses a distinct risk. Under this new lens, it appears that almost anyone could be classified as suffering from a mental illness at some point—creating a different kind of stigma altogether.

When someone experiences a difficult life event, such as a breakup or job loss, emotional reactions may be intense, but they are also normal, valid, and expected. If these reactions are situational and don't create significant lasting dysfunction, they may not be signs of mental illness, trauma, or an emotional disorder—even if the person feels awful, finds it difficult to function for a few hours or days, or realizes that support is needed to overcome the challenge. It's simply part of the human condition to feel pain, to feel threatened or hurt, to struggle, to need and doubt, and to grieve.

To ensure that individuals receive the right support, it's necessary to understand their full story before assigning a mental illness label. Such information includes their situation, environment, culture, challenges, values, and physical health. Keep in mind that diagnoses are primarily tools for treatment guidance and insurance reimbursement rather than ultimate truths or life sentences.

At its core, dysfunction is what distinguishes mental illness from the normal ups and downs of mood, behavior, or cognition. By dysfunction, I mean **a sustained level of impairment that disrupts multiple areas of life**—such as being unable to hold down a job because of overwhelming anxiety, losing close relationships due to persistent anger or paranoia, or neglecting basic responsibilities like caring for children due to chronic emotional or cognitive difficulties.

It's when internal states become persistent and unmanageable, consistently interfering with daily functioning, that a mental health issue may be considered.

So, adapting and surviving, are they actually different things?

This question opens the door to understanding why we behave the way we do, including those behaviors we would rather eliminate. Here's the distinction that is at the core of understanding how deep the wound is: surviving is about immediate protection from threat, while adapting is about learning and adjusting for long-term success. Adapting is what our brain does every minute from the moment we are born.

Modern developmental and evolutionary psychology recognizes that human beings enter the world equipped with inborn systems that help us survive, connect with caregivers, and learn from our surroundings. These systems are part of our emotional architecture, which has two major components that directly relate to our survival-adaptation question. The first component encompasses **adaptive emotions** for navigating daily life and social situations. The second manages **survival-oriented emotions** designed to protect us from immediate threats.

FOR ADAPTATION	FOR SURVIVAL
Investigating	Defending
Learning	Reacting
Regulating	Protecting
Connecting	Eliminating
Thriving	Numbing

Main Functions of the Emotional System

Both systems begin operating early in life. For instance, infants cry to signal distress, visually track faces to engage with caregivers, and naturally seek social contact when upset—**core adaptive strategies** shaped by evolution over millennia. We possess many such innate mechanisms, guiding us to respond effectively to our surroundings.

These adaptive strategies reflect our built-in capacities—such as attachment-seeking, exploration, and social interaction—that help us navigate everyday challenges and equip us with the essential tools for a better future. When infants seek comfort from a reliable adult, they greatly increase their chances of receiving care and protection. As children grow, they refine these early strategies into more sophisticated skills: seeking emotional support from grandparents when parents seem overly strict or learning to "read the room" by observing a parent's mood.

These behaviors aren't random. They're guided by adaptive mechanisms that promote learning and build resilience—capacities we all share and use throughout our lives.

Recently, some popular psychological approaches have minimized these inborn capabilities, portraying infants and children as entirely defenseless—easily wounded or traumatized by any adversity. But for centuries we have observed that it typically takes significant and prolonged hardship to overwhelm a child's deeply embedded adaptive systems. These systems are designed to help us adjust to life's challenges, strengthening our ability to thrive in diverse and ever-changing environments. We are far better equipped for adverse circumstances than we often give ourselves credit for. Just consider this list of some of our built-in adaptive capabilities:

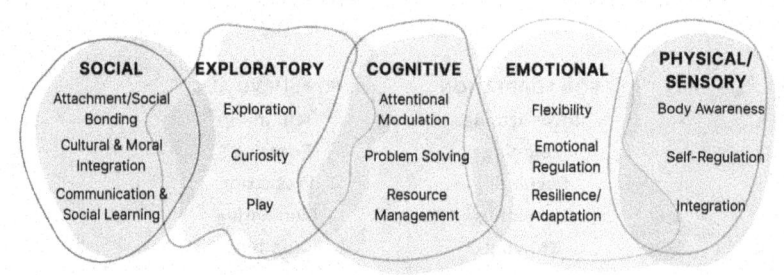

SOCIAL	EXPLORATORY	COGNITIVE	EMOTIONAL	PHYSICAL/SENSORY
Attachment/Social Bonding	Exploration	Attentional Modulation	Flexibility	Body Awareness
Cultural & Moral Integration	Curiosity	Problem Solving	Emotional Regulation	Self-Regulation
Communication & Social Learning	Play	Resource Management	Resilience/Adaptation	Integration

Adaptive Capabilities

Besides adaptation, survival responses are governed by a distinct set of functions—the survival system—specifically designed to protect us from immediate harm or death. In our hyperconnected, fast-paced modern world, it's become common to confuse survival reactions with adaptive responses, as though every challenge were life-threatening.

You may have observed and probably experienced that in typical environments—where there may be emotional ups and downs but not relentless threats to our safety—our inborn adaptive strategies are enough to help us manage, grow, and adjust. *For example, a parent who is strict or moody but remains loving and present might cause a child stress or confusion, yet it rarely triggers survival-level fear if the child perceives no real threat of harm. The child's system continues to develop naturally, integrating these experiences into their evolving understanding of relationships and the world.*

How can we distinguish between a genuine threat and a mere challenge? Key indicators include whether the situation feels escapable, whether we have any sense of control or agency, whether the emotional intensity completely overwhelms our ability to cope, and whether we find support from others. Genuine threats typically involve feelings of helplessness and overwhelming intensity that exceed our capacity to respond adaptively—often because external resources are unavailable or internal resources have been depleted. In contrast, challenges—while difficult—typically allow some sense of agency, maintain hope for resolution, and don't exceed our capacity to use our resources.

By the way, in case you're wondering, "having agency" means recognizing that you have choices—even in the midst of difficulty—and feeling able to take actions that influence your situation. It's the internal sense that your decisions matter and can shape the outcome. When agency is present, we're more likely to interpret hardship as a challenge to be navigated; when it's absent, we're more prone to experience distress as a threat because we feel powerless in the face of it. Sometimes, developing agency is the first step on the way to recovery.

Someone with agency perceives challenges as opportunities, while someone without it may label difficult situations as traumatic, assuming that emotional distress means inability to deal with them. Understanding the vital difference between challenges and genuine threats may be the beginning of developing a healthier perspective. Learning to trust our adaptive systems is a fundamental first step.

This understanding doesn't contradict the fact that there are circumstances that are truly overwhelming and impossible to resolve. That's why we have a survival system that can respond with extreme measures if needed. Fortunately, it usually remains dormant during everyday challenges.

WHY DO WE SOMETIMES PERCEIVE REALITY TO BE SO DARK?

It may be just inertia from ideas developed before neuroscience helped us understand how our system works that we've placed disproportionate emphasis on memory while overlooking the powerful role that perception plays in our emotional struggles. Another reason may be the difficulty in clearly understanding what perception actually is.

Perception is how the brain interprets and makes sense of information from the senses—what we see, hear, smell, taste, and touch—as well as internal signals like emotions and bodily sensations. But perception isn't purely objective. Our mind shapes perception by drawing on past experiences, beliefs, expectations, and emotions to assign meaning to what we experience. This is when the mind's power becomes evident—while the brain processes raw information, the mind actively influences how that information gets interpreted. All these factors shape our emotional responses and establish the basis of our emotional existence.

Do you think those dots are different color?

For instance, I'm sure you perceive the circle on the right as darker than the one on the left. Try covering the surrounding areas with your fingers or a piece of paper—then you'll see that they're actually the same shade of gray. This exercise, like other optical illusions, shows us that we often see what we're programmed to see—not what's truly there. These are the mysteries of perception, but we can learn to shape it. While our automatic perceptual habits are deeply ingrained, we're not powerless to influence them.

When we've endured significant emotional pain without resolution, the brain often responds by heightening its threat detection system. It becomes more sensitive to potential dangers, disappointments, or failures. While this protective mechanism is meant to keep us safe, it can also distort our perception. We begin to notice more of what confirms our insecurities and overlook what might bring relief or hope—especially if we've been conditioned to view the world through a lens of threat.

As a result, life can start to feel darker, riskier, or more hopeless—not because reality has changed, but because our interpretation is biased toward hazard and pessimism. It's like experiencing a difficult event that leaves a lingering gray filter over everything that follows. We might not even realize we're looking through this filter, yet our entire perspective becomes subtly tinted by its shade.

Recognizing that our perception may not reflect what's actually happening—and actively questioning our interpretations—is key to taking in new, healthier experiences and gradually changing our emotional story. When we notice that an old wound is coloring our view, we can address it directly and begin to shift to a clearer view.

For example, someone who experienced rejection or criticism might perceive neutral facial expressions as disapproving or hostile. When a coworker has a focused, concentrating expression during a meeting, they see judgment or annoyance directed at them. Their threat-detection system distorts visual information, making them literally see rejection in faces that others would perceive as simply thoughtful or neutral.

The Observer Reframe Technique. Let's practice a quick reframe exercise to work on your perception.

Bring to mind a recent situation that triggered strong emotions—especially one you suspect might be colored by past wounds. Rather than just thinking about it, actually see the scene unfolding before you. Notice the colors, sounds, and physical space where it happened.

As this memory surfaces, pause and scan your body from head to toe. Where do you feel tension? Perhaps tightness in your throat, a knot in your stomach, or heat in your face? Place your hand on that area and acknowledge, *"I'm feeling this reaction in my body."*

Next, ask yourself, *"What story am I telling myself about what happened?" "What meanings am I attaching to this situation?"* Observe this narrative and then question it: *"Is it possible that I'm reacting more to past events than to the current situation?"*

Now, physically change your position—stand up if you were sitting, or move to a different chair. This physical shift helps trigger a mental one. From this new position, imagine you're watching the scene unfold on a screen.

Notice details you missed before—facial expressions, tone of voice, and surrounding context. Take three slow, deep breaths. With each exhale, imagine releasing your emotional connection to your original interpretation. From this calmer state, ask, *"What would someone who doesn't share my history see in this situation?" "What details might they notice that I overlooked?"*

Return to your original position. Notice any shifts in your body sensations. Has your breathing changed? Has tension diminished anywhere? Acknowledge these physical changes as evidence of your perception shifting. Say to yourself, *"My initial perception is just one possible interpretation. I can hold multiple perspectives at once."* Notice how this statement feels in your body.

Try this exercise whenever strong emotions seem disproportionate to a situation. With practice, the ability to shift perspectives will become more natural, creating space between trigger and reaction.

LEARN TO SEE EMOTIONAL PAIN AS A SPECTRUM, FROM "HURT" TO "TRAUMATIZED"

"We can't escape pain, but we can decide what story it tells."

Life's journey is full of beauty and light, but it's also paved with challenges and pain. From your first breath, you faced discomfort—hunger, cold, fatigue, and loneliness ache. Even the most devoted caregivers can't shield infants from these primal afflictions—the raw cost of growth. In adulthood, emotional pain may feel different and possibly heavier—perhaps because it is uncommon for us to be taught how to transform it into adaptive skills. Coping is the concept most people have learned about how to deal with pain: manage it to make it bearable. I have shifted from the idea of merely managing pain to the understanding that every ache is a call for care and an opportunity for us to build resilience. This is our inherent nature.

Pain—whether physical or emotional—is the body's immediate response to something being out of balance, signaling that **something needs our attention**. While pain can't always be avoided, we can often manage it by addressing its root cause. But suffering? That's a different story. Suffering comes from holding onto distress beyond its useful purpose, from the stories we tell ourselves about it, and from the meanings we attach to it.

Pain is meant to be a temporary response tied to a specific occurrence, asking to be resolved as it happens. Suffering lingers when our mind keeps feeding itself harmful narratives like *"I deserved this"* or *"I'll never recover,"* when we continuously relive the situation by replaying arguments or rehashing what went wrong, or when we wait for someone else to fix it—expecting apologies that may never come or hoping others will change so we can feel better. That type of mental activity sends the wrong message to the brain—that we are powerless—and therefore, to its functioning.

This distinction matters because the brain is constantly learning to better adapt, and challenging experiences are even more helpful to this task. Emotional pain is part of our growth process; the more intense the experience, the more it influences development. We have the tools to avoid making the same mistakes over and over, but we have to put some effort into learning the lesson. While we can't always avoid pain, we can learn to prevent unnecessary suffering by shifting our perspective, reaching out for support, finding our way out of the hurt, and developing healthy ways to process difficult emotions. This section is a guide to get there.

What Counts as an Emotional Wound?

At first, it may be surprising to learn that **emotional wounds are far more common than trauma.** But once you think about it, you'll see how obvious it is. Emotional wounds happen when our need for connection or validation is unmet or violated, especially during moments of vulnerability. These wounds can also form when our sense of trust is betrayed, when our authentic self-expression is repeatedly dismissed, when our emotional needs are ignored, or when there's a stark disconnect between what we experience and what others acknowledge. Unfortunately, these are pretty common occurrences.

For instance, imagine a child eagerly sharing an accomplishment with a parent who dismissively says, "That's ok, but why not an A+?"—a moment where genuine excitement meets minimization, creating a small tear in the fabric of emotional security. What distinguishes these experiences from everyday frustrations is not just their emotional intensity but how they challenge our fundamental understanding of ourselves in relation to others and the world around us. They wound our sense of being inherently valuable and worthy of unconditional love.

An emotional wound is the lingering hurt from a painful experience we haven't fully processed. This unresolved pain leaves our mind caught in cycles of distress and doubt that interfere with letting it go. One of the reasons these wounds persist is the unconscious hope that the person who hurt us will somehow repair the damage—the child hoping to meet the father's expectations and receive his approval—rather than taking responsibility ourselves to transform the experience into knowledge that helps us adapt and grow. The child, evidently, doesn't have the capacity to see how the father may just want the child to be their best, but as they grow older, they can find a different meaning, avoiding years of resentment and self-doubt and letting the wound go.

Imagine a man experiencing sudden tightness in his chest after receiving criticism. He feels hurt and thinks, "I'm disappointed; I believed I could trust that person." If that single event takes over his emotions with rigid thoughts like *"I'm always at fault,"* his body might stay tense and hypersensitive, keeping his mental space occupied with negative thoughts. As a result, his emotional state shifts toward constant pain, doubt, or defensiveness. In that mode, even small challenges feel hurtful because his perception directs the system to protect him from disappointment rather than help him see them as opportunities to investigate and reconnect.

If instead, he recognizes this pattern and deliberately recalls positive interactions—with that person or others—he can begin to soften his defensive stance. He might see criticism as feedback rather than an attack or understand that the other person's judgment might come from their own hurt. This broader perspective helps prevent a single painful moment from defining the entire relationship.

The tendency to fall into defensive cycles demonstrates why resilience is so crucial. Resilience is the ability to adapt and recover in the face of adversity, drawing on cognitive, psychological, and social resources to help us stay grounded, maintain perspective, and move through challenges. This capacity doesn't mean a person never struggles; it means they can navigate difficulty with flexibility and preserve—often strengthen—their emotional well-being, sense of self, agency, and overall functioning.

Take the person who was harshly criticized—resilience means they can choose to respond constructively: maybe seek clarification, set boundaries, or learn from the feedback. Their emotional system files it away as a difficult but manageable experience, actually strengthening their ability to handle future criticism. Or think of the child who didn't get the A+ they worked so hard for. With support and some repair work either from the father or someone else, they can learn to value effort over outcome, build self-compassion, and bounce back with motivation instead of shame or insecurities.

What Makes Trauma Different from Other Emotional Wounds?

The word "trauma" comes from the Greek term for "injury," which is why I find it helpful to compare trauma to a bone fracture—a classic and commonly understood physical injury. Just as a fracture is a break in the bone's structure and function that requires stabilization, protection, and time for the bone to properly solder, trauma represents a break in our emotional functioning. The quality of care it receives determines whether the bone heals properly or remains a lasting problem.

An emotional wound, in this analogy, would be equivalent to the bruise that shows up alongside the fracture. Along with the broken bone, there may be damaged tissue, blood vessels, or swelling in the surrounding area. The bruise causes pain or discoloration, but it usually heals on its own with time and minimal intervention because it's just a sign of the blow. Similarly, emotional wounds can still be painful, but they don't necessarily involve the same disruption to core functioning that trauma does.

Once a bone mends, we no longer call it a fracture; it becomes a past injury or a healed bone—evidence that recovery has occurred, even if some sensitivity or limitations remain. But if the fracture goes untreated—if the bone remains broken or heals incorrectly—the injury stays active, causing pain and limiting function. This is how I describe **trauma: an injury that remains active and creates dysfunction.**

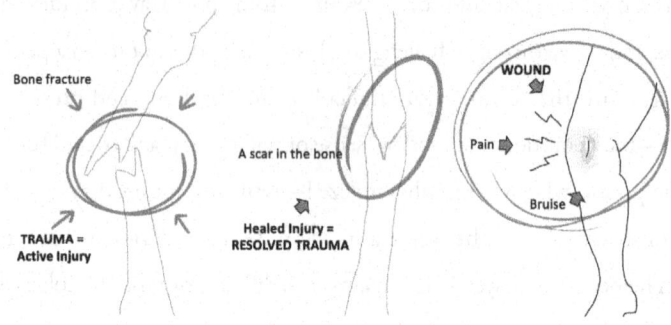

A Wound, a Scar, and an Active Injury

An emotional wound might sting in the moment, but with awareness, the proper support, and a healthy approach, it can be processed and resolved—whether it arose from a significant disappointment or a minor setback. Once properly integrated, like a healed fracture, it doesn't cause ongoing disruption.

Trauma, however, is like a fracture that hasn't been properly set or treated. It remains an active injury, continuing to cause pain, limiting mobility, and interfering with regular functioning. It typically requires more specialized attention—professional support, specific therapeutic approaches, or structured healing processes—to address its aftermath.

How do you know where emotional hurt ends and trauma begins?

Being traumatized and being emotionally wounded are distinct responses to different types of challenging situations. We get traumatized from situations perceived by the nervous system as immediate threats to our life, body, or core integrity—our fundamental sense of wholeness and safety.

We get emotionally wounded by relational injuries: betrayal by someone we trusted, public humiliation that damages our sense of self, significant losses that disrupt our sense of meaning, or the slow accumulation of small hurts that gradually erode emotional well-being and confidence. These experiences do not activate survival defenses, yet they can leave us feeling hurt, confused, or in pain in subtler but significant ways.

While both trauma and emotional wounds can leave lasting imprints, their neurobiological signatures—and thus their resolution—are different.

Traumatization is primarily fear-driven. When the nervous system perceives life-threatening danger, it heavily involves the **brain's survival system**, leading to responses that push us to fight, escape, or shut down. This includes surges of adrenaline and the imprinting of fear memories in what's known as the "fear network."

Emotional wounds are about social pain and self-awareness. Emotional wounds, by contrast, occur when events engage brain regions associated with relational distress and the processing of self-relevant emotional experiences. These are the same regions activated during experiences of physical pain, which is why rejection, shame, or heartbreak can feel as if we were punched, stabbed, or slapped. The pain is genuine—just not wired to the same survival circuitry as trauma.

What's interesting and worth considering is that when an emotional wound remains unresolved and is fueled by fear, it can evolve into psychological trauma—just as a neglected cut can fester and trigger lasting complications. That's why distinguishing between them isn't just helpful—it's critical. Timely intervention can prevent years of dysfunction and suffering.

What's all the buzz around the "nervous system" about?

Yes, there is definitely a buzz, isn't there? I've noticed that many people—from life coaches to fitness gurus to spiritual mentors—are promoting the nervous system as the "master switch" for all our problems, promising to "rewire" it and banish stress or trauma in just a few steps. There are even watches and rings that claim to monitor your emotional state through nervous system activity.

On one hand, the excitement makes sense. Modern neuroscience has shown that many so-called "bad" behaviors—like shutting down emotionally, overreacting, procrastinating, or dramatizing—aren't moral failings or personality flaws. They're the body's built-in responses managed and directed by the autonomic nervous system

(ANS). That's a big deal. It shifts the conversation from *"What's wrong with me?"* to ***"What's my nervous system trying to protect me from?"*** It opens the door to self-compassion and true resolution.

On the other hand, this knowledge is often oversimplified. People are sold the idea that they can "reset" their vagus nerve or "hack" their stress response with cold plunges or breathing apps. While some of these practices help, the nervous system isn't a gadget to tweak. It's a deeply intelligent system connected to all other systems in our body and shaped by connections with our history, relationships, thoughts, and environment. And it doesn't just need to "calm down"—it needs to **regain coordination, flexibility, and balance** so we can adapt, engage, and recover more effectively.

Let's not forget that our nervous system isn't just responding to emergencies—it's behind everything we feel and do. It regulates our heartbeat, digestion, sleep, attention, and emotions—whether we're resting, making a decision, having an argument, or falling in love. When it's out of balance, our experience of life narrows. We lose access to reflection, empathy, curiosity, and presence. That's why nervous system awareness is central: because it determines how much of our full self is available at any given moment.

In my work, I don't just aim to calm nervous system hyperactivation. I focus on redistributing the brain's energy to optimize its functioning. When our survival systems are monopolizing internal resources, the solution is to redirect that energy toward curiosity, reflection, decision-making, creativity, and connection. That shift alone can change how we experience ourselves and the world. Genuine nervous system regulation offers something many people have searched for desperately: relief from suffering that relies on activating the prefrontal cortex—the brain's executive center—rather than consuming our brainpower in surviving ghosts.

So yes, the nervous system matters—especially in trauma, emotional pain, anxiety, sleep, attention, and even identity. It isn't the entire answer, but it is the gateway. Let me highlight key elements of the ANS as a foundation for the rest of the book:

The autonomic nervous system (ANS) is your body's built-in, automatic control center that runs continuously behind the scenes, regulating everything from heart rate and digestion to your emotional responses—without conscious effort. It has two main branches that work together to maintain balance:

Sympathetic Nervous System: The energizing branch that handles action-oriented tasks: movement, alertness, energy production, and defensive responses. I call it the "get-into-action system" to avoid the misleading tendency to label it the "fight-or-flight" branch. Although it does activate during emergencies, it's equally responsible for everyday energy mobilization—from walking to helping us focus during a work presentation or enjoy an engaging conversation.

Parasympathetic Nervous System: The restorative branch that handles rest-oriented tasks: digestion, sleep, healing, and overall restoration. It's also involved in protective shutdown during crisis when other strategies aren't available.

These two branches function like a dynamic seesaw, constantly adjusting to keep us in balance. This ongoing calibration determines not only our physical health but also our emotional resilience and capacity to engage with life's challenges.

I HEAR THE TERM "OVERWHELMED" A LOT. IS IT ALWAYS CONNECTED WITH TRAUMA, AND WHAT ARE ITS CONSEQUENCES?

"Overwhelm" is another one of those terms that trauma-focused discussions have popularized, often with unnecessary pathologizing. But in reality, overwhelm isn't always a sign of something pathological or even traumatic. It occurs frequently in everyday life, especially when one emotion becomes too intense to handle—like when we get furious. It also happens when multiple emotions collide at once, such as feeling relief, guilt, anger, and sadness simultaneously. In both cases, it becomes hard to process and make sense of what we're feeling.

In these instances, we temporarily lose our **capacity to integrate**—to bring all the pieces together, make meaning of what's happening, stay grounded, and respond intentionally. That loss is often brief. Once the nervous system calms down—whether through rest, reflection, support, or simply the passage of time—we can usually regain access to our integrative functions and sort through what happened with a clearer mind.

Many descriptions of trauma characterize overwhelm as the moment when the autonomic nervous system activates to combat danger. As a result, many people assume that if they get overwhelmed, they may be traumatized. But **overwhelm is just the initial reaction**. It's not until overwhelm is coupled with a sense of helplessness that survival circuits get activated to deal with the crisis. This doesn't mean either the survival circuits will stay activated or that the person is now permanently in survival mode. It simply means there may be a temporary shift toward protection, because the brain can't allocate resources to complex thinking when it believes it needs to immediately stop in its tracks, fight, flee, or collapse to stay safe.

While overwhelm can trigger trauma responses, it's typically adaptive. It signals the need to pause, reset, or seek support, rather than being a sign of dysfunction. It only becomes a problem when it's chronic, unresolved, excessive, or reactivates unresolved trauma patterns.

What does it mean to be hyperactivated? Is it the same as broken, dysregulated, or stuck in survival mode?

While these terms are related, they refer to different aspects of nervous system function. **Hyperactivation** describes a state of increased arousal in the nervous system, while **dysregulation** refers to a condition where the system loses its ability to return to balance—often resulting from repeated or prolonged hyperactivation. **Survival mode** describes a broader process in which the system becomes oriented entirely toward threat detection and self-protection, often bypassing reflective thinking or emotional flexibility.

None of these states alone mean you're **"broken."** They represent your nervous system working to protect you, just not optimally. Unfortunately, the "broken" narrative has become too common in our current conversations about mental health, but let's focus on the serious issues this question raises.

When someone says they're **"hyperactivated,"** they usually mean heightened arousal in the nervous system, which could be perceived as increased energy, vigilance, anxiety, or emotional intensity. Conversely, when the shutdown part of the parasympathetic system is overactivated, it leads to **"hypoactivation."** When hyperactivated, we might feel impatient, angry, loud, or abrupt. Conversely, when hypoactivated (dorsal vagus), we might come across as absent, apathetic, aloof, or unemotional.

Considering the different levels of activation—especially of the sympathetic branch—will help clarify what's "normal" and what might be linked to survival mode.

Throughout this book, I'll use the term **"activation"** to describe how the system dials up energy to meet life's demands, with a focus on how intensely or quickly the sympathetic branch gets "revved up." Below is a simplified range of sympathetic activation, from our typical awake state to the extremes of a survival crisis. Please keep this in mind to avoid assuming that all activation is pathological or indicates something negative.

Sympathetic Levels of Activation

Awake: Even when we're resting or sleeping, the sympathetic branch doesn't fully "shut off." It maintains a baseline level of activity (called sympathetic tone) to regulate essential functions like heart rate, blood vessel tone, and breathing. During sleep, especially in deeper stages (like slow-wave sleep), its activity drops significantly, but it's never completely inactive. For example, it can spike briefly during REM sleep (dreaming) or in response to stressors (e.g., a loud noise). As we wake up and start our day, it gradually increases into a steady gear, providing the energy to move, work, focus, and connect with the world.

Eustress: Sometimes called "good stress," eustress is healthy sympathetic activation that energizes us to meet challenges—like pushing to meet a deadline, learning something new, or staying alert in a busy environment.

Stress: When demands increase and tension builds, the "get-into-action" system dials up. The body secretes more cortisol—our main stress hormone—than usual. If this heightened state is short-lived, we can break down the extra hormone and quickly reset. At this stage, there's no perception of immediate danger—the system simply tenses and prepares for increased demands. Problems may arise when this activation happens too frequently or stays on too long. Stress itself can go up and down along a continuum, from manageable to potentially problematic.

Anxiety: With constant sympathetic over-activation, the body learns to maintain this heightened state, remaining flooded with stress hormones beyond what's helpful. The get-into-action response can shift into persistent worry. This heightened state can gradually become the "new normal," leaving us in a condition of ongoing tension and energy depletion.

Distress: This stage emerges when stress or anxiety intensifies and begins to disrupt daily life significantly. Stress chemicals continue to build, overwhelming our usual coping abilities. We might experience persistent worry, agitation, or irritability that feels harder to control, pushing the system closer to a crisis point.

Panic: Panic is an extreme spike of sympathetic arousal. The body releases so many stress hormones—adrenaline, cortisol, etc.—at once that they overwhelm the system, sometimes producing symptoms that feel like a physical illness (chest tightness, racing heart, dizziness, etc.) and force the brain to prepare for a calamity. While intensely uncomfortable, panic episodes are typically brief, and the system can return to baseline once the hormone surge subsides.

Terror: Terror is an escalation beyond panic where the sympathetic system becomes so intensely activated that it feels life-threatening. Unlike panic's brief surge, terror involves prolonged flooding of stress hormones, creating extreme symptoms like severe trembling, difficulty breathing, and a sense of imminent doom.

Survival: This is where a sudden surge in the sympathetic branch brings the system to extreme levels, either during an actual threat or when triggered by past trauma, as though facing imminent danger. Hypervigilance may get activated to maintain constant scanning for threats, sacrificing rest, digestion, and restoration for the sake of perceived danger. This state is exhausting and can lead to severe mental and physical strain. Constant activation at this level causes dysregulation.

In essence, I wanted to show how hyperarousal reflects the degree to which the sympathetic branch can move along a wide spectrum—from everyday functioning to extreme states of alarm. When activation spikes, it can rise so high that a person may become intensely keyed up, appearing paranoid or even temporarily "out of touch." This highlights the importance of recognizing and tracking such escalation.

This system also participates in positive states—there's a parallel activation that ranges from calm engagement to enthusiasm and even euphoria. Happiness, motivation, and excitement also rely on sympathetic arousal; it's the intensity, **meaning of the experience**, and context that determine whether the activation is detrimental or favorable and adaptive or overwhelming.

In a similar way, there is also a form of overactivation in the parasympathetic nervous system, commonly considered the "shutdown" or "rest-and-digest" response. In that state, the body tries to conserve energy by drastically slowing down, making people experience fatigue, numbness, or a sense of disconnection. The body uses this excessive parasympathetic activation as a protective strategy, but it should only last briefly. When it persists, it can lead to feelings of helplessness or lasting dissociation, which delays healthy participation with life's demands or even complete disengagement and fainting.

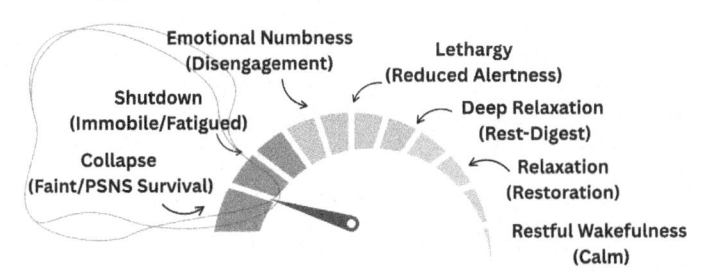

Parasympathetic Levels of Activation

Of course, our real-life responses aren't always sequential. For instance, someone might jump directly from a calm (awake) state into panic due to a sudden threat without going through anxiety or distress stages first or move directly from restful relaxation into emotional numbness or shutdown if faced with an overwhelming emotional shock or traumatic event.

As you can see, hyperactivation is not the same as being dysregulated or chronically relying on the same response. It's a state—often intense and prolonged—but one that the nervous system can shift out of with the right conditions and support. Being in **survival mode** is one possible outcome of extreme and prolonged hyperactivation, since problems arise when these protective responses don't deactivate. That's when symptoms become chronic.

Part of healing from all emotional and psychological issues involves recognizing when we're moving up these activation levels, learning ways to bring our nervous system back toward balance, and developing self-regulation skills to avoid those painful peaks.

> **Sympathetic Downshift Practice.** When you feel stress or anxiety rising, try this simple practice to keep sympathetic activation down.
>
> Stand or sit in a quiet, comfortable place. Take a moment to gently scan your body. Where do you feel tension in your body—your shoulders, chest, or stomach? If you feel tense, gently wiggle your fingers and toes to connect with your body.
>
> Take a slow, steady breath in, letting your ribs expand. As you exhale, imagine releasing just a bit of that tightness. Notice if the tension softens even slightly with each breath. Continue this gentle breathing pattern for a few more cycles, allowing your nervous system to gradually shift toward calm. Remember, the goal isn't to eliminate all stress immediately but to give your system permission to downregulate naturally.
>
> Now, raise your arms slowly to shoulder height, palms up, as if lifting a soft wave, then lower them gently, like the wave receding. Move with your breath—inhale up, exhale down—for 4-6 slow cycles. Feel your shoulders soften and your chest open as physical tension releases.
>
> Close your eyes or lower your gaze and picture a calm ocean wave washing over you, carrying away stress or fear. As you move your arms, imagine the wave dissolving tightness wherever you hold it—chest, jaw, or shoulders. Silently say, *"This wave carries my stress away,"* linking mind and body.
>
> Finish by breathing deeply twice, feeling warmth under your hands. Say softly (or think), *"I'm safe, and my body is calming."* This grounds you, reinforcing peace. Notice how your body feels—lighter, softer? If it's still tight, keep going.
>
> Repeat daily or during stress to retrain your nervous system.

WHAT DOES DYSREGULATION REALLY MEAN FOR SOMEONE THAT WANTS TO HEAL FROM TRAUMA?

"Dysregulation" is another term that's been adopted to casually describe someone's intense emotional reactions. The true meaning of dysregulation goes deeper than just being angry or loud, moody, or "very emotional." Those states are usually temporary spikes in sympathetic activation or strong emotional reactions rather than true dysregulation. I prefer to call them emotional surges, activation spikes, or emotional instability.

For decades, psychology implied that our behaviors were either fully within our control or predetermined by genetics, leading to interventions aimed at changing behaviors through persuasion or teaching coping strategies. The concept of dysregulation has transformed this perspective, helping us understand behavior and emotions from a more holistic and compassionate standpoint.

Dysregulation is a serious issue that includes disruptions in behavior caused by a combination of psychological and physiological factors. Put simply, dysregulation describes a system operating chaotically because it has lost its internal organization or equilibrium. Like trauma—and as part of the phenomenon—dysregulation also implies **a persistent state with significant consequences**, indicating we've lost our ability to effectively manage or balance our physiological responses, and therefore our emotional ones. This results in reactions that feel overwhelming, out of control, or inappropriate relative to the situation on a constant basis.

But why would this happen? When the brain is functioning optimally, it operates like a well-oiled machine—the brain structures that manage emotions work in natural, coordinated rhythms and regulatory mechanisms.

Dysregulation happens when our body's systems stop working normally due to factors like chronic stress, constant hypervigilance, insufficient sleep, inflammation, hormonal imbalances, and elevated stress hormone levels. These disruptions can cascade through multiple systems, affecting everything from emotional regulation to basic bodily functions.

The consequences of this persistent lack of coordination can range from mild to severe disturbances in mood, cognition, or physical health, depending on the intensity and nature of the disrupting events.

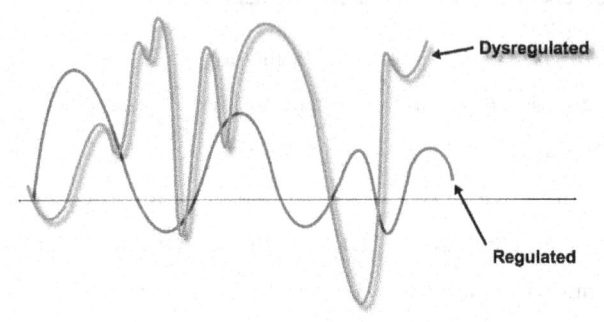

Regulated vs Dysregulated Activation

But don't get me wrong—intense emotional moments can certainly interfere with how some brain structures work together. However, we shouldn't be calling it dysregulation when someone has just brief emotional spikes or is temporarily struggling. The key difference is separating normal overreactions (like jumping at the sight of a scorpion) from actual incapacity to calm down for hours after a minor event. Imagine not sleeping for days after you see a spider, getting into a huge fight after a slight disagreement, having panic attacks in everyday situations, or feeling completely disoriented over small frustrations. These are patterns that show ongoing problems with emotional and cognitive stability, not just isolated reactions to stressful events. **Dysregulation is a chronic state that can significantly impair daily functioning and quality of life.**

But something that most people ignore is that dysregulation isn't an all-encompassing term. There are two main types commonly associated with psychological issues: autonomic dysregulation and emotional dysregulation. Both can occur separately or together, even without obvious symptoms.

Autonomic dysregulation refers to disruptions in how the autonomic nervous system manages core bodily functions—such as heart rate, digestion, and stress responses. This type of dysregulation can lead to a broad range of symptoms, including irregular heartbeat, chronic fatigue, and heightened emotional reactivity.

Recent neuroscientific research highlights how closely interconnected all organ systems are, suggesting that autonomic dysregulation may contribute to more physical and medical problems than traditionally recognized. As a result, medicine is gradually shifting toward a more systemic view of illness, acknowledging that imbalances in the nervous system can reverberate throughout the entire body. Psychology is following this shift by understanding emotions as systemic processes. By the way, autonomic dysregulation is not readily apparent and is essentially impossible to detect with the naked eye.

Emotional dysregulation, on the other hand, involves a persistent difficulty in managing and responding to emotional experiences in adaptive ways—and the inability to return to a stable state afterward. This condition is often visible to others, which creates its own challenges. When we can't control the intensity or expression of our emotions, we may feel confused, ashamed, vulnerable, or even "crazy"—feeling as if caught in a storm without any solid ground.

This dysregulation often arises from unresolved emotional wounds—not only trauma—and is rooted in how the brain processes and interprets distress. An overactive amygdala can amplify emotional responses, while an underactive or overwhelmed prefrontal cortex struggles to regulate and calm them. In short, dysregulation isn't just about reacting too much—it's about a system that has not learned how to manage challenges.

While emotional dysregulation can occur independently, autonomic dysregulation typically leads to emotional dysregulation. Dysregulation doesn't just affect one aspect of a person's life; it permeates every facet, from relationships to digestion. People suffering from dysregulation may feel either too much or nothing at all. Frequently swinging between extremes, such as hating one moment and loving the next, can fragment a dysregulated person's sense of self, leading them to doubt their identity or question the validity of their experiences, ultimately lowering their tolerance for distress. Recognizing that this dynamic exists is often the first step toward resolving it.

Feel the Effect of Becoming your Own Ally

"Healing starts with a single, hopeful decision to move forward. As you heal, your light touches everyone around you—family, friends, strangers—creating waves of change that reach far beyond what you can see."

Resolving emotional pain is not a linear path but a type of discovery—one that involves seeing your emotions differently, embracing discomfort and pain as part of the process, and investing in making sense of your experiences. The key to finding a way out lies in expanding your capacity to tolerate distress, not by avoiding it, but by facing it head-on. Think of it like strengthening an emotional muscle: the more you practice navigating life's challenges without being crushed by them, the stronger and more resilient you become. This growth isn't about becoming immune to pain but rather developing the ability to weather it, adapt, and emerge wiser from it.

Even in academic circles and across cultures, healing is understood to be rooted in wisdom—the ability to respond to life's ups and downs with greater understanding and grace. This means drawing insights from both pleasant and difficult experiences, using each one to refine how you approach future challenges. Your emotional resilience grows as you face, process, and transform suffering, giving you the tools to navigate emotional struggles more effectively.

What screams "mentally healthy"?

For decades, we have primarily focused on diagnosing and defining mental illnesses, but what if we shift our attention to understanding and cultivating being mentally healthier?

Have you noticed the transformation in physical health awareness—where people now actively pursue overall wellness? For example, insurance companies offer discounts when people exercise regularly or give incentives to develop healthy habits before they pay for medical bills. It may be time to apply this same proactive approach to emotional well-being. Instead of waiting for emotional struggles to become severe, you could benefit from recognizing the importance of building psychological resources and maintaining emotional wellness proactively.

You can look to mentally healthy individuals as examples of how to navigate life's challenges. Allow me to share some of the characteristics they tend to demonstrate:

Remarkable flexibility and adaptability. They bend without breaking, adjusting to change while maintaining their core stability. Their versatility means they can adapt to different situations without losing themselves in the process. They know when to hold firm and when to let go, understanding that their energy is better spent on what they can actually influence rather than trying to control everything. While this level of emotional well-being isn't yet the norm, it offers a compelling model for what we might all strive toward—which is what I want to promote in this book by explaining our adaptive innate characteristics.

Relationships. They have the ability to stay generous with their emotional energy, even during tough times. They can still show up for others while dealing with their struggles and keep smiling. Watch how they handle people they don't like—instead of acting out or being nasty, they maintain their serenity, set appropriate boundaries, and observe with an open mind. They approach relationships with patience and maintain hope for positive connection, even when it's challenging.

Purpose and joy. They stay productive, not from anxiety but by leveraging their sense of purpose, whether they're gardening, reading, or creating something new. There's this consistent forward momentum in their lives, even during setbacks. They can get genuinely excited about simple pleasures—like the smell of fresh coffee or a beautiful sunset—while keeping their bigger life goals in focus.

Self-awareness. Very importantly, **they look inward for validation** rather than constantly seeking approval from others. When things go wrong, their first instinct isn't to blame others but to reflect on what they can learn and how they can grow.

Overall balance. It's not about being perfect—it's about maintaining this dynamic balance between acceptance and growth, empathy and boundaries, present joys and future challenges. Mentally healthy individuals aren't just surviving or complaining; they're actively creating their lives with purpose and enthusiasm.

| Flexibility and adaptability | Let go of control | Stay productive | Look inward for validation | Dynamic balance | Positive & healthy habits |
| Excitement for simple pleasures | Purpose and enthusiasm | Good boundaries | True to their values | True to themselves | Reflect, learn, grow |

Mentally Healthy Characteristics

Staying mentally healthy doesn't mean there will be no problems—it's the presence of constructive, life-affirming patterns and habits that help people navigate both good and challenging times while staying true to themselves and their values. It's understanding that we all face difficulties and that relationships can be complex, but approaching them with self-awareness, enthusiasm, and acknowledgment of our own constraints.

> **Taking In the Good Exercise:** This exercise helps you actively notice and absorb positive experiences, strengthening your capacity to find balance even during difficult times.
>
> Throughout your day, pause when something good happens—no matter how small. This might be a moment of physical comfort (warm sunlight, a comfortable chair), a brief positive interaction (someone's smile, a kind text), a small accomplishment (completing a task, helping someone), or a pleasant sensation (the taste of tea, a favorite song).
>
> When you notice something positive, stop for 30 seconds. Don't rush past it. Let yourself really experience it instead of immediately moving to the next thing.
>
> Deliberately enhance the experience by taking a deeper breath, noticing physical sensations associated with the good feeling, letting yourself smile or relax your shoulders, and thinking, *"This feels good,"* or *"I'm grateful for this."*
>
> Imagine this positive experience settling into your body and memory. Visualize it as warmth spreading through your chest or light filling a space inside you. Tell yourself, *"I'm taking the moment in,"* and allow it to get in.

> Start with just one positive moment per day, then gradually increase. The goal isn't forced positivity—it's learning to fully receive the good that's already present and allow your system to benefit from it.

WHY ARE SO MANY PEOPLE AFRAID OF BEING VULNERABLE?

Vulnerability is often misunderstood as weakness, being easily hurt, being overly emotional, or lacking boundaries—essentially, a liability. More recently, however, vulnerability has been reframed as the willingness to be seen fully, especially in relationships—imperfections and all—a form of courage rather than a weakness.

In its truest sense, and from a more metaphysical standpoint, **vulnerability means openness**—one of humans' greatest gifts. Vulnerability embodies a high level of authenticity and the willingness to face uncertainty with acceptance and tolerance, to let others in, and to be fearless in recognizing and accepting one's qualities as well as shortcomings.

Vulnerability is the embodiment of trust and hope—and an essential element in developing a strong sense of self. It can strengthen relationships and foster personal growth. When we explore what true openness means, we discover that vulnerability offers far more than just courage—it opens a realm of possibilities.

When you embrace openness, you connect to the shared thread of life itself, what some cultures call "chi" or **life energy.** Opening to suffering and imperfections also allows you to experience the joy of weaving into the systemic dynamics of existence. Chi flows through this duality, like yin and yang—suffering's quiet weight (yin) and joy's vibrant surge (yang) aren't opposites to conquer but currents to ride. Vulnerability lets you tap into this flow, risking pain to feel life's pulse. When we view vulnerability through a purely threat/avoidant, survival-mode lens, we only perceive it as weakness.

But what I hear more often from people, especially younger ones, is that vulnerability is the readiness—or sometimes necessity—to uncover themselves, whether emotionally, physically, or socially. Vulnerability becomes almost synonymous with "exposing" your most intimate truths and feelings. And it seems that this type of vulnerability occurs without any certainty of protection. Depending on how the person and others respond to this complete exposure, vulnerability can become the gateway to an emotional wound or, in some cases, a stepping stone toward trauma.

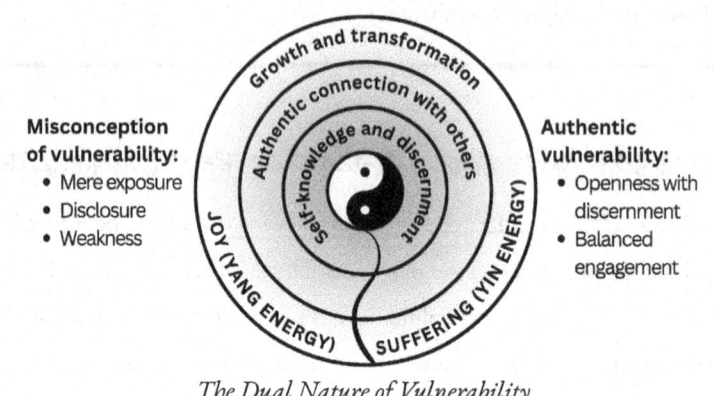

Misconception of vulnerability:
- Mere exposure
- Disclosure
- Weakness

Authentic vulnerability:
- Openness with discernment
- Balanced engagement

The Dual Nature of Vulnerability

Vulnerability, seen simply as revealing wounds or sharing difficult experiences, can be confusing and debilitating. Authentic vulnerability involves discernment about what to share, with whom, and for what purpose. It requires the courage to be seen in your humanity—including your strengths, aspirations, and capacity for growth—not just your suffering or flaws. But it requires no expectations about the response. And for that, you need to know yourself pretty well, which is a genuine challenge. Additionally, if your sharing is driven by what you expect from others, it may not be an indicator of vulnerability but of insecurity.

Some people share traumatic stories while remaining emotionally defended, perhaps seeking sympathy or validation without opening themselves to deep connection.

Others overshare without considering how their disclosures might impact the listener, inadvertently creating an emotional burden rather than a bridge—and sometimes shame. Neither approach embodies the transformative power of vulnerability.

At its essence, vulnerability isn't just about exposure—it's about engagement, which starts with yourself. Full engagement carries both benefits and risks, including the potential for exploitation, boundary violations, and emotional dysregulation.

If you want to use vulnerability as a strength, you must begin with self-knowledge because you need to be willing to risk disappointment for genuine connection, face uncertainty for growth, and acknowledge limitations while remaining open to feedback.

Knowing yourself makes these expectations more realistic.

> **Graduating Vulnerability Practice.** This is a simple exercise to build your vulnerability muscle gradually.
>
> Begin with a neutral observation about your day: *"Work was busy today,"* or *"I had three meetings back-to-back."* Proceed with a concise sentence that reveals a hidden aspect: *"Today's work was hectic, and I noticed I felt a little invisible in the meeting."* Choose something authentic but not your deepest insecurities.
>
> Take one slow, deliberate breath. This creates space between sharing and judging. Notice your physical response: What sensations arise? Do you experience tight shoulders, a flutter in your stomach, or a warmth in your chest? These are your body's reactions to your own truth, which could bring up some emotions and thoughts. Notice them.
>
> Check if any critical thoughts arise *("I shouldn't feel this way")* without engaging them. Simply acknowledge, *"That's judgment appearing."*
>
> Take another breath and ask, *"Can I allow this truth to exist without judgment?"* Feel what shifts when you release criticism. You may feel warmth towards yourself or have a sudden deep sigh.
>
> Openness, the basis of genuine vulnerability, is the gentle acceptance that may emerge.
>
> Try this daily for a week. The second week you can either journal or practice with someone you trust. Start with smaller truths and gradually work toward more significant ones as your comfort grows.

WHAT'S THE MAIN REASON WE COULD BELIEVE IN HEALING FROM SUFFERING IF MOST PEOPLE SPEND MOST OF THEIR LIVES STRUGGLING WITH PSYCHOLOGICAL PAIN?

It's true that humans experience a great deal of emotional pain. Still, we can remain optimistic because we've learned that brains can rewire themselves, that the alterations caused by traumatization are treatable, and that our capacity to understand and work with emotions can be developed. We are also learning more about our innate capacity for healing, how to work with our nervous systems, and how to transform suffering into wisdom.

There are many examples of individuals who dedicated their lives to showing us the way forward. For example, Buddha Shakyamuni, upon attaining enlightenment, taught four core principles known as the Four Noble Truths—a condensed expression of the full truth about suffering and liberation.

The first truth he shared, *"Life involves suffering,"* explains that struggle, dissatisfaction, and pain are inherent parts of human existence. **Yes, some pain is inevitable!** The second Noble Truth states that suffering is primarily caused by grasping—we suffer because we want things to be different than they are, cling to what we desire, and resist what we don't. In other words, we could suffer less if we let go of the belief that things must align with our preferences and stop trying to control everything in the hope of feeling more satisfied—an approach that simply doesn't work. Things don't always go our way, and not accepting this fact makes suffering worse.

Consider a breakup: you may suffer deeply, longing for the other person to return, to act in ways that please you, and to remain in your life forever. The more you resist accepting the situation as it is—or the way it has evolved—the more pain you create. But when you begin to accept that the relationship may be over, regardless of the reason, your suffering can start to soften.

The third of those Four Truths asserts that suffering can end. Buddha said it's possible to overcome this cycle of craving and wanting, finding peace by changing how we relate to our experiences.

For instance, if you frame a breakup as a defeat, your suffering will continue. But if you see it as a lesson—about what to do next time, how to choose your next partner, how to improve yourself, or how to grow from it—your suffering transforms, your system functions better, and more energy becomes available for moving forward. Nobody knows the future, but you will be more prepared for a better one.

The Fourth Truth is about the method—a path of practices and perspectives that lead to liberation from suffering. This path requires effort, discipline, and a commitment to working on your well-being, which is part of what we will be exploring throughout this book to resolve emotional pain.

- **Life is suffering**
- **Suffering comes from grasping/craving**
- **It's possible to eliminate suffering**
- **Needs discipline and the right mindset**

The Four Noble Truths of Suffering and Healing

If you want a "translation" of these ideas into more scientific terms, we could say that humans are wired for resilience and are equipped with resources. Neuroplasticity, for instance, shows the brain can rewire itself no matter how dire our circumstances have been—new neural pathways form when people engage in therapy, mindfulness, or even just headstrong persistence.

Your brain is never static; it reorganizes in response to new experiences. Yes, chronic stress and disconnection can wire the brain for heightened reactivity and threat detection, but positive experiences, consistent emotional support, and various forms of interventions can increase internal resources and help reverse or moderate these patterns. Even when some pain persists, opportunities for relief, insight, or transformation continue to emerge.

Resilience doesn't always mean returning to life exactly as it was before. It means discovering, transforming, or gaining strengths and values through adversity. This capacity for growth mirrors what you see in nature—flowers continue to offer their scent, and birds still sing and display their colors even after storms. All you have to do is look up to notice the peace that's waiting for you.

How does mindfulness work in healing everything? Is it really the cure-all?

Don't we all wish for a magic pill or enchanted wand to end our pain and struggles? Many people carry this wishful thinking when searching for solutions—like assuming that money fixes everything or that a psychedelic trip will erase the past. Wealth may bring happiness for some, but certainly not for everyone. MDMA may open doors to awareness or bring demons to the surface. The same goes for mindfulness: it can work wonders for many, but it doesn't help everyone in the same way.

Mindfulness has proven effective in many studies and across its various forms. It works by rewiring cognitive, emotional, and physiological responses through deliberate, nonjudgmental attention to the present moment. That simple principle—being present without judgment—can create powerful shifts, even if you don't call it "mindfulness" or maintain a formal practice.

A consistent mindfulness practice can go even further. It helps strengthen the prefrontal cortex (PFC), which is essential in this quest since executive function and emotional regulation depend on it. It also reduces overactivity in brain regions associated with stress and fear. By interrupting the stress response, mindfulness helps lower cortisol levels and reduces heart rate and blood pressure. It also disrupts ruminative thought loops and stimulates the release of endorphins and oxytocin while increasing serotonin levels—"feel-good" chemicals that support mood regulation and emotional stability

Even though many people remain skeptical, research shows that observing thoughts and emotions without judgment enhances metacognition, reduces emotional reactivity, improves resilience, and heightens interoceptive awareness—which can even modulate the perception of pain.

However, these benefits depend not only on regular practice but also on individual temperament, commitment, and even the quality of instruction. Many people struggle with mindfulness due to attention difficulties or cultural misunderstandings. Some assume it's a religious practice tied to specific beliefs, while others teach it that way—framing it through rituals or fixed expectations that may feel inaccessible or alienating.

Still, I'm a firm believer in its power. No, it may not resolve everything—but it significantly supports neuroplasticity and helps the brain function more efficiently. The key is understanding that mindfulness doesn't require elaborate techniques; it simply asks for focused attention on what's happening right now, paired with acceptance.

Throughout this book, you'll find exercises that apply this principle in practical ways: intentionally focusing on your body or sensations without judgment and then using that present-moment awareness to reflect, resolve, imagine, and visualize better outcomes. While mindfulness may not be a panacea, healing without it could be a paradox.

> **Essential Awarefulness Practice.** To practice "Awarefulness," keep in mind a few essentials.
>
> Unlike the simplified mindfulness often described elsewhere, authentic mindful awareness demands three specific elements:
> - somatic engagement (actively feeling it in your body and engaging with the present),
> - experiential presence (fully being in the moment, not only thinking about it),
> - intentional choice (consciously deciding to engage and focus).
>
> Without this trinity, you may be practicing mere attention, just thinking about it, or you may fall asleep.
>
> The type of participation that I suggest for most of the exercises in this book (I like calling it Awarefulness) requires all three elements.
>
> Gently bring your awareness to the present moment as often—and for as long—as you can, even if only for a minute or two. The goal is to make these responses your default state over time.
>
> Approach whatever you notice with **curiosity, not criticism.**
>
> Anchor your attention to something tangible—your breath, a sound, or a sensation—so the mind has a steady base.
>
> Let's try using color. Bring the color red to mind. Imagine it filling your mental space—bright, bold, and expansive. Let it saturate the inside of your awareness. Notice how your body responds to red. Stay with it for at least 30 seconds. Let it move through you, fill you, and energize you.

> Now gently shift your focus to the color yellow. Picture it spreading into your mind, growing brighter and softer. Let it expand until yellow fills your inner terrain. Notice any changes in your body—your breath, your posture, your energy. Stay with it. Focus on it. Be yellow.
>
> You can continue this practice with other colors—or return to the one that feels most nourishing and stay there longer. Let the color hold you, and allow yourself to be fully immersed in its presence.
>
> Finally, meet lapses with patience.
>
> Returning to the present is the practice and creates "muscle."
>
> It doesn't require a special posture, setting, or belief—just the willingness to redirect your attention to what's happening around you when needed and to tend to your inner experience when that feels right.

How do you heal an emotional wound?

Healing emotional wounds isn't always straightforward because our hurts can arise from countless different situations. I may even say that emotional wounds don't need to be healed but resolved. **Resolving a wound** suggests processing and integrating an experience, finding meaning and learning from it, moving forward without ongoing disruption, and ensuring that the wound no longer actively interferes with functioning. The "lesson" was taken.

When we talk about **healing,** we might imply restoration to a previous state—that the wound disappears entirely. Healing is a more medical/physical recovery model and may raise expectations to unrealistic highs. That's why I'd rather talk about resolving emotional pain. I'll include specific ways to deal with certain wounds in the upcoming chapters, but if I had to summarize an overall approach, I'd say:

Resolution calls for a mindset in which, rather than letting one event define your entire emotional landscape, you tap into existing resources—like memories of how you've successfully handled challenges before, supportive relationships, or overlooked personal strengths. If those resources truly weren't available before, you can begin creating them by adopting realistic yet affirming perspectives.

For example, saying *"I've handled tough feedback before"* is more constructive than saying *"All criticism is an attack."* You might tell yourself, *"I'll maintain some distance from overly critical people and stop taking comments personally,"* or *"I might read a book to better understand what happened."* For example, saying *"I haven't managed this well in the past, but I can start handling things differently now"* can help shift our mindset toward resolution.

> Resolving emotional wounds involves self-awareness, deliberately processing what happened, finding meaning that brings peace and closure, and integrating any lessons it offers.

When you're able to **integrate both the negative and positive aspects** of painful experiences, the once-isolated wound no longer interferes with your emotional life; you continue moving toward connection, well-being returns, and your system stays in balance. I don't like to sound alarmist, but if too many wounds remain unattended, your system can lose the ability to distinguish emotional hurt from actual threat, which can develop into trauma.

Emotional Resource Integration. There are many different ways to help ourselves resolve emotional wounds. Here is a simple exercise that covers one way to integrate your emotional resources.

Begin by acknowledging the emotional wound. Sit quietly for a moment, allowing yourself to think about the hurt you're experiencing (a boss's disapproval, a fight with your partner, a criticism). You can do this exercise with your eyes closed to have the chance to go deeper inside, or, if you prefer, write down the event or emotion that triggered this pain. Allow yourself to feel the emotions involved and notice the sensations in your body.

Next, notice the negative impact this wound has had on you (feeling inadequate, anxious about keeping the job or the relationship). Does it make you feel insecure, angry, or alone? Be specific about how this wound has affected your mental and emotional state, and connect with how your body reacts when you stay on the impact.

Please take a moment to consider a mental list of resources that may assist you in your journey. These can be memories of past successes, strengths, relationships, or new perspectives that help you manage difficulties, especially if they are connected to how you are feeling (like getting a recent promotion and praise from the boss or how you have resolved fights before). If you can't think of any, challenge yourself to imagine resources you could develop moving forward (e.g., learning to set boundaries, finding support groups, reading helpful books, making new friends). Notice how your body responds when you think about your resources.

Based on your list of resources, bring to mind some affirming statements. These could sound like *"I have navigated difficult moments at work before"* and *"I've been able to resolve past fights, and I know we love each other."* Or *"I can approach this challenge from a place of strength."* Connect these thoughts with your body as well.

Finally, reframe the emotional wound by considering how you can integrate both the pain and the learning. What lessons can you draw from the experience? How can this experience become part of a larger story of resilience rather than a defining chapter of hurt? You could see a negative comment as a chance to improve rather than a failure. You can reframe it as, *"While the comment was difficult to hear, it reminds me that I can always learn something I didn't know, and I can use feedback to make my work even better."* Notice the sensations that come up.

Repeat (or read) your affirmations and reframed perspective several times. Focus on internalizing the balance between the emotional hurt and the positive resources you've identified. Allow yourself to feel the original sensations with the new ones, and you will notice you have space for both.

This exercise encourages both processing the pain and creating new perspectives that allow emotional wounds to become part of a larger healing narrative.

Chapter Two

EMOTIONS

HOW TO UNCOVER THE TRUTH ABOUT WHY FEELINGS HURT SO MUCH

"The more we learn how emotions work, the more they work for us."

Have you ever wondered why some people seem to bounce back from challenges while others struggle more? Or maybe you've wondered what happens inside your brain and body when anger flares or sadness lingers? The answers lie in understanding the inner architecture of your emotions—the wiring that shapes how you feel, react, and manage the ups and downs of your emotional life. What many people don't realize is that emotions are part of a system we actively help build over time, often unconsciously. Until recently, we simply didn't have the tools or understanding to see how this emotional architecture actually works.

Research is finally explaining how your emotional patterns determine not just how deeply you feel but also whether a fleeting moment of frustration fades quickly or ignites a day of irritability, depending on the neural pathways that have formed in your brain through repetition, the information you have absorbed, and the way you stored that information.

We will learn in this chapter why some emotions pass naturally while others intensify and persist, and why trauma or unresolved wounds can alter our emotional blueprint, turning protective signals into patterns of reactivity or confusion. We'll explore why what once was supposed to serve you can keep you at its mercy, as if you were navigating life with a faulty internal compass.

Too often, we misread our emotions, mistaking normal stress for dysfunction or ignoring signs of deeper dysregulation. The distinction between "just frazzled" and "trauma's shadow" becomes vague, leaving us uncertain about our resilience and when to seek help. My hope is that understanding your emotional architecture can give you the tools to rebuild your emotions as they are meant to be and work for you.

Let's begin by exploring your own patterns. We'll start with a brief exercise to experience firsthand how your emotions take shape. Then, we'll dive into why emotions are more than feelings—they're predictive signals—how your body strives for balance, and what happens when that balance becomes disrupted.

Kick Off With a Step-by-Step Guide to

Deconstructing Your Emotions

"To understand our emotions is to reclaim authorship over our own story."

I'd like to invite you to try an exercise that can help you better understand your emotions. It offers an insightful starting point, revealing how complex the process is—how your mind and body constantly work together to construct emotional responses. The goal is to discover why emotional situations can feel so overwhelming or unpredictable. The exercise will give you a glimpse into how emotions are constructed—something I'll explore in more detail later. I recommend trying it once before reading the explanation and again afterward.

So, will you join me in beginning this journey with an experiential moment—before we cover the theory?

This isn't a meditative mindfulness exercise, nor is its purpose relaxation—though you may choose to do it with your eyes closed. Instead, the goal is to fully engage with your body and mind in the present moment so you can directly observe how your emotions are constructed through your physical sensations and mental processes. It's an internal journey!

If you're ready, please follow these instructions:

> **Deconstructing an Emotion.** Bring to mind a recent event during which you experienced one distinct emotion—something fresh, clear, and easy to recall. Clearly identify the emotion you'll be working with. For example, maybe you felt anger when someone interrupted you, sadness after receiving disappointing news, or joy while reconnecting with a friend. Pick just one.
>
> Once you've chosen the emotional experience, vividly picture it in your mind as though it were happening right now, and allow yourself to fully reconnect with that emotion. Keep this image firmly in mind and remain connected to the feeling while you reflect and answer the questions around the following aspects of your chosen emotion:
>
> **Bodily Sensations.** Notice any physical sensations arising in your body as you continue holding the image and staying connected to the emotion. These sensations might include tension in your shoulders, heaviness in your chest, warmth in your face, or chills running down your spine. Below, I've included a table listing possible sensations to help guide you, especially if you're having trouble identifying what you feel. With practice, recognizing these bodily cues will become easier. Rather than trying to mentally guess or decide what you should be feeling, bring gentle, patient attention directly to your body. Simply notice whatever sensations naturally arise. This kind of embodied awareness is part of what we want you

to develop through this and other exercises. So, no rush—take your time. If the image has faded, bring it back into your mind until it becomes more vivid. Add sensory details—light, temperature, color, sound—whatever helps anchor you in the moment.

Once a sensation (or several) comes into focus, ask yourself, *"Is it calming or arousing?" "Is it pleasant, unpleasant, or neutral?"* This moment of noticing helps you understand how emotions live in the body, not just in the abstract.

Tightness (chest, throat, shoulders, stomach)	Dry mouth or throat
Heaviness or pressure (head, chest, limbs)	Shortness or shallowness of breath
Lightness or ease	Deep or relaxed breathing
Warmth or heat (e.g., face, neck, chest)	Dizziness or faintness
Coolness or chills	Energy surge or increased alertness
Tingling or pins-and-needles sensations	Weakness or fatigue
Shakiness or trembling	Nausea or queasiness
Numbness or lack of sensation	Restlessness or agitation
Fluttering sensation (e.g., stomach, chest)	Itchiness or skin sensitivity
Racing heart or pounding heartbeat	Relaxed muscles or softness in the body
Clenched jaw or fists	Pain, discomfort, or aches (joints, stomach)
Sweating (e.g., palms, forehead)	Expansion or openness (chest, shoulders)

Body Sensations Table

Labeling or Naming. While connecting with the sensations and image, think of the name of the emotion you first identified, and see if it still matches. Sometimes, connecting to the sensations brings more information and helps better identify the type of feelings we are having. Try to find a name that matches your experience. Notice the words or thoughts that pop into your mind that better describe what you are feeling. You can choose any emotion as long as you can connect it to the event. You can also choose not to label your feelings if you cannot find a name that fits them.

Value: Notice the experience's emotional value—how negative or positive it feels and whether it's calming or activating. Try rating it on a scale from minus 10 to 10, where -10 is extremely unpleasant and 10 is the most positive it could be.

```
-10 -9 -8 -7 -6 -5 -4 -3 -2 -1  0  1  2  3  4  5  6  7  8  9  10
|----|----|----|----|----|----|----|----|----|----|----|----|----|----|----|----|----|----|----|----|
Most unpleasant                        Neutral                          Most pleasant
```

Interpretation or Meaning. Now that you've connected to your physical sensations, named the emotion, and assigned a number to its effect on you, let's explore the deeper context behind it. Let's call it the emotion's **"storyboard."** This step focuses on uncovering the stories, memories, cultural influences, or beliefs you've accumulated that guide your emotional reactions.

Keeping your chosen emotion and event clearly in mind, ask yourself the following questions and write down your answers. Consider that if, for instance, the emotion you chose is fear, your storyboard might contain messages such as *"I have to be careful because people can't be trusted"* or *"I was taught that unfamiliar situations always bring trouble."* If it's shame, you might identify a message like *"I learned that mistakes mean I'm not good enough."* If it's contentment, you may recognize that the message is *"Life is wonderful"* or *"When you work hard, there is reward."* Please take your time to find your answers.

"What do I believe about this emotion?"

"What memories come to mind when I think of the emotion alone?"

"What did I hear as a child when others mentioned this particular emotion?"

"Can I recognize past events or learned beliefs that shaped my interpretation of this emotional experience?"

"What do I believe about myself in relation to experiencing this emotion?"

"What past experiences might be influencing how I interpret this moment?"

"Are there any beliefs or messages I've repeatedly heard or learned from family, friends, or culture that come to mind when experiencing this emotion?"

Do you notice yourself automatically labeling certain situations as *"dangerous,"* *"unacceptable,"* *"hurtful,"* *"exciting,"* or *"rewarding,"* even before fully evaluating them?

"What assumptions or expectations are guiding my reaction in this particular scenario?"

Now that you've explored the physical sensations, labeled the emotion, rated its impact, and unpacked the personal meanings tied to it, take a moment to summarize your **emotional storyboard.** For example: *"My storyboard about anger says that expressing it makes me unlovable, so I try to suppress anger or not show it—even when it's justified"* or *"My storyboard about joy includes the belief* *that I must earn happiness, so I rarely trust when I feel it."* Write your summary below:

"What does my storyboard about this emotion tell me?"

Read your summary and reflect on how your storyboard differs from someone else's, noticing that your emotional responses are influenced by your unique history, learning, and experiences. Once you write this description, you can continue with the following step.

Reaction or Response. Now, let's take a closer look at the actions or reactions these scripts prompt in real life. For instance, if your internal storyboard for disappointment says, *"Being let down is unbearable," your response might be to withdraw, end relationships prematurely, or avoid taking risks altogether.* But if your storyboard says, *"Disappointment happens, but it can be managed,"* your reaction might include openness, reflection, or communicating to resolve the issue. Similarly, if your anger script reads, *"I won't allow anyone to abuse me,"* the instructions might range from yelling, slamming doors, or pounding your fist on the table to calmly asserting your boundaries and asking to be treated with respect.

Keep your chosen emotion and situation clearly in mind as you reflect on the following questions:

"What specific actions, behaviors, or reactions does this emotion typically trigger in me?"

"How do I respond externally? Do I act immediately, retreat into silence, express my feelings openly, or perhaps hide them?"

"Do I notice an immediate urge or reflex when I experience this emotion? (For example, pulling away, arguing, avoiding eye contact, speaking louder, shutting down, or seeking reassurance.)"

"Are my responses similar across situations, or do they vary depending on who I'm with or what's happening?"

"Are these responses helpful and adaptive, or do they sometimes make things worse?"

"Do I recall if my responses are something I learned from others (parents, friends, partners) or developed through personal experience?"

Please take a moment to clearly describe your typical responses to this emotion. Describe what you usually do or feel compelled to do when this emotion arises. Notice whether your response feels proportionate and helpful—or if it sometimes escalates, lingers, or amplifies your discomfort.

After writing it down, tag each response using the **Reactivity Scale** below. This is not about judging yourself but about understanding the tone and pattern of your reactions so that change becomes possible.

Level of Reactivity	Description of the Reaction
Overextended (**OE**)	Emotion spills into other areas, prolongs distress, affects unrelated domains.
Exaggerated (**EX**)	Emotion drives dramatic reactions; relief is sought through expression.
Disproportionate (**DP**)	Reaction exceeds the situation; hard to self-regulate.
Charged (**CH**)	Emotion is strong but there's some awareness or control.
Measured (**MS**)	Emotion is proportionate and helpful; guided by reflection.
Muted (**MU**)	Emotion is vague or underplayed; hard to identify or express.
Suppressed (**SU**)	Emotion is denied, numbed, or disconnected from experience.

Reactivity Scale Table

Tag each response with the word that best describes it. This step helps you see exactly how your emotional scripts translate into real-life actions, giving you insight into which responses support your well-being and which might benefit from thoughtful revision. For instance, let's say your storyboard around **anger** instructs you to suppress it entirely—shutting down, staying silent, or pretending everything is fine—which, over time, makes you feel resentful, emotionally distant, or even have physical symptoms like tension or fatigue. Take your time responding to and tagging this question:

"How does my storyboard tell me to act and respond when I feel this emotion?"

Understand Your Emotionality (Overall Emotional Pattern): In this final step, we'll observe how your emotional experiences, storyboards, and responses come together to form your overall emotionality—the general pattern or style of your emotional life. For example, if you had highly reactive emotionality around disgust, you may not only feel repulsed by unpleasant food smells but may also frequently feel disgusted or uncomfortable in many unrelated situations—such as interacting with people, encountering unfamiliar environments, or experiencing minor inconveniences.

Still keeping the same emotional experience clearly in mind and the connection with the emotion that by now may feel even more vivid, reflect on and respond to the following questions:

"How intensely and quickly do I usually feel this emotion?"

"Does this emotion often linger, influencing my mood and decisions long after the triggering event?"

"Are there recurring patterns across different emotions or situations that suggest I have certain tendencies—such as heightened sensitivity, easy frustration, rapid escalation, or persistent worry?"

"Do these emotional patterns help me live better, more fully, or do they tend to limit my choices, relationships, or life satisfaction?"

If you find that you have heightened sensitivity around this emotion, you could notice how it limits your ability to enjoy diverse experiences, creating a sense of being controlled or overwhelmed by emotions. Considering your emotionality around the emotion you have been deconstructing, answer these questions:

"Does my overall pattern reflect a balanced, adaptive emotion that informs and supports me?"

"Or have rigid, negative, or fearful storyboards created overly intense or disproportionate emotional reactions?"

I hope you have given yourself the minutes you needed to write down how this particular emotion works. Thinking about how your usual feelings—anger, joy, stress—affect your days, your choices, and your relationships will help you be more aware of how you see yourself. Just noticing these patterns can show you what you might want to change or build on.

Now that you've got this insight, let's dig into why understanding your emotional setup matters. It's not just about healing old hurts—it's about seeing how deep they go. Later, we'll come back to the emotion you worked on here and learn how to turn it into a tool for growth.

Find Out How Emotions Work for and Against You

"Emotions are not what disrupt our system—they are part of a system we've failed to understand."

You may not notice it, but emotions silently orchestrate much of your life. They shape decisions you believed were rational, color relationships you thought were consciously chosen, cloud your objectivity, and influence your sense of self in ways you rarely recognize. Modern neuroscience now confirms what some have long suspected: emotions aren't disruptive intruders—they're essential guides in human experience.

This insight reveals a long-standing disconnect. For centuries, psychology and behavioral science often treated emotions as interruptions to be managed or suppressed, while many spiritual and philosophical traditions viewed them as obstacles on the path to wisdom. Both views missed a key point: emotions are not just reactions to the world; they help us interpret it. Understanding how we experience emotions isn't just a matter of self-improvement—it's an act of self-recognition.

What's intriguing is that despite centuries of inquiry into human behavior and decades of advanced brain research, psychologists have continued to struggle with one basic question: what exactly are emotions? This persistent uncertainty reinforces the mistaken belief that emotions are unpredictable, disruptive forces rather than natural expressions of our biology. In this chapter, I'll present a framework that addresses this fundamental gap.

WHAT'S ACTUALLY HAPPENING WHEN WE GET EMOTIONAL—IS SOMETHING CONTROLLING IT?

Isn't it noteworthy that our standard models of human biology lack the formal concept of an "emotional system"? We understand symptoms like salivation or diarrhea within the digestive system and blood pressure within the cardiovascular system—but we haven't applied that same systematic logic to emotions. This gap is more than academic oversight—it shapes how we conceptualize, diagnose, and treat emotional well-being, leaving blind spots in our approach to mental health.

Recently, trauma-related research has helped close that gap. The deep connection between our emotions, nervous system states, perceptions, and actions has revolutionized our understanding of human behavior. Behavior is no longer considered simply the product of conscious thought or genetic predisposition but as what emerges from the dynamic interaction between emotions and experience—creating survival responses, emotional patterns, and perceptual filters. This new framework is transforming treatment approaches and forcing us to reconsider long-held ideas. Long viewed as secondary or problematic, we now recognize emotions as central to psychological health. What we need now is a comprehensive system to help us understand how emotions work, what manages them, and how we can influence their function.

One way to describe **an emotional system is as a complex network of physiological responses, brain chemicals, thoughts, and feelings that links body and mind as partners.** This partnership constantly adapts to our experiences, producing emotions—how our whole system reacts to the world.

That sophisticated interaction includes how emotional pain activates many of the same neural circuits as physical pain, highlighting how deeply emotional wounds are experienced in the body. This overlap suggests that our emotional system monitors not just what's happening outside us but also what's happening within, signaling when something threatens our social safety, identity, or sense of connection. Emotions help us detect what matters, prioritize our responses, and influence how we relate to others and our environment. Emotions are not distractions from our functioning—they are a central part of it.

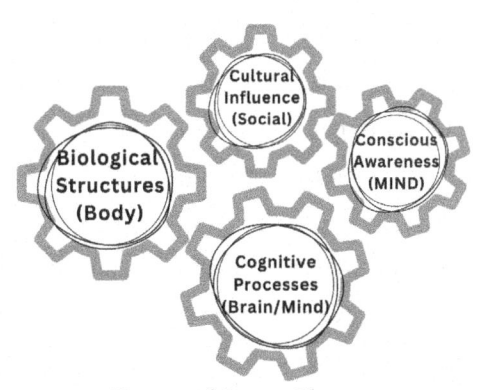

Emotional System Elements

The emotional system I'm proposing here includes the following elements:

Biological structures: This includes regions of the **brain,** the autonomic nervous system, the endocrine system (which produces hormones), and the pain-processing network that overlaps with emotional pathways. Together, they set the physical and chemical groundwork for our emotions, from stress responses to feelings of calm.

Cognitive Processes: These involve **mind/brain** interactions that label, interpret, and appraise the raw signals from our bodies and connect them with stored information and meaning. Our thoughts, memories, and learned associations should help us identify and decide whether a racing heart signals excitement, fear, or anger.

Social and Cultural Influences: Emotions don't develop in a vacuum. Family norms, cultural traditions, peer feedback, and societal expectations shape which emotions we consider appropriate, how strongly we feel them, and how we choose to express them.

Conscious Awareness (the "Mind" Aspect): Beyond purely automatic or learned responses, our reflective mind can notice, evaluate, and regulate emotional states. This self-awareness allows us to transform a fleeting feeling into a deliberate action (or inaction), modulate intensity, and guide emotional learning over time. As I mentioned before, the mind includes energy in the form of electricity, and its power goes beyond words or concepts. This element enables us to step back from automatic reactions and consciously shape our emotional future through deliberate choices and sustained awareness. How? We can utilize the electrical nature of consciousness as a bridge between our individual awareness and the vast energetic field of human knowledge and universal intelligence.

You may notice that I'm including the nervous system as part of the emotional system, but I want to clarify that I'm not suggesting it's a subset. Because the nervous system has recently taken center stage in discussions about emotional life, I include it here to highlight that it's not the sole driver. Both systems are deeply interwoven—much like the circulatory and respiratory systems. Each has distinct organs and functions, yet they intersect in fundamental ways. The nervous system and the emotional system have unique components as well but overlap heavily. Emotions depend on brain circuits, hormones, mental states, and physical sensations, while the nervous system orchestrates the signals that flow throughout the body—including those that underpin our emotional experiences.

In this emotional system structure, our conscious thoughts, past learning, and social context feed back into the system, shaping how emotions are constructed, interpreted, and acted upon. Each component interacts continuously with the others.

Biology sets the stage → Cognition interprets the signals → Social context shapes our responses → Conscious mind refines the process → Feeding back to influence our biology

This interaction enhances the brain's ability to **predict future events** by drawing on past experiences—**a key function of emotions.** This predictive process then sets the tone of our reactions, increasing the likelihood of success in our endeavors, mitigating risk, and helping us adapt to our environment and survive danger. I'll use this emotional system concept throughout the book to define emotions in a way that lets us use them to our advantage, rather than continuing to suffer from how poorly we sometimes manage them—or how intensely they manage us.

WHAT ARE EMOTIONS SUPPOSED TO BE DOING FOR US? ARE THEY HELPFUL IN ANY WAY?

Only in the 19th century did we begin to use the word "emotion" as a psychological category. Before that, mental states were classified in various ways, such as "appetites," "passions," "affections," or "drives." Notice how negative and loaded those terms are. This historical bias toward viewing emotions negatively was something I experienced firsthand in my formation. Early in my training as a Buddhist teacher, I learned that emotions are "delusions" that mask our true nature. Later, in the Tantric tradition, I learned to see emotions as energy—something that can be transformed. Eventually, through the Dzogchen tradition, I discovered how to recognize the wisdom within emotions themselves.

This evolution mirrors what modern psychology is beginning to affirm: emotions are part of our system's intelligence. They serve as messengers—alerting us to potential opportunities or threats, shaping our responses, and motivating us to act in service of our well-being. When understood and integrated, emotions don't cloud the mind—they guide it. But when ignored or suppressed, confusion takes hold, and suffering follows, as I explained in the example of the child being ignored by their mother that escalates the calling of *"MOM."*

The language itself encodes this understanding. The word "emotion" derives from the Latin "emovere," meaning "to move out" or "to stir up." This connection to movement is also present in the word "motivation," which shares the same Latin root, "movere" (to move). This etymology suggests we have always known they are not just passive feelings but forces that move us to action. I sometimes think that in the past, when we knew much less and science was more flexible, we were wiser.

In any case, over the years, many theories have tried to describe emotions in terms of facial expressions, survival mechanisms, social judgment, or personal traits. While each perspective offered valuable insights, none provided a complete picture. Only now—with advances in neuroscience and contributions from leading researchers—are we coming closer to the Dzogchen view of what emotions are and their important role in our lives.

New scientific studies indicate that emotions are not universal and automatic responses, as previously believed. Instead, **they are actively constructed by our brains in real time,** shaped by the experiences we accumulate, the cultural norms we learn, and the context of our situations—making them highly individualized, adaptable, and open to change. This viewpoint emphasizes that how we interpret our sensory experiences guides our actions. It also suggests we have more control over our emotional responses than we might have thought. Far from being random, negative, or unnecessary, emotions are integral to understanding ourselves and, when properly recognized, can become powerful allies.

What's the purpose of having emotions that make us feel so bad?

The reason emotions sometimes make us feel awful is actually part of their protective design. I know this is hard to believe, but I urge you to use emotions as they were meant to be used. *For example, fever is actually a manifestation of how hard our body is fighting infection for us. Yet our instinct is often to immediately take a pill to lower it, potentially interfering with this natural healing process.* Something similar happens with emotions. They're trying to alert us to important information about our situation, but we feel compelled to control or eliminate them immediately and believe they are part of the problem— *"You are making me angry," "I just want this sadness to go away,"* or *"I can't feel envy. It's wrong!"* for example.

This misunderstanding extends beyond emotions to how we view our brain's responses. I often come across content online that says something like, *"Trauma wires our brain to expect what hurt us last time."* While it is true that trauma can certainly leave a strong imprint, it's not just traumatic events that shape our responses—**every significant experience does!**

Our brain never stops learning the best way to navigate daily challenges and situations. Because our brain functions fundamentally as a prediction machine, it continuously stores relevant information—whether pleasant or unpleasant—and develops corresponding responses to help us navigate future situations. This predictive process doesn't apply only to threats; it also supports our ability to handle challenges, achieve goals, and maintain meaningful connections.

It's important that we shift our recent tendency toward catastrophizing, or seeing everything as damaging, into understanding that **the brain never really stops adapting;** it updates its mental map with each new, meaningful experience, whether it's a painful event, a major triumph, or even a subtle shift in our environment. If something was pivotal—positive or negative—the brain keeps a record of it, adjusting our perceptions and reactions accordingly.

When our emotions function for adaptation, the emotional system behaves like a learning algorithm that gradually refines our emotional responses based on new experiences. Think of how Google Ads learns from clicks and conversions, constantly adjusting which ads to show for better results. Similarly, our emotional system uses repeated exposure, healthy thinking patterns, and hopeful outlooks to integrate new knowledge and shape increasingly balanced, nuanced responses.

For instance, someone who was once criticized for a presentation might learn to prepare more thoroughly—an adaptive response—without developing a debilitating fear of public speaking. The shame or frustration from that experience motivates them to prepare better next time. Similarly, consider a scenario where a person experiences disappointment with a close friend yet uses this understanding to establish healthy boundaries instead of perceiving all new acquaintances as potential betrayals. In both examples, the conscious mind engages with presence and objectivity, helping the individual interpret each setback in context rather than as a generalized risk.

It's also true that emotions play a critical role in survival. Survival-focused emotions are designed to assist us in immediate threats. When faced with a truly dangerous situation—such as narrowly avoiding a car crash—our system goes into high alert. The body undergoes a series of intense physiological changes to help us respond. While these reactions are essential for getting us out of harm's way, they're not designed to become our baseline. These survival responses are powerful but **useful only when they're short-term**—they exist to help us protect ourselves from on-the-spot danger.

However, when fear is left unchecked—when we continue stacking reasons to feel unsafe or staying on high alert—a reactive script drowns out its original message, trapping the system in unnecessary distress.

Ultimately, adaptive emotions help us learn, grow, and respond to life's demands in a measured way, while survival emotions kick in when genuine danger looms, prompting us to act quickly and decisively.

Some emotions feel way more important than others—is that true?

It's true that some emotions have more influence over us than others. I'll walk you through the key emotions that shape our experience, exploring what each one is designed to do. We'll look at those that help us survive immediate threats and those that support our ability to adjust, connect, and thrive. Every emotion carries useful information—and once we understand their purpose, we can respond with clarity rather than confusion. Later, we'll explore how these emotions can change over time.

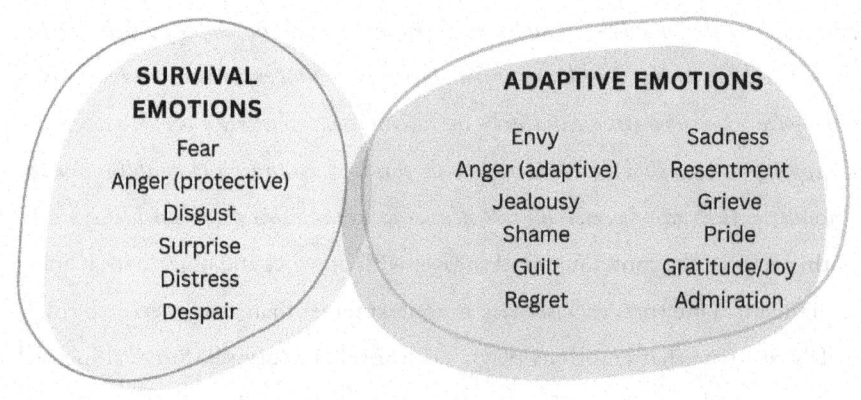

SURVIVAL EMOTIONS	ADAPTIVE EMOTIONS	
Fear	Envy	Sadness
Anger (protective)	Anger (adaptive)	Resentment
Disgust	Jealousy	Grieve
Surprise	Shame	Pride
Distress	Guilt	Gratitude/Joy
Despair	Regret	Admiration

Survival and Adaptive Emotions

Survival Emotions

These arise when our senses or internal detection system perceive potential threats—real or assumed—triggering protective responses like mobilization (run or punch) or immobilization (disappear or shut up). Designed to motivate us to act in ways that keep us alive, they can be intense, often involving surges of adrenaline and heightened vigilance. Survival emotions, while crucial in emergencies, can become overwhelming when activated too frequently or in the absence of an actual threat. The clearest defensive emotion is fear, but there are others as well.

FEAR: Heightens our awareness of **potential danger,** prompting us to consider how we can protect ourselves and prepare for what lies ahead. It exists on a spectrum of intensity, with different layers manifesting as trepidation, alarm, dread, horror, panic, or terror—depending on the level of activation. It's not the same as feeling insecure. We'll see later how insecurity is not an emotion but a perception of inadequacy that contributes to various emotional responses and defensive behaviors.

ANGER (protective): Alerts us to situations where we feel wronged, abused, or threatened, encouraging us to consider how we might assert boundaries and address injustices. Anger, at its core, is a protective emotion that is also adaptive.

SHAME (protective): Evolved as a social survival emotion. In early human groups, social exclusion could threaten physical survival, so shame became a deeply visceral response to potential rejection or failure to meet group norms. It signals, *"I've done something that could get me cast out."* From this lens, shame protects social bonds and belonging—critical for survival in a tribal context.

DISGUST: Helps protect us from potential contamination—whether physical (like spoiled food) or moral (taboos we find repellent). The reflexive aversion and revulsion serve an immediate protective purpose, much like fight-or-flight responses do for physical threats. It protects us by steering us away from disease-carrying substances or behaviors that might undermine social cohesion.

SURPRISE: Forces us to pause and gather more information, which can be lifesaving if a threat emerges unexpectedly.

DESPAIR: Emerges when we feel overwhelmed or unable to change our circumstances. Although it can be deeply painful, it also serves an adaptive purpose by pushing us to pause and acknowledge the gravity of what we're facing. This mental circuit breaker can help conserve emotional energy and signal profound need, prompting us (and those around us) to consider new sources of help or entirely different approaches.

Adaptive/Social Emotions

These emotions support our growth, connection, and fulfillment in everyday life. When these emotions flow freely, we feel resilient and equipped to handle challenges without cycling through fear or defensive reactivity.

ANGER (adaptive): Motivates us to take corrective action; it sharpens our focus on what's unjust, galvanizes us to stand up for our rights, and signals to others that a limit has been reached. In evolutionary terms, this burst of energy and clarity was essential for self-defense and asserting one's place within a social group. When used skillfully, anger becomes an ally rather than a liability, prompting us to address problems head-on, advocate for ourselves, set boundaries, and prevent further harm or disrespect.

SHAME (adaptive): Draws our attention to actions or qualities we believe misalign with our values, prompting us to consider how we can grow and reconnect with our best selves. Shame becomes destructive when it becomes chronic, toxic, or internalized as identity *("I am bad"* rather than *"I need to improve")*.

ENVY: Drives us to reflect on what others possess that we desire, encouraging us to consider how we might attain similar achievements or possessions.

JEALOUSY: Encourages us to protect and appreciate what we already have, especially when we feel it might be threatened by others.

GUILT: Motivates reparative action when we harm others (apologizing, fixing). Under normal circumstances, guilt helps maintain relationships and moral behavior.

SADNESS: Helps us process loss and change, inviting us to appreciate what we once had, recognize what we have now, and accept we need comfort, connection, and closeness. When we experience loss or failure, sadness makes us withdraw and conserve energy. It signals to others that we need help or comfort (think of a child crying—it elicits caregiving). Sadness also prompts reflection: we slow down to adjust to new realities (life without a loved one or after a setback). In evolution, this might help with learning (so we don't repeat mistakes) and with social bonding (drawing support from others).

RESENTMENT: Signals that we feel overlooked, oppressed, or unfairly treated, encouraging us to consider and express our boundaries and needs and to seek ways of addressing unresolved conflicts.

REGRET: Motivates us to reflect on choices we wish we had made differently, guiding us to learn from our mistakes, realign with our values, and make more intentional decisions moving forward.

GRIEF: Arises in response to loss—whether the loss of a loved one, a cherished opportunity, or any other important attachment. While it may include sadness, yearning, and even anger, it ultimately helps us process the reality of what's gone. By allowing us to mourn and share our pain with supportive others, grief acts as a bridge to gradual healing, making space for both remembrance and adaptation to a changed life circumstance.

PRIDE: Encourages us to recognize our own accomplishments or positive qualities. By highlighting personal success, it boosts self-confidence and motivates us to persist in challenging tasks or to set new goals. When channeled constructively, pride drives continued growth and self-improvement.

GRATITUDE: Shifts our focus to what we have received or achieved—often due to others' efforts or support—and inspires us to reciprocate kindness or maintain supportive relationships.

ADMIRATION: Arises when we witness qualities or achievements in others that we respect or aspire to. It prompts us to learn from their example and sparks self-development.

JOY: Emerges when something goes well or aligns with our hopes and values. It naturally rewards behaviors and situations that benefit our well-being, reinforcing positive choices. On a social level, expressions of joy can strengthen communal ties by spreading a shared sense of delight and optimism.

As you can see, each emotion—whether survival-focused or adaptive—carries important information about our internal state and external circumstances. Rather than viewing emotions as problems to solve, we can begin to see them as an intelligent guidance system designed to help us navigate life's complexities. The key is learning to listen to their messages without being overwhelmed when they grow in their intensity—and developing the ability to regulate that intensity when needed.

So apparently everything I learned about emotions is outdated. What's the real story?

Emotions have been studied for decades, yet there is no single, universally accepted definition that captures their full complexity and diversity. Much of the work focused on how emotions relate to one another—investigating whether certain core emotions exist and whether emotional expressions are universal across cultures. This work includes cross-cultural research examining similarities and differences in how people label, experience, and interpret emotions. However, debates continue about how to define, categorize, and measure the multitude of emotional states people report. A notable contemporary view of emotions—the Theory of Constructed Emotion (TCE)—by Lisa Feldman Barrett regards them as constructed experiences, offering a significant shift in how we understand and address emotional struggles.

I use the TCE because it offers one of the most promising frameworks available—integrating both scientific evidence and clear reasoning. It proposes that each of us builds our own emotions over time. Since its emergence, it has been an inspiration to explore how this constructed experience relates to the way we emotionally interact with the world and how it connects to our suffering.

We can now say that **emotions are the day-to-day expressions of how our emotional system coordinates its many components.** This system includes our brain's limbic circuits, our physiological feedback loops (like heart rate and breathing), and—very importantly—our learned storyboards, which together shape how each emotion unfolds in real time.

We'll see throughout the book that **emotional construction** is especially relevant to understanding trauma manifestations. Traumatized individuals often struggle to make sense of their emotional reactions and overwhelming internal states. Through the TCE lens, it becomes clear that the construction of emotions—especially fear—doesn't simply stop with the traumatic event. Their meaning and instructions can continue unfolding, sometimes intensifying to the point where emotional reactions feel disproportionate or irrational. After all, what keeps the survival circuits active is fear, and what makes fear so powerful is that it keeps accumulating reasons to explain the lack of safety.

But let's be clear: all emotions—whether linked to survival or adaptation—involve the activation of brain circuits, the release of neurotransmitters, changes in the body (like shifts in heart rate), and behavioral reactions. They are, first and foremost, internal experiences felt as either pleasant or unpleasant, calming or arousing. This perspective helps us recognize that **nearly every experience activates an internal emotional response and that unpleasant feelings are a natural, hardwired, unavoidable part of human experience.** These automatic responses aren't something we consciously create or choose. Still, we *can* learn to interpret and respond to them in ways that reduce unnecessary suffering.

Constructed Emotions Architecture (CEA).

The construction of emotions is actually quite complex. Emotions are constructed by the brain through a combination of bodily sensations, previous experiences, and social context. The brain pieces together emotions rather than simply letting them arise. Each emotion includes not only a feeling but also a set of internal instructions that guide how we react. Understanding these elements gives us the opportunity to reshape emotional responses by changing how we interpret and relate to what we feel.

The construction process is ongoing—every new encounter can add depth or complexity to how we perceive, express, and engage with our emotional life, evolving organically through each significant experience. I call this constant updating our "emotional architecture," which can be broken down as follows:

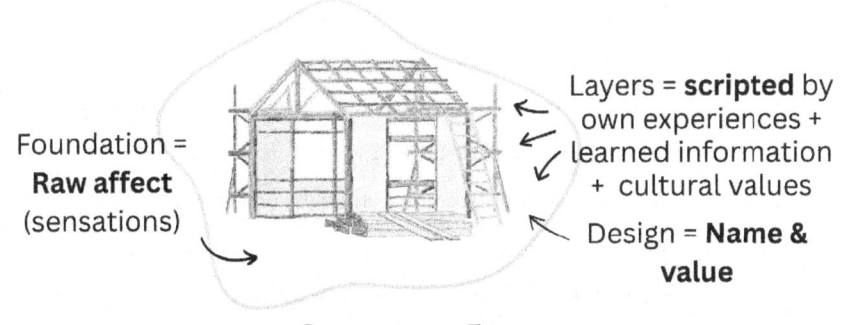

Foundation = **Raw affect** (sensations)

Layers = **scripted** by own experiences + learned information + cultural values

Design = **Name & value**

Constructing our Emotions

I) Bodily Sensations (Raw Affect): The first element of an emotion emerges from our body's reactions to stimuli, thoughts, perceptions, or values. This activity might be the innate seed of what will eventually become a specific emotion, carrying the essential qualities I described earlier for each emotion type. Just as when we're hungry our stomach rumbles without needing the conscious thought, *"I should eat,"* when we encounter rotten food our stomach tightens and we may feel a wave of nausea—immediate sensations that occur long before we consciously register, *"This is disgusting."* These sensations are rooted in biology, as our brain and body cooperate to prepare us for potential action, threats, challenges, or rewards.

II) Labeling: The next step in creating each emotion involves the brain assigning a label or name—such as "sadness," "fear," or "gratitude"—to the raw bodily sensations, along with an overall sense of whether the experience is pleasant or unpleasant. Most people recognize these labels in similar ways, much like shared concepts in language. For instance, we learn that "disgust" refers to the tightness and nausea experienced when smelling rotten food.

Just as our brain distinguishes whether an emotion is "disgust" or "joy," it also determines whether the situation calls for adaptation (managing everyday challenges) or survival (responding to genuine danger). Based on this assessment, the brain decides in an instant how much conscious, cognitive participation is needed or whether an automatic response should take over. In essence, it determines whether the emotion represents an emergency or an opportunity to engage (and learn).

III) Value: The name is stored along with the experience's value—how negative or positive it turned out to be. For example, if your encounter with the rotten food made you violently ill, your brain might store disgust with an extremely high negative value. But if you simply avoided the food and felt relieved afterward, the same disgust label might be stored with a moderate negative value—unpleasant but bearable. If our labeling skews overly negative, or if we learned early on to label cognitively harmless stimuli as threatening, we risk misinterpreting otherwise useful signals. The result can be unnecessary rejection or avoidance instead of a measured response. This is precisely why understanding how emotions are constructed—and learning to build them in a balanced, organic way—matters.

IV) Emotional Scripts: The next stage in constructing emotions involves personal experience and cultural learning, which makes your emotional response different from mine. Perhaps your parents repeatedly warned you that *"any food with a strong smell is bad for you."* That view may have become part of your mental storyboard, labeling any intense odors as dangerous. You might react negatively to pungent cheese, while in my culture it's considered a staple and labeled "delicious," triggering no alarm. What's disgusting to you isn't necessarily disgusting to me.

By taking on the values and meanings others attach to experiences—especially regarding safety/danger or benefit/detriment—we develop scripts (storyboards) that dictate how we respond when an emotion surfaces. As these scripts continue to accumulate negative value and meaning, whether from actual experiences, imagined scenarios, or influence from others' beliefs, we lose sight of the emotion's original purpose—to protect or guide us. Instead, we let the scripts dominate our responses, causing us to avoid experiences or interpret them as damaging, even when they aren't.

V) Emotional Responses: Our emotional scripts ultimately shape our real-world actions and reactions. Although I am discussing them separately here, these responses and their instructions are also components of the emotion's storyboard. For instance, if your disgust script indicates that a strong smell equals a hazard, it may instruct you to push the plate away, urgently warn others, or refuse to stay near the food. Meanwhile, someone with a different script might just shrug and calmly discard the questionable item or even taste it first.

This is what often happens in real life. Without knowing why, certain emotions become heavy and taxing, and we lose control over how we behave. This occurs because we may not realize we need to be **active participants** in constructing our emotional responses.

This construction process—combining bodily sensations, learned scripts, and contextual meaning—gives us the fundamental components of any emotion. From there, these components can create brief emotional reactions (like a flash of anger), longer-lasting moods (like feeling irritable all day), or persistent emotional patterns (like chronic anxiety), depending on factors like how intense the trigger is, how long it lasts, and our personal history with similar situations.

Bodily Sensations → Labeling → Value → Scripts → Responses

Should we just let emotions play out or try to manage them?

I once had a client who believed she had never felt anger, having been taught that it was an inappropriate emotion for a "lady." Yet instead of acknowledging her anger, she often found herself fantasizing about hurting the people who treated her poorly. In her case, "acting out" her anger didn't look like yelling or confrontation—it meant doing nothing externally while channeling that emotion into vivid internal fantasies.

We often assume that "acting out" means dramatic outbursts, yet emotional expression can be just as powerful in quieter forms—withdrawal, silence, or fantasy.

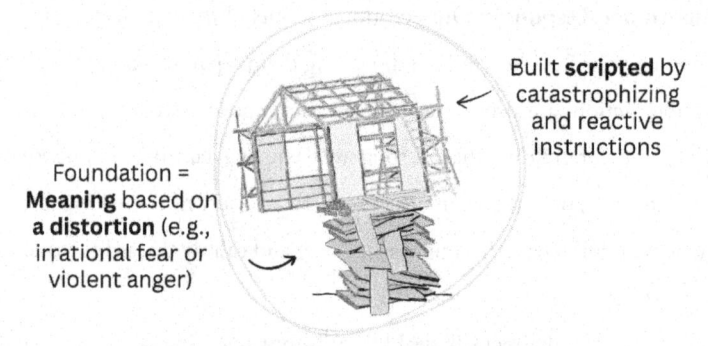

Built **scripted** by catastrophizing and reactive instructions

Foundation = **Meaning** based on **a distortion** (e.g., irrational fear or violent anger)

Emotion Built on a Distorted Script

As we've discussed, emotions begin as raw affective states. That raw affect doesn't offer detailed instructions—only an initial signal, like an urge to run or strike. Most of what comes next depends on how we interpret those sensations shaped by past experiences—even those that weren't real threats—or information absorbed through media (movies, news, social platforms, etc.).

If we pause and reflect on our impulses—and revisit the scripts we've built, as we did in the earlier exercise—we can begin to transform them. But most of the time—and perhaps because a few of us are taught how to work with our scripts proactively—our interpretations become hardwired into the storyboard that defines how emotions should be handled and what behaviors should follow. Scripts can serve us well when they're flexible and context-aware. But when they're rigid, outdated, or rooted in traumatic memories, they may lead us to react in ways that no longer fit the present.

For example, someone whose anger script was shaped in a turbulent environment—or influenced by exposure to violent movies or video games—might escalate a minor frustration into physical aggression, believing on some level that hitting is the best path to safety or respect. Another person might respond to anger by going quiet or walking away if their past experiences taught them this was the most adaptive option. In both cases, the underlying emotion of anger isn't the problem; it's the storyboard that can either help or harm, depending on how accurately it reflects current reality. Aggression might be an effective response in one situation but not in another. Likewise, staying quiet may have been adaptive in the past but may no longer serve in the current context.

Ultimately, whether or not we act on emotional impulses should depend on the context—including our safety, social norms, and overall well-being. Emotions provide vital signals, but once negative experiences accumulate, the behaviors they inspire may need to be assessed, reassessed, and, when necessary, rewritten. As we move through life, our scripts can evolve—with new insights, new experiences, and better guidance.

Do we experience emotions one by one, or do we experience several at the same time?

We've been exploring emotions and how they're constructed and updated by focusing on one emotion at a time. However, real-life emotional experiences seldom occur in isolation. Research suggests we don't always experience emotions strictly one by one, nor always multiple at once—it can be a mix, depending on the situation.

Most often, we feel several emotions simultaneously because our brains process multiple stimuli and internal states at the same time. *For example, you might experience joy upon seeing a loved one and, at the same time, anxiety about an upcoming conversation with them.* This reasoning makes sense from a neural standpoint: emotions share common physiological and neurological pathways. Neuroscience shows that the amygdala, for instance, doesn't simply signal fear—it responds to anything emotionally significant, potentially contributing to multiple emotions (joy, sadness, anger) at once, depending on the context. In intense situations, one emotion may dominate—think terror during a near-accident—but that doesn't mean all other feelings vanish; they're just overshadowed in the moment.

Moreover, key processes like detecting the importance of an event, labeling, regulating, and processing bodily sensations remain active across various emotions. A single situation—like receiving bittersweet news (say, a promotion that involves moving away from loved ones)—may trigger multiple bodily responses concurrently: a racing heart (arousal), a tight chest (sadness), and a warm flush (excitement). **The brain doesn't box these signals into a single emotion; it processes them in parallel.**

When faced with something complex, the brain doesn't always settle on one label. Instead, it generates multiple interpretations—sometimes contradictory, sometimes complementary. Take reuniting with an old friend: it might spark joy *("I've missed them!")* and regret *("Why didn't I stay in touch?")* simultaneously. Higher-order thinking lets us juggle these mixed reactions.

This parallel processing means that every stage of emotional construction—bodily sensations, labeling, assigning value, scripts, and responses—can reflect multiple emotional themes at once. During the labeling stage, for example, we might tag bodily signals with overlapping or even conflicting descriptors, like "both sad and excited" or "both relieved and anxious." Our scripts can diverge as well, leading to behaviors that reflect a mix of competing impulses. This internal complexity often fuels emotional conflict, leaving us feeling polarized and uncertain about how we truly feel.

Some frameworks describe these mixed facets as "parts," treating them as distinct sub-personalities, each with its own perspective and emotional narrative. While evocative, this approach can sometimes deepen confusion, fragmenting our sense of self further. What I'm trying to do in this chapter is propose a simpler path: addressing each emotion individually to organize our emotional system. Understanding each emotion and how it has been built around our most significant events could be the key to managing them more effectively. When we've been emotionally wounded, those experiences often hijack the construction process, causing us to build emotions around protection and avoidance rather than accurate assessment of current reality.

Discover Where All That Emotional Pain Comes From

"Pain yells when we stop hearing what it's trying to say."

Now that we've explored the construction and development of emotions, we can examine why they sometimes hurt so much. Emotions begin as guides that motivate us to take action. But after difficult or overwhelming experiences, they change big time. Instead of motivating us to act, they become intense and confusing, causing pain that lingers longer than it should.

These newly programmed emotional reactions accumulate layers of maladaptive reactivity, making our responses harder to manage and, ironically, less protective. In this section, we'll explore why emotional pain can feel so overwhelming and how these shifts in our emotional responses can trap us in cycles of hurt.

Why Do Emotions Make Us Suffer So Much?

Let's take hunger and thirst as examples to explore why we suffer. For adults, these sensations are usually manageable and not inherently painful. But for babies, hunger or thirst can be deeply distressing. Once we learn to recognize these sensations and know how to respond—by drinking water and eating—we're able to ease the discomfort. A baby, however, has no awareness that the feeling is temporary or easily resolved. That's why they cry—because they rely on someone else to soothe the discomfort they can't yet understand or manage.

We can think of emotions in a similar way. We suffer when we don't realize that emotions are transient signals—messages indicating that something needs attention—and that we can work with them skillfully to find resolution. Emotions themselves don't inherently cause suffering. The distress comes from how emotions are constructed, interpreted, and managed within our emotional system, as well as our lack of awareness that they can be redirected or even reprogrammed.

We experience distress because we often attach meanings that weigh heavily on us, shaped by how we've interpreted our experiences (such as seeing criticism as proof we're worthless)—yet we're rarely taught to frame these interpretations in more constructive or less damaging ways (understanding that others' reactions often reflect their own struggles rather than our flaws).

Almost by default, we brace for negative outcomes, believing, for instance, that staying hypervigilant will protect us more effectively than letting our guard down or that yelling when we're angry will earn others' respect, without ever stopping to question these assumptions and their consequences for our well-being. In doing so, we let our emotions grow like ivy, gradually winding around everything in their path. Over time, the tangled vines become harder to trim back, obscuring our original perspective and making it nearly impossible to see what's underneath. If we never stop to prune or guide this growth, it can choke out healthier ways of feeling and thinking—turning our natural emotional responses into something unmanageable and overwhelming.

Our emotions directly influence perception by changing how the brain interprets incoming information. When strong emotions are present, our brain filters sensory input differently, prioritizing cues that match the emotion while muting contradictory information.

For example, if you think *"I'm ugly"* and feel disgust, your brain shifts into an emotional state where you may become afraid of being rejected, which will make it look for evidence to confirm that risk. Instead of seeing the whole picture—your genuine smile, kind eyes, or how others respond positively to you—your attention becomes laser-focused on perceived flaws: that small blemish you're convinced everyone notices, the way your face looks when you're concentrating, or imagining that you smell bad when you don't. Your brain essentially creates a filter that blocks out contradictory information and amplifies anything that seems to confirm the threat.

The process isn't just psychological—it's biological. Stress-related chemicals like cortisol and adrenaline affect how our pupils respond to light, how quickly we scan our environment, and even how memory retrieves information. Over time, this emotional filtering shapes our perception more powerfully than external facts, creating habitual patterns that become difficult to break without conscious intervention.

Think of someone who struggles with self-image and weight. They might find themselves constantly noticing other people who are overweight, unconsciously scanning for comparison or reassurance. But instead of finding relief, this habit reinforces the idea that their weight defines them—deepening their focus on the issue and feeding the very insecurity they're hoping to escape.

These value judgments directly influence our perception and lead us to interpret experiences more positively or negatively based on how we initially construct the emotion. We often strengthen these interpretations through the thoughts and beliefs we revisit frequently. Over time, these interpretations begin to feel unquestionably real.

When this perceived reality becomes particularly negative, we experience emotional distress and the painful consequences of that mindset—reinforcing the mistaken belief that the emotion itself is causing our suffering.

Is Emotional Pain Just In Our Heads?

No, emotional pain isn't "just in our heads"—it's processed by the same brain networks as physical injury. While our thoughts can influence how we experience it, that doesn't make it less real or important.

Emotional wounds primarily activate our pain system—the complex network in the body and brain responsible for detecting and responding to potential disconnection or hurt. This pain system responds to events that challenge our confidence, well-being, sense of self, social bonds, or deeply held beliefs, creating subjective experiences of distress that feel very real because they are real.

It has been proposed that because social bonds and acceptance are crucial for mammals, the brain evolved to treat emotional pain as seriously as physical injury—signaling that something essential, like potential alienation, may be at stake. Feeling emotional pain physically motivates action: to seek support, to rejoin the pack, or to move away from harm.

For humans, emotional pain often stems from interpersonal situations (e.g., rejection, loss, betrayal), internal conflicts (such as shame or guilt), or unmet emotional needs (like loneliness or lack of appreciation). These experiences push us to modify our behavior, re-evaluate relationships, or reconsider our choices and values in ways that support adaptation and improve our chances of success in the world. Because emotional pain shares neural circuits with physical pain, the same principles of tolerance and subjectivity apply. Pain—whether physical or emotional—is always subjective.

It wasn't until the 1980s that a pharmaceutical company introduced the idea of using a 0-to-10 scale to guide pain medication dosage by simply asking patients how much pain they felt. If we had such a scale for emotional wounds, it would be just as personal—and just as "real."

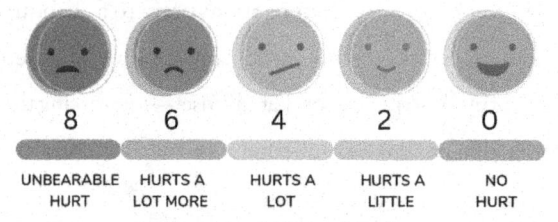

Emotional Wound Scale

As you can see, this approach isn't strictly scientific. You choose a number—or a face—based on your personal perception of pain and your current tolerance for discomfort, making the rating entirely subjective.

But here's the fascinating part: if you consciously introduce a more positive or reassuring thought into your mind, your rating can immediately change. This shift illustrates just how powerfully our mental state influences our experience of pain—and how managing discomfort is possible.

> **Tolerating Pain Practice.** Here's an exercise you can try to lower emotional pain.
>
> Bring to mind a memory or thought that feels emotionally painful.

Take a moment to tune in and notice where any physical discomfort arises in your body. Stay with that sensation, and briefly rate its intensity on a scale from 0 to 8 (or a face from the illustration)—just to establish a starting point.

Keep your attention gently focused on the area of discomfort for a few seconds. Then, shift your awareness to a part of your body that feels neutral or even pleasant. Perhaps your hands are warm, your feet feel grounded, or your breath is moving smoothly. Settle into that sensation of ease, breathing into it slowly and intentionally for about a minute.

Now, return your attention to the original area of discomfort and rate it again. Has the intensity changed?

You may find that the discomfort has softened—even slightly—demonstrating how a small shift in attention can ease pain. This simple redirection highlights the mind's ability to reshape our experience of distress.

Practice this often to gradually increase your emotional pain tolerance and strengthen your trust in both the power of your mind and the wisdom of your system. Each time you do, you're reinforcing your inner capacity to heal and adapt.

Does Emotional Pain Change Someone Mentally?

Indeed, emotional pain can alter a person's mental state, often in unexpected ways. Our mind—less bound by biological reflexes than our body—is uniquely capable of shaping, amplifying, or numbing our emotional experiences over time. Just as positive emotions like joy, love, and accomplishment can expand our sense of possibility and resilience, painful experiences can alter fundamental assumptions about trust, safety, and self-worth, influencing how we perceive our abilities, relationships, and life possibilities. As a result, people may become more cynical, avoidant, or emotionally reactive after extended periods of emotional pain. To better understand how this shift happens, it helps to look at how emotions operate across different layers of time and intensity—starting with emotional states, then moods, and finally emotionality itself.

Emotional States (Short-Term Context). Emotional states are brief, situation-specific reactions to immediate events or triggers. They're what emotions look like in action, shaped by context. They can be intense but typically fade once the stimulus is gone or is processed. However, when emotional states are repeated frequently—or paired with unresolved pain—they can reshape how we interpret similar situations in the future, influencing our scripts and emotional values.

For example, someone who once felt joy around dogs may develop fear after a single painful bite—reinterpreting "future encounters with dogs" as dangerous. This can evolve into a new emotional script that replaces the previous association (joy with dogs) with a fear-based construct. As a result, future encounters with dogs may automatically trigger emotional states of fear, even in safe contexts, until the person consciously participates in modifying the emotional response.

Mood (Sustained Emotional Backdrop). Moods are more prolonged and less intense than emotional states, often emerging without a clear trigger. They influence how we filter our experiences. Persistent emotional pain can lower our mood baseline, coloring everything we encounter and making us more susceptible to negative interpretations—even when the moment itself is neutral.

A person experiencing a low mood may perceive a neutral conversation as criticism or interpret a delayed reply as rejection. These interpretations then reinforce the emotional pain, shaping how future events are felt and remembered.

Emotionality (Higher-Level Perspective). Over time, repeated emotional pain doesn't just affect our moods—it can reshape **emotionality**—the tendency to feel emotions more intensely, frequently, or unpredictably. People with heightened emotionality often have more reactive nervous systems and may struggle with emotional regulation, especially when past pain has distorted the scripts associated with their emotions.

For instance, someone who experienced rigid or shaming reactions to their emotions growing up may now interpret even mild sadness or anger as unacceptable, triggering overwhelming responses.

When emotional pain is left unprocessed, it doesn't just sit in memory—it modifies how our emotions are built and expressed, affecting their very architecture. That's how emotional suffering can reshape perception and identity over time.

In other words, emotional pain—if left unresolved—can change the value, script, and reactivity of our emotions, making our emotional life feel more overwhelming and difficult. Using the language commonly found nowadays, "it rewires the brain"—not as severely as trauma, but significantly nonetheless.

> **Perspective Shift Check.** If you repeatedly find yourself stuck in negativity, or if emotional or physical pain becomes overwhelming, practice this exercise:
>
> Ask yourself while focusing on a recent emotional wound, *"Am I reinforcing this emotional wound by continually focusing on its negative meaning, or am I actively seeking alternative perspectives that might help me feel better?"*
>
> Simply by posing this question, you may already notice a reduction in your discomfort and prevent further negative consequences.

Why are therapists always asking, "Where do you feel it in your body?" Are we supposed to feel something?

It's increasingly common to take a somatic perspective when discussing emotions, especially in the context of trauma. Yes, the question, *"Where do you feel it in your body?"* is very common in therapy. While many people have become comfortable identifying physical sensations that accompany emotions, others operate more cognitively and remain unsure of what the question really means.

Building the ability—or "muscle"—to identify bodily sensations is extremely useful, as it's one of the most accessible ways to anchor yourself in the present moment and connect with the "seed" of the emotion. With that in mind, I'm providing a guide to how different emotional pains often show up physically, commonly manifesting in distinct areas of the body.

Where do you feel it in your body?

Head: stress, worry, confusion, mental overload, overthinking, lack of intuition

Shoulders/neck: chronic stress, overwhelm, emotional burden, responsibility

Jaw: Frustration, anger, anxiety, suppressed expression

Chest: grief, rejection, loss, isolation, difficulty giving/receiving love

Throat: sadness, grief, helplessness, suppression of emotions, no expression

Stomach: anxiety, worry, dread, fear

Pelvis/genitals: fear (survival and abandonment), insecurity, lack of stability, shame, disconnection from self

Limbs: helplessness, exhaustion, vulnerability, fear of action or moving forward

Sensations Felt in the Body

Chest: Tightness, heaviness, or aching near the heart often relates to grief, rejection, or loss. When emotionally distressed, our breathing patterns change, heart muscles tense, and stress hormones increase—creating physical sensations that match the emotional experience. This is why rejection or heartbreak can feel like a literal physical ache in your chest. In many energy-centered traditions, this area contains the **Heart Chakra**, which relates to love, compassion, and emotional connection. It's believed by many that blockages in this energy center manifest as difficulty giving or receiving love, grief, or feelings of isolation. Blockages in this area can be rooted in unprocessed pain or unresolved grief.

Stomach/Gut: Anxiety, worry, and dread often show up as tightness, knots, or "butterflies" in the stomach. The gut-brain axis plays a central role here: emotional distress and stress hormones like cortisol can quickly disrupt digestive functions. Blood flow is redirected away from digestion during stress, causing the smooth muscles in the stomach to tighten or spasm. These reactions can lead to queasiness, churning, or the sensation of having a stomach in knots. From an evolutionary perspective, digestion is deprioritized during stress or danger, which is why we often feel tense or nauseous when we're anxious or afraid. Additionally, the **Solar Plexus Chakra**—believed in energy-based traditions to govern our sense of identity and personal agency—is associated with this area. Emotional pain tied to shame, powerlessness, or fear of judgment is thought to especially impact this region.

Throat: Feelings of sadness, grief, or helplessness can manifest as a "lump" in the throat, sometimes making speech difficult. This lump sensation often arises when we're suppressing or controlling strong emotions. It's an instinctive physiological reaction in which the throat muscles contract to prevent crying, screaming, or other emotional vocalizations. From an evolutionary perspective, briefly stifling these expressions might have protected individuals from drawing unwanted attention during vulnerable moments, which helps explain the link between throat sensations and emotional pain. Energetically, the throat area houses the **Communication Chakra**, governing self-expression and truth-telling. Difficulty expressing emotions or speaking one's truth is thought to create constriction in this energy center.

Head: Stress, worry, and confusion can translate into headaches or pressure around the temples and forehead. Mental strain leads to muscle tension, particularly in the face, jaw, and scalp. The more we ruminate on concerns, the more these muscles tighten, creating sensations of heaviness, pressure, or throbbing. Additionally, the **Brow Chakra** at the forehead and the **Crown Chakra** at the top of the head are associated with intuition, wisdom, and higher consciousness in various traditions. Mental overload, overthinking, or disconnection from intuition may be experienced as tension in these areas from an energetic perspective. You may even notice that in some people, the vein in the forehead becomes evident, showing how more blood is trying to navigate through compressed blood vessels, as chronic tension restricts normal circulation in the head and face.

Shoulders and Neck: Chronic stress and responsibility often accumulate as tension in these areas. When we feel overwhelmed or burdened by life's demands, we literally carry that weight in our upper body, resulting in stiffness and pain. While not a primary chakra location, this area sits between the heart and throat chakras and can reflect challenges in balancing emotional expression (throat) with vulnerability (heart).

Jaw: Frustration, anger, and anxiety commonly appear as jaw clenching or tension. Many people unconsciously tighten these muscles when suppressing difficult emotions or facing situations where they feel they cannot express themselves freely. The jaw is related to the **Throat Chakra** and may tense when there's resistance to expressing difficult emotions or speaking authentically.

Limbs: Feelings of helplessness, exhaustion, or vulnerability might manifest as heaviness, weakness, or tingling in the arms and legs. These sensations reflect how emotions influence our readiness to act in the world, though tingling can also be perceived as life energy with a very positive tone. In some energy medicine traditions, extremities are viewed as extensions of our power to act in the world, with arms relating to giving/receiving and legs to moving forward in life. Sensations here might reflect challenges in these aspects of living.

Pelvis/Genitals: Emotional pain in the pelvic region is often tied to feelings of fear, shame, and vulnerability, particularly around issues of safety, survival, and sexuality. This area is the physical home of the **Root Chakra** in energy-centered traditions, associated with grounding, belonging, and basic trust in the world. When we experience early instability, abandonment, violation, or chronic stress, this region can hold tension, numbness, or a sense of disconnection. People may report tightness in the pelvic floor, avoidance of physical closeness, or a lack of sensation in this area—not always from overt trauma, but sometimes from subtle or prolonged experiences that made them feel unwanted. Energetically and somatically, this part of the body reflects our relationship with the most primal aspects of being: our right to exist, to be supported, and to feel at home in our body.

These physical manifestations occur because emotional and physical pain share many of the same neural pathways and chemical messengers. Our brains and bodies don't maintain strict separation between emotional and physical discomfort—they're part of the same integrated system designed to help us respond to our environment. Also, emotions literally "move" something in our system, which is part of what they're trying to indicate needs attention.

How can you tell if someone is hurting emotionally?

Most of us haven't learned to view our emotional struggles in a healthy light or to care for them appropriately. We often resist acknowledging emotions as a natural part of our experience, and many of us feel ashamed—not only of what we feel, but of our difficulty managing those feelings. That's why, when someone is hurting emotionally, they might not express it directly. However, their pain often reveals itself through noticeable changes in behavior and physiology.

Sometimes, accumulated emotional pain can reach such intensity that it creates overwhelming episodes. Take shame, for example. When shame builds up over time and combines with other difficult emotions like fear, disappointment, or anger, it can trigger what feels like an emotional avalanche. These **"shame attacks"** feel so unbearable that the person desperately wants to disappear—to hide from the world or escape their own awareness through whatever means available, whether that's isolating completely, numbing through substances, or dissociating from the overwhelming feelings entirely. The pain becomes so intense that the mind seeks any form of relief, even temporary oblivion.

Consider Lena, who was struggling with deep insecurities and decided to "borrow" a designer dress from a friend's closet to impress people at an important social event. The friend discovered it and confronted her publicly, calling her out in front of the very people she was trying to impress; the resulting shame attack was beyond her tolerance. The combination of humiliation, being exposed, and terror of judgment created such unbearable emotional intensity that Lena rushed to hide, desperately wanting to escape her own skin, and even had thoughts of harming herself just to make the crushing feelings stop. The result was a shame attack in action—emotional pain so severe it feels genuinely life-threatening.

A particularly positive trend is the growing willingness among younger generations to discuss mental health and emotional struggles openly. However, there's sometimes a distinction between discussing emotional pain intellectually and actually feeling and processing those emotions. Some people can articulate their struggles with remarkable sophistication, using therapeutic language and mental health terminology, while remaining disconnected from the actual emotional experience. They may understand their patterns cognitively but haven't developed the capacity to sit with and integrate difficult emotions. This intellectual approach, while valuable for awareness, can sometimes become another way of staying removed from the deeper work of emotional resolution.

Someone dealing with ongoing, unresolved emotional pain may begin to withdraw from friends, family, or social activities without understanding why. Others might notice a loss of interest or joy in things they once enjoyed. They may seem more irritable, impatient, or reactive to minor frustrations. Other signs can include changes in sleep or eating habits, declining self-care, and trouble concentrating. Emotional distress can also manifest physically—through headaches, muscle tension, or other unexplained discomfort.

This internal struggle often leads to physical strain, as the person remains mentally preoccupied with pessimism, regret, or despair. When we're emotionally hurting, we tend to replay the situations that caused our pain, and the more we mentally circle the wound, the more it hurts. You may notice that what I'm describing may sound like the descriptions of trauma you find everywhere. It doesn't have to be.

What can make these episodes particularly distressing is that too much emotion can cause us to panic about feeling out of control, creating a perfect storm that can feel genuinely life-threatening to the person experiencing it, even though there's no external danger present.

It's not unlike a physical injury—if you keep pressing on a sore spot, the pain intensifies. The system is asking for attention, signaling that something needs care, but dwelling on the pain only worsens it.

When the pain becomes extreme, the person may disconnect from it entirely. However, when we disconnect from pain, we often lose access to joy and other emotions as well, diminishing our capacity to "listen" to what our system needs.

A common reason emotional wounds remain unresolved is the belief that healing requires involvement from the person who caused the hurt. In reality, the pain itself can obscure a deeper truth: the path to resolution lies within, not in the hope that someone else will undo the original damage.

In my experience, the one who "stabs" you rarely stitches the wound they caused. Those who hurt others are often either incapable of taking responsibility for what they did or are simply not interested in repairing it. That realization sometimes hurts even more than the original offense, especially if you have been waiting for them for a long time before moving on.

One way to recognize when someone is emotionally stuck is by noticing if they're caught in an unending narrative—repeatedly revisiting the same story without moving toward resolution. They may constantly explain how they were wronged, insist on reparations, or focus on why they can't forgive. This loop can prevent emotional processing and keep the wound unresolved.

> **"Am I Carrying Emotional Pain?" Quiz.** Here is a self-assessment quiz to help you recognize emotional suffering that may be active beneath the surface.
>
> Try to respond based on a recent experience.
>
> Consider **Rarely as** once a month or less, **Sometimes as** a few times a month to weekly, and **Often as** multiple times per week to daily.
>
> **Emotional Energy**
>
> ☐ Rarely ☐ Sometimes ☐ Often — *I feel emotionally drained, even without clear reasons.*
>
> ☐ Rarely ☐ Sometimes ☐ Often — *I feel disconnected from joy or a sense of aliveness.*
>
> ☐ Rarely ☐ Sometimes ☐ Often — *I avoid situations that might make me feel too much.*
>
> **Inner Dialogue**
>
> ☐ Rarely ☐ Sometimes ☐ Often — *I find myself stuck on past hurts or rehashing old conversations.*
>
> ☐ Rarely ☐ Sometimes ☐ Often — *I feel ashamed of something I haven't been enable to move past.*
>
> ☐ Rarely ☐ Sometimes ☐ Often — *I often question whether I'm overreacting or being dramatic.*
>
> ☐ Rarely ☐ Sometimes ☐ Often — *I wish someone would finally acknowledge how much something hurt me.*
>
> **Body and Nervous System**
>
> ☐ Rarely ☐ Sometimes ☐ Often — *I notice physical tension, fatigue, or tightness I can't easily explain.*
>
> ☐ Rarely ☐ Sometimes ☐ Often — *My sleep or appetite has changed, even if I don't feel "upset."*

☐ Rarely ☐ Sometimes ☐ Often — *I feel keyed up or numb for long periods, without a clear trigger.*

Behavior and Functioning

☐ Rarely ☐ Sometimes ☐ Often — *I keep myself busy to avoid feelings I can't name.*

☐ Rarely ☐ Sometimes ☐ Often — *I struggle to care about things I normally value.*

☐ Rarely ☐ Sometimes ☐ Often — *I've pulled away from people without knowing exactly why.*

☐ Rarely ☐ Sometimes ☐ Often — *I react more strongly than usual to small stressors or criticism.*

Self and Relationships

☐ Rarely ☐ Sometimes ☐ Often — *I find it hard to be fully open with others, even those I trust.*

☐ Rarely ☐ Sometimes ☐ Often — *I sometimes feel like I'm carrying something others can't see.*

☐ Rarely ☐ Sometimes ☐ Often — *I worry that my pain is a burden.*

☐ Rarely ☐ Sometimes ☐ Often — *I minimize my struggles even to myself.*

If you answered **Often** to several items, you may be carrying emotional pain that hasn't been fully seen, processed, or supported.

If **Sometimes** dominates, it might be a sign that something unresolved is lingering just below awareness.

Even with mostly **Rarely** answers, revisit this if symptoms reappear, but for now, you can trust in your adaptability.

Emotional pain can resurface in subtle ways—and deserves your attention without shame.

This isn't a diagnostic tool. It's a mirror—a way to help you recognize and name pain that may be shaping your experience quietly and consistently.

WHY CAN SOMEONE BE ATTRACTED TO EMOTIONAL PAIN?

There are individuals who seem to live their lives immersed in drama, right? It might appear that they find emotional pain appealing. I doubt it's actually based on an attraction to pain itself. Some people may find the dynamics that create the pain attractive, or they may find some benefits. Let's see if we can understand this distinction before we judge them.

Many individuals are drawn to the heightened emotional interactions and conflicts that often characterize troubled relationships (drama) because they feel familiar, especially for those raised in turbulent environments. When emotional intensity was the backdrop of childhood, even distressing emotions can feel like home. There could be a sense of competence in navigating familiar emotional storms—knowing the unwritten rules of engagement provides an illusion of control in otherwise chaotic situations.

This familiarity creates a paradoxical comfort in discomfort. The nervous system becomes wired to expect and respond to emotional turbulence, making calmer, healthier dynamics feel strange or even boring by comparison. What others might see as harmful patterns, these individuals may experience as familiar territory where they understand the landscape—even if that landscape is ultimately damaging to their well-being.

Another possibility is when individuals have low self-worth and emotional pain reinforces their internal narrative. If someone deeply believes they don't deserve happiness or love, they may unconsciously seek out relationships and situations that confirm that belief. These patterns often stem from internalized criticism or early messages that conveyed a lack of worth.

You may also encounter individuals who form a relationship with emotional intensity as a way to counteract numbness. Those who learned to disconnect from their feelings may later find that even painful emotions provide a sense of aliveness they otherwise lack. The contrast between emotional void and emotional pain makes the latter feel preferable, as in *"at least I feel something."* There's a psychological component to this attraction as well. Emotional turmoil triggers the release of stress hormones like cortisol and adrenaline, creating a biochemical response that can feel energizing.

Attention and care dynamics play a significant role too. When someone consistently receives attention only during moments of crisis or pain, they may unconsciously learn that suffering is the price of connection. This conditioning is particularly powerful when it develops in formative relationships.

If you recognize yourself in these patterns, consider rewriting your narrative to find healthier ways to meet your underlying needs. The validation or intensity gained through emotional pain ultimately exacts too high a cost on your mental and physical health.

WHY EVERY TIME I FEEL SAD, I ALSO FEEL ANGRY?

This question points to an important phenomenon that doesn't get enough attention: **coupled emotions.**

When one emotion consistently triggers another—like sadness automatically leading to anger—it usually reflects how the brain has learned to process emotional experiences. This is not uncommon and can create significant roadblocks to emotional healing.

When one negative emotion becomes coupled with others, it can block the learning and adaptation that would otherwise help us resolve emotional wounds. That's why it's so valuable to become aware of these emotional pairings and to work on uncoupling them so each emotion can be understood and processed on its own terms.

Emotional pairing develops through one of these pathways:

- Emotional learning happens early in life **when our brain forms connections between different feelings and experiences.** If you repeatedly experienced situations where sadness and anger occurred together (perhaps family conflicts where sadness was quickly followed by frustration), your brain may have wired these emotions together.

- This pairing can also serve as a **protective mechanism.** Anger often feels more empowering than sadness, which can feel vulnerable and helpless. Your brain might automatically shift to anger as a defense against the vulnerability of sadness—it's easier to feel angry at someone or something than to sit with painful feelings of loss or hurt.

- Past experiences may have taught you that expressing sadness wasn't safe or acceptable. Some families or environments tolerate anger more than tears. If you learned that sadness led to rejection but anger got results, **your emotional system adapted** accordingly.

Uncoupling Emotions Practice. Try this exercise if you've observed that a certain emotion, like anger, frequently coexists with another emotion, like sadness:

First, pause and take three slow breaths.

Now, bring into your mind any moment where you can recognize the primary emotion (i.e., sadness) without the coupled response (i.e., anger). It might be a distant memory or a fleeting recent experience. As you hold this memory, notice how it feels to experience this emotion on its own. What sensations appear in your body? Where do you feel they are? Allow yourself to simply observe without judgment.

Next, without pushing, notice if the coupled emotion is present. Notice the transition point—that moment when one emotion began shifting into the other. Was there a thought, a physical sensation, or an image that triggered this shift? Place one hand over the area where you most strongly feel this transition. With gentle curiosity, ask yourself, *"What is this second emotion protecting me from or trying to do?"* Notice the thoughts that come after the question, and see if you can find the adaptive function.

Tell yourself, *"I can feel sad without needing to feel angry right now."* See if you can visualize each one as separate and create some type of division between them, like a screen. Allow yourself to experience each one without the other.

If the secondary emotion is still present, visualize it as smaller or farther away and go back to the primary one. Or ask the second emotion to please give you the space to experience the other emotion before you come back to it. This "asking for permission" to feel demonstrates respect for all parts of your emotional experience while creating the space needed to understand each emotion's unique message. It acknowledges that both emotions may have important information, but that

> experiencing them separately can provide clearer insight into what each one is trying to communicate.
>
> Continue practicing the exercise until you feel more empowered to notice each emotion separately and until the secondary emotion feels less intertwined with the primary one.

Change Your Emotions (Yes, It's Possible)

"We have a responsibility, and indeed a profound obligation, to heal our wounds."

Now that you have a solid understanding of how we construct, evaluate, and activate our emotions, it's time to put that knowledge to work. We will first explore how our brain regulates emotions using the same emotional architecture we'll be applying in the upcoming exercise. Understanding these regulatory mechanisms will set the stage for the practical work ahead, giving you the tools to reshape and manage your emotional responses more effectively.

A crucial point to take away from this chapter is that emotional construction is deeply tied to memory. We often make memory the centerpiece of emotional healing, yet memories merely inform the system about what to pursue or avoid; it is emotions that actually drive our actions. Memories aren't the enemy—they're prediction tools. Once an emotion is heard and balanced, the brain no longer needs to wave the memory as a danger flag; the signal has done its job. That's why engaging with emotions is more effective than fixating on memories, regardless of whether the goal is healing or adaptation.

Is my brain actually in control of my feelings?

It's not a surprise that with all the new information about the nervous system circulating, we imagine that our brain controls our emotions as if it had a switch. But that's not exactly how it works. Our feelings are part of a set of experiences that emerge from the interaction between our brain, body, nervous system, and environment—with some responses happening too quickly for conscious control. The key is understanding how this system maintains balance. Let's learn how our system works to restore balance when emotional regulation is disrupted.

Our nervous system is constantly working to regulate our functions and reactions. Effectively managing emotions requires coordination between brain networks that respond rapidly to emotional stimuli and regions that help interpret and modulate those responses. Emotional regulation, then, is the process of harmonizing these complex neurological systems so we can respond appropriately to everyday experiences.

The human brain regulates a broad spectrum of emotions—including joy, sadness, disgust, excitement, and anger—through mechanisms far more nuanced than simply avoiding danger. Using the CEA framework I previously introduced to explain how emotions are constructed, it becomes easier to see how we can regulate—or even deconstruct—problematic emotions at various levels. Let's begin by exploring the most immediate level.

Regulating Automatic Bodily Responses (Raw Affect). Before we're even consciously aware of a sudden sound or movement, the brain begins rapidly adjusting our bodily state—shifting heart rate, breathing, and muscle tension. If the brain determines the stimulus is non-threatening, it dials down arousal and returns the body to baseline. Think of jumping at a pan tipping over in the kitchen and how your body settles once you catch it.

But when the system becomes dysregulated—due to chronic stress, trauma, or repeated overwhelm—these automatic responses can spiral. **Regulation at this stage means pausing to notice these sensations and updating your interpretation.**

Tuning into these signals and labeling your state helps you calibrate your response to the real situation instead of letting a false alarm hijack your system. This process activates your prefrontal cortex, which can then guide adaptive responses.

> **Becoming Familiar With Your Emotions Exercise.** To practice gaining some control over how you feel and react, this exercise provides a series of quick instructions.
>
> **Quick Instruction (Raw Affect):** When you notice a sudden physical reaction—like a jolt, tightness, or rapid heartbeat—pause and tell yourself, *"This is my body talking to me."* Pause, listen, and then ask, *"What exactly am I feeling?" "Is this reaction to a threat, or a fear I developed in the past?" "Is this alarm justified, or can I return to what I was doing?"* This simple check-in helps your brain recalibrate, restore balance, and prevent unnecessary stress responses. Go in to make the experience more integral.

Interpretation, value, and creation of scripts. Just as with bodily responses, the brain automatically evaluates and assigns meaning to stimuli before we're consciously aware of it. This interpretation system rapidly categorizes experiences based on similarity to past events, creating immediate assumptions about what's happening or could happen. If the brain's prediction systems function well, they accurately assess situations—distinguishing a friendly joke from an insult, or a constructive suggestion from criticism—without conscious effort.

When this automatic interpretation system becomes dysregulated, our meaning-making can become biased, rigid, impaired, or threat-focused. The brain may begin defaulting to negative interpretations, seeing rejection in neutral expressions or criticism in casual comments. As your mind begins processing a social interaction—like a coworker's ambiguous comment or a partner's change in tone—your brain activates interpretive frameworks, triggering immediate assumptions about intentions and meanings.

Emotional regulation at this level means catching yourself in the act of judging and considering whether your default response still serves you. If you notice that you always assume the worst or snap at people when surprised, regulation involves pausing before accepting your first interpretation.

> **Quick Instruction (interpretation):** When you catch yourself reacting emotionally to a situation, pause and ask, *"What am I assuming right now—and is it the only possible explanation?" "What exactly did they mean?" "Am I assuming negative intent based on past experiences rather than present evidence?" "What other explanations could account for this interaction?"* This moment of reflection creates space to question automatic interpretations and shift toward a more flexible, accurate understanding. Go in, connect with the experience, and notice how you feel when you reflect in this way.

Regulating the overt response. Like bodily regulation and interpretation, our emotional and behavioral responses have automatic components that the brain manages without our awareness. This system quickly selects emotional reactions and behaviors based on context—laughing at a joke, showing sympathy for suffering, or pushing back when annoyed—without deliberate planning, yet following previous learning that has been imprinted in our emotional scripts.

When this response system becomes dysregulated, our reactions may become disproportionate, rigid, or context-inappropriate. The brain may struggle to moderate emotional intensity or select behaviors that match the situation. As your emotional response begins—like irritation building during a difficult conversation or anxiety spiking before a presentation—your brain activates action tendencies, priming specific behaviors like withdrawal, aggression, or people-pleasing.

Intentionally regulating at this stage means noticing your emotional trajectory and behavioral impulses. *"Is my anger building too quickly for this situation?" "Am I about to react in my habitual way rather than in a way that's effective here?" "What would a proportionate response look like?"* Tuning into these emotional currents and recognizing your behavioral patterns helps you modulate your expression to match the actual circumstances, preventing overreactions or unhelpful habits.

A question that comes up frequently is, *"Can I ever really stop reacting?"* The truth is, not reacting at all is nearly impossible—emotional responses are part of being human. What truly matters is the intensity, appropriateness, and duration of the reaction. I've had clients who remained extremely angry for days because their partner ignored a traffic light—an incident that not only caused a rupture in the relationship but also spoiled several days over something ultimately minor. That kind of prolonged, disproportionate overreaction is what we want to eliminate.

Regulating at this stage means observing your emotional progression and evaluating whether your behavioral impulses align with your goals. That engages executive functions that help you pause automatic reactions, assess situations more accurately, and gradually rewrite your emotional storyboards with more adaptive instructions.

> **Quick Instruction (regulating):** Before you act on a strong emotion, pause and ask, *"Is this reaction helpful—or just familiar and habitual?"* That moment of reflection allows you to choose a response that fits the situation rather than defaulting to old scripts. Feel the response of your system and the shift of your mental state. Over time, this practice helps create new neural pathways for more adaptive responses.

How can we change an emotion?

As you learned at the beginning of the chapter, you need to deconstruct an emotion first in order to reconstruct it later. The reconstruction happens by updating the beliefs and meanings you've attached to your emotions.

Just as we learn the language and accent of our caregivers—our tongue adapting to move and flex in precisely the ways our family speaks—our emotional system learns the feeling-language of our environment. We unconsciously absorb not just what emotions are acceptable, but also how to express them, when to hide them, and what they mean about people. The remarkable thing is that, like spoken language, our emotional patterns can be updated. While traces of our original emotional "accent" may remain, we can learn new ways of feeling and responding.

To change an emotion, do the exercise from the start of the chapter, but in reverse. Instead of deconstructing it, you'll reconstruct it. (A planned workbook for this title will provide every step you'll need to reconstruct any problematic emotion.)

You can work on reconstructing an emotion by revisiting a charged memory, identifying the bodily sensations, labels, and beliefs that originally formed around it, and then deliberately updating that "storyboard."

First, notice the trigger and name the primary feeling—along with any physical cues that signal it's active. Next, surface the old beliefs attached to that feeling *("I'm unsafe," "People always leave")* and ask whether they still fit present-day reality.

Finally, substitute any rigid or outdated message with a more accurate, flexible one, and then imagine responding to that new script. Revise that old, conflicted script with a new one that appears both feasible and more effective for your needs. In doing so, you preserve the emotion's useful warning or guidance signal but free it from the past constraints that once locked it in place. The result is an emotion that still guides you, yet no longer overwhelms or misdirects you.

> **ARCO: Exercise to Diminish Reactivity.** Despite their power, emotional scripts are remarkably adaptable and modifiable. After experiencing traumatic events that disrupted your emotional scripts, you can learn to create less reactive patterns by deliberately practicing the four simple steps represented by the acronym **ARCO:**
>
> > **A**wareness: Notice trauma-based reactions as they happen. You feel a surge of anger and find yourself clenching your fists or about to slam a door when someone disagrees with you. Catching that impulse is the first sign of awareness—recognizing that something old may be triggered.
> >
> > **R**eflection: Ask, *"Is this truly a threat, or is my extreme script kicking in?" "Am I mixing past events with the present situation?"*

A colleague interrupts you in a meeting, and you suddenly feel dismissed and invisible. Pause and consider: *"Is this moment really about being unworthy, or am I reliving an old experience of being silenced?"*

Choice: Opt for a calmer, more balanced response instead of the automatic fear-based one. Instead of yelling or withdrawing completely, you take a breath and say, *"I'd like to finish what I was saying,"* signaling self-regulation and a shift from reaction to intention.

Options: Observe positive outcomes—reduced conflict, less anxiety, or a renewed sense of control—and let these successes strengthen healthier neural connections. After choosing a calmer response, you notice the conversation goes more smoothly, and you feel respected rather than regretful. This success strengthens the pathway to safer, more constructive responses.

Each time you choose a more adaptive path, the brain rewards that choice, making it easier to repeat. By engaging your reflective capacities rather than reacting impulsively, you gradually rewrite your scripts. While traumatic incidents can powerfully influence how you respond, they don't have to dictate your reactions forever.

Chapter Three

TRAUMA

HOW TO ACHIEVE A FULLER UNDERSTANDING OF THE RELATIONSHIP BETWEEN FEAR AND EMOTIONAL INJURIES

"Trauma is an active, ongoing injury—one that continues disrupting our regular capacity even after a perceived danger has passed because the threat remains emotionally alive."

What began in the 1980s as a breakthrough—finally giving voice to thousands of traumatized people who had long been ignored or misjudged—has, in some ways, evolved into a narrative that now risks doing them a disservice.

Many authors are already talking about how the overgeneralization of the term "trauma" is blurring its true meaning and diluting its significance, reducing our capacity to adapt, encouraging some people to adopt a victim identity in response to mild adversity, and obscuring the true consequences of deep emotional injuries.

I explored several of these issues in my book *Traumatization and Its Aftermath* (Routledge, 2023). In that work, I argued that imprecise language distorts our understanding of emotional life and blocks healing. That book offers clear explanations of the neurobiology of traumatization and its full range of consequences, including the domains where serious alterations occur and the specific mechanisms involved in developing various trauma syndromes. Trauma is a genuine phenomenon, and traumatization significantly hinders our mental health—but not every hurtful experience qualifies as trauma.

This book aims to clarify what trauma is and how it differs from emotional wounds to help normalize and attend to the wide spectrum of human emotional experience. This chapter puts fear under the microscope, showing how it drives trauma disorders. Understanding whether fear has created a surface wound or a deep injury determines how you resolve it.

TURBOCHARGE YOUR TRAUMA EDUCATION

"Trauma lasts only as long as fear keeps us from feeling capable. Once safety returns, any injury transforms into a scar—just a mark of what we went through, a testimony of life!"

What qualifies as trauma? How does it impact you? And why do some people seem to carry its weight much longer than others? What invisible line separates a difficult experience from one that fundamentally alters how you function? And perhaps most importantly—is trauma about what happens to you or how your system processes what happened?

Understanding trauma goes beyond mere academic knowledge; it provides insight into your biology, behavior, suffering, and the interconnections among these aspects. When you grasp how your nervous system responds to perceived threats, you gain insight into your most perplexing behaviors and reactions. This is why I want you to explore the survival mechanisms that initially protect you but can eventually imprison you. You'll understand the process of traumatization itself and discover why trauma's impact varies so dramatically from person to person.

Why must we all deal with trauma on this planet?

This question reflects a common belief: that no one can escape the devastating consequences of trauma and mental health struggles. While trauma awareness has undoubtedly enriched our understanding of mental health, it has also led to labeling ordinary pain, disappointment, parenting challenges, or even adaptive discomfort as trauma. This fact unintentionally reinforces a disempowering narrative that can cause emotional pain to linger indefinitely or, worse, activate survival circuits meant to protect us from real danger—not from fear itself.

Unlike physical health conditions—where clear markers distinguish between diabetic, pre-diabetic, and non-diabetic states—mental health lacks such definitive thresholds. That's why we often rush to apply damaging labels to a wide range of behaviors, from merely irritating to truly destructive, without adequately considering their origins or context. We call a child who struggles to sit still in class "ADHD" without first asking whether the teaching style suits their learning needs. We label someone "OCD" simply because they like things orderly, ignoring the crucial difference between a personal preference and a seriously debilitating compulsion. These labels risk not only misrepresenting the individual's experience but also short-circuiting our efforts to understand the root causes and the level of dysfunction—and thus effective paths to resolution.

Adversity certainly exists, and it can be challenging to go through. But assuming that every form of hardship inevitably leaves lasting psychological damage is both inaccurate and unhelpful. A major source of confusion may be rooted in labeling trauma as the cause (the event) rather than the effect (the consequences) and in assuming that all difficulties have uniform effects. This way of thinking diminishes our resilience, overlooks our innate capacity to adapt, and neglects the body's natural tendency toward resolution and healing. As I've said before, we've forgotten or dismissed how wise our system already is.

Those who believe in this overly deterministic view—like the one implied by the question—may find themselves living in a negative and defeatist mental state, which can become an obstacle to addressing their issues at the root or finding ways to overcome them.

The phenomenon of trauma has proven to be much more than just a bad experience, a painful memory, a severe reaction, or an uncomfortable interaction. Trauma is an active, open injury that remains unhealed due to factors preventing its resolution, which in turn creates obstacles for normal living. However, we've been approaching this new paradigm with an outdated framework. Simply talking about our negative experiences—the approach early therapy believed would heal—does not resolve the confusion and instability in our nervous system.

Transient Signal	Emotional Response	Emotional Wound	Emotional Trauma
Brief discomfort	Temporary distress	Recurring pain	Persistent suffering
Clear cause	Identifiable trigger	Negative meaning given	Identity-defining
Adaptive purpose	Mixed interpretations	Affects multiple contexts	Distorted worldviews
Easily resolved	Manageable impact	Requires processing	Significant life impact

Emotional Pain Spectrum

Just consider that if instead of "trauma," we used the term "emotional pain" in the question, the statement would become undeniably true—yes, we all must experience emotional pain on this planet. Why? Our intricate minds can't help but ache with longing, grief, or regret. It's part of being human. Think of emotional pain like muscle soreness after intense exercise: temporary discomfort that comes with stretching beyond your current capacity and a sign that your system is adapting and becoming stronger. Once you've allowed time for healing and integration, the soreness fades—but while it's present, that persistent ache reminds you that you've pushed beyond familiar limits and that some development is occurring. Negative feelings, shaky reactions, broken relationships, and gloomy thoughts? Like muscle soreness after a challenging experience, these unavoidable effects are signs that you're stretching beyond your comfort zone and that greater emotional strength and resilience are developing.

Trauma, by contrast, is like a torn ligament that won't heal properly because it keeps stretching. A torn ligament represents an active process of damage that begins when normal recovery mechanisms fail to work. Instead of the natural soreness that fades with rest and care, an active injury festers, disrupts daily functioning, and keeps the nervous system operating as though the source of damage is still occurring. In other words, everyday hurts are like muscle soreness—uncomfortable but evidence of growth—while trauma is the torn ligament that demands specialized treatment before any healing can begin.

The world's challenges demand greater adaptability than ever. Assuming everyone experiences trauma and adopting a victim mindset puts us at risk of becoming hopeless. Viewing ourselves as permanently damaged serves no one. Instead, let's nurture hope and trust in our built-in capacity to adjust, overcome, and improve—especially in difficult times.

WHAT, IN YOUR OWN WORDS, IS THE DEFINITION OF TRAUMA?

Many existing definitions fall short in accurately describing the trauma phenomenon. An effective definition of trauma can allow individuals suffering from psychological injuries to focus not only on having their pain acknowledged—wait, that on its own may keep them stuck in the problem—but also on charting a path toward resolving the fears, building resilience, and encouraging transformation.

Psychological trauma is a neuro-bio-psycho-social phenomenon. It starts with the crisis-mode activation of the nervous system's anticipatory response to perceived danger or life-threatening events. That activation is designed to protect the individual from assumed imminent harm. Once the initial protective response fails to resolve even after the threat has passed, disruptions in neurobiological, psychological, and social functioning become lasting. Trauma means that the system continues operating under the false assumption that maintaining these defensive responses is necessary for survival, even when they now cause harm rather than protection. Therefore:

Trauma is essentially a condition where unresolved fear/insecurity keeps survival circuits activated, forcing the system to operate suboptimally because it believes this dysfunction is the only way to stay safe.

WHAT DOES IT ACTUALLY MEAN WHEN PEOPLE SAY YOU'RE IN "SURVIVAL MODE"?

In well-informed circles, when we talk about survival mode, we're talking about trauma. I say "well-informed" because I've seen chatbots describe survival mode as the body's response to a current threat—as if it were a momentary reaction—which reflects a huge misunderstanding and oversimplification. The fact that AI can repeat such a popular but inaccurate explanation shows just how widespread the most pathologizing interpretation is. So, be cautious about believing everything you read on popular platforms or even from ChatGPT or other bots.

Survival mode occurs after our brain shifts into emergency programming, interrupting normal operations to focus on survival, and stays there. This doesn't mean that survival mode kicks in whenever there's a perceived risk or stress. Survival mode doesn't activate or deactivate easily—it's a serious, sustained, and chronic shift indicating our system has abandoned its normal state of internal balance and efficiency because there is no better alternative.

Think of the survival mode as the "eject" button in a fighter jet: pressing this button is a drastic, last-resort measure. Once the pilot is ejected, the jet cannot be controlled by the pilot. It might have an automated emergency protocol guiding it temporarily, but it lacks the pilot's conscious, logical direction. Similarly, when our nervous system enters survival mode, our mental pilot—our rational thinking, perception, and deliberate decision-making—can become partially blocked or severely limited. Emergency programming takes over, driven solely by the imperative to survive.

TRAUMA   117

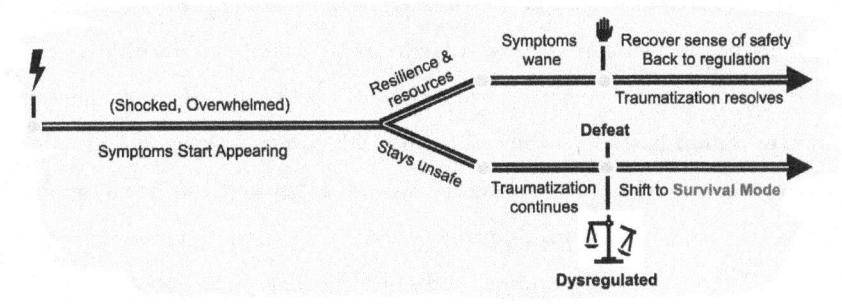

Progression to Survival Mode

Even though it's not uncommon to see "survival mode" used to name a temporary acute stress response, a shift into survival mode often happens gradually, unfolding over weeks or months, as the system progressively activates one protective mechanism after another. When these mechanisms are no longer sufficient to manage the perceived threat, the system makes a critical trade-off: it opts for a suboptimal mode of functioning that prioritizes survival above all else—even if that means deactivating, suppressing, or neglecting other essential processes like emotional regulation, digestion, or connection with others.

Reversing survival mode is also a gradual process, typically unfolding over weeks or months for a single event or several months for more complex cases—depending on factors that help the system regulate.

So is everything trauma now, or are there actual rules?

This is one of the most important questions in mental health today. As a trauma therapist, professor, and former co-director of one of the top postgraduate trauma studies programs in the U.S., I've spent years emphasizing that not everything is trauma—and that making this distinction accurately is essential for resolution and complete healing.

To help shift our perspective, it's important to remember that concepts and constructs are constantly evolving. We may remain attached to a "truth" we once learned, even if it's no longer valid—or perhaps only partially so. We can also become loyal to popular, generalized ideas that overlook critical details and nuances, ultimately altering the meaning entirely. New findings make it essential to stay current. That's why new books continue to emerge. While earlier work laid important foundations, our understanding of trauma has evolved significantly since those early discoveries.

It's surprising that even among leading trauma experts, the definition and explanation of trauma haven't yet fully caught up with current insights into its nature. Many continue to rely on older classifications such as "small t" and "big T" trauma, approaches that define trauma primarily by the event itself or imply its impact can be judged by the perceived magnitude of the incident. This perspective is profoundly flawed.

For example, labeling ongoing bullying as a series of "small t's" implies that each incident is minor, which risks downplaying the potential severity of individual events and failing to acknowledge the cumulative psychological and physiological toll of sustained intimidation and emotional humiliation. Additionally, labeling stress at home as mere "small t's" without assessing whether the situation is traumatic or just challenging might either downplay a genuinely severe threat or over-pathologize typical childhood experiences.

But then what is it? At this point, it becomes much clearer to talk about trauma as a set of different but interconnected aspects. We can either say that trauma is an active injury that has not resolved and affects all of those aspects or identify it as the condition that results from that unresolved injury, but definitely not as the event, and even less, a scar.

If we see all the areas that get affected by the internal process after the traumatic event, then we can see how trauma is a serious issue, not just a narrative or a term we could throw around to get sympathy. Consider how this plays out in clinical diagnoses like PTSD. There is a fallacy in its definition. If someone develops PTSD, it's because that one event sent the system into a series of responses that remain active long after the event is over. Only when the symptoms persist or intensify for at least a month can we diagnose PTSD. It's during that process that PTSD unfolds. Most symptoms don't occur during the traumatic event; rather, they develop as the activation of crisis responses persists.

Observing trauma as a phenomenon shows that while external events often initiate trauma responses, internal factors can be just as influential (if not more so) in shaping how an individual responds to an event and processes it, and whether they resolve it or not. When we acknowledge that trauma exceeds the sum of its parts, we see why fixating on a single aspect complicates efforts to create a unified definition. Essentially, remember that trauma means:

**Trauma =
Threatened + Overwhelmed + Unsurmounted +
Defeated + Dysregulation + Persistent + Failed to Adapt**

**Trauma =
Unresolved Sense of Threat + Unsettling Fears =
Active Injury**

If some argue that trauma is not the event, how do we define what is and isn't trauma?

The question creates a delicate situation in the current conversation. If someone has been saying they have trauma because they went through traumatic events, hearing that it may not be trauma can feel invalidating. But affirming that it is trauma without considering the whole picture could give them the wrong impression about the nature of their suffering. See the conundrum?

Referring to the event itself as trauma is at the root of much of the confusion around who is truly traumatized and who is not. I remain hopeful that simply shifting our language—saying "traumatic event" instead of "trauma"—could resolve many of these misunderstandings. The reality is that many trauma-related concepts are still evolving. As we saw in the previous chapter, we can now differentiate *"I'm traumatized"* from *"I'm emotionally wounded"* to start with. Then we can recognize whether our experience left us with lasting dysfunction or not.

What defines trauma in simpler terms? In my view, one of the clearest ways to determine whether trauma has been resolved—or is still governing someone's nervous system—is by examining **the relationship** a person has developed with what happened to them. That relationship is the key factor in assessing whether the event continues to damage the system.

This relationship is primarily psychological, but it's deeply shaped by social and cultural influences. How a person interprets the event, the meaning they assign to it, and the way they integrate it into their sense of self and life story all play pivotal roles. It also depends heavily on the fear script.

For instance, someone who loses their job might interpret the event as evidence of personal failure—"I'm worthless and unemployable"—which brings a sense of threat that can trigger responses that affect many areas of their system. Conversely, someone else might view the same experience as an unfortunate but manageable setback—"It's tough, but I can learn from this, find a new opportunity, and move forward"—which is more likely to support healthy adaptation and emotional recovery. The external event is identical in both cases—what differs is the relationship each person develops with that experience.

What Does Traumatization Do to a Person?

Despite numerous explanations of what trauma involves, one key element is often missing: what happens after the stressful event ends but before a trauma disorder fully develops?

Even when a few symptoms are present shortly after a traumatic event, a full-blown disorder typically unfolds gradually—over one to six months in the case of a single event and possibly over years in cases of prolonged exposure. During this critical window, the mind can either begin to regain a sense of control and hope—or lose faith entirely. If hope is lost, the mind continues to send signals of danger to the brain, keeping it in emergency mode. The system keeps clinging to those high-cost defenses—even when they no longer provide protection (when the threat is over). Everything that happens inside of us—from the initial shock to the ongoing effort to survive—is part of what traumatizes the system. That's what traumatization means.

Traumatization is the neurobiological and psychological process the system enters upon perceiving or anticipating danger—one that doesn't end until our fears are resolved and our sense of safety is restored.

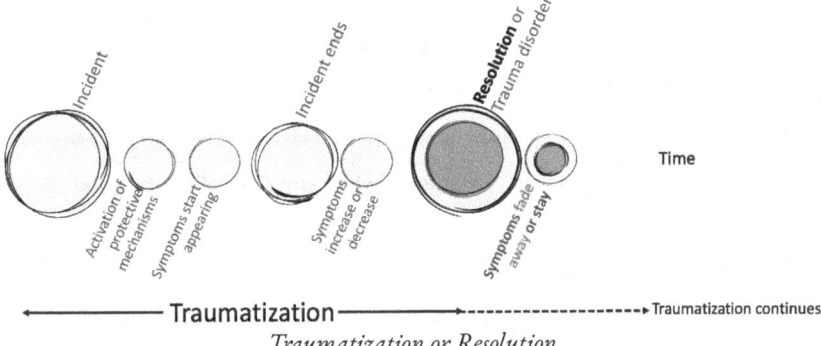

Traumatization or Resolution

Traumatization begins the moment our protective responses are activated in crisis mode and prove insufficient in eliminating the threat, and it can persist long after the threat is gone, depending on how the mind continues to interpret the situation. When we remain frightened and overwhelmed—even in the absence of real danger—the process continues, and this prolonged state amplifies the effects of the original response, potentially manifesting as a mental disorder.

So how does this traumatization process finally end? It's only when the cortex (the brain's outer layer responsible for higher-level thinking and reasoning) signals that the threat has passed that our system can begin returning to its normal regulation. However, for the brain to trust and accept this signal, we must genuinely feel safe—meaning **our mind needs sufficient mental space to allow for hope, reassurance, and favorable outcome anticipation.** Without this sense of safety, the system remains skeptical, continuing to activate fear responses. Because the brain naturally seeks balance rather than chaos, it eagerly awaits clear signals of safety and will respond strongly to bring us back to normal as soon as our hope is reestablished.

WHY DO SOME PEOPLE STAY TRAUMATIZED MUCH LONGER THAN OTHERS?

Since we've placed so much emphasis on the event that hurt us, we've also implied that the responsibility for our suffering lies entirely with whatever—or whomever—caused the damage. In reality, internal factors influence the way a person's system reacts. These include negative core beliefs, distorted perceptions, a defeatist or victim mindset, heightened rejection sensitivity, persistent rumination, and overly rigid emotional scripts for shame, anger, sadness, and fear. All of these influence the relationship a person develops with the traumatic event.

These internal elements influence whether resilience is nurtured or depleted, whether recovery takes place or crisis lingers, whether we assimilate the good and bad of the experience and subdue the fears, and ultimately whether well-being is restored or remains compromised over time.

Throughout this book, I emphasize how important our role is in our healing—but I must also point out that **our role is equally significant in our traumatization.**

For instance, someone who repeatedly tells themselves, *"My parents broke me,"* or *"My childhood trauma will never allow me to become who I was meant to be,"* may unknowingly reinforce a victim identity, focusing more on validating their pain than on exploring strategies to resolve their fears and move toward resolution. This mental state sends a clear signal to the brain: *"I can't handle life on my own."* In response, the system remains in survival mode.

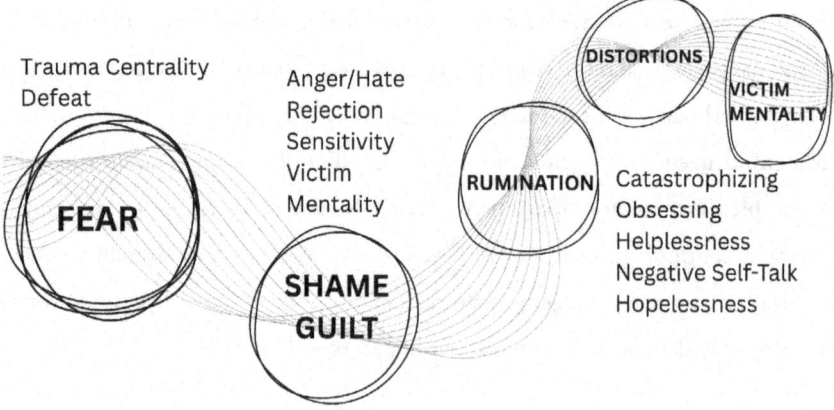

```
Trauma Centrality      Anger/Hate           DISTORTIONS
Defeat                 Rejection                            VICTIM
                       Sensitivity                          MENTALITY
                       Victim         RUMINATION  Catastrophizing
       FEAR            Mentality                  Obsessing
                                                  Helplessness
                                                  Negative Self-Talk
                            SHAME                 Hopelessness
                            GUILT
```

Internal Traumatizing Agents

We know that external traumatizing agents—such as ongoing stressors like an abusive relationship, financial insolvency, or systemic oppression—initiate the problem; however, internal traumatizing agents can be even more detrimental because they prolong it and affect us in our most private spaces—specifically, the thoughts, beliefs, and fears that continue to activate our survival responses from within. We might be physically safe, but these agents keep our system on high alert through constant "what if" thinking, shame about our reactions, or beliefs that we're permanently damaged or destined to fail.

Think of it like this: external traumatizing agents are like intruders who break into your home. Internal traumatizing agents are like a security system that's become so hypersensitive it treats every shadow as a threat—sounding alarms for family members, delivery drivers, and even your own reflection in the window.

Does trauma make someone less resilient?

Resilience is one of our most valuable capacities for navigating, adapting to, or overcoming life's challenges. Resilience depends on both inner strengths and outer resources, but—like any resource—each person has a limited supply. Internal resources might include self-esteem, hope, or emotional regulation skills, while external resources could be supportive relationships, financial security, education, or access to professional help. High resilience means being able to handle difficulties by adapting relatively quickly, whereas low resilience means having a harder time managing both big and small challenges.

Trauma definitely reduces our resilience, and traumatization strains it significantly. This capacity can be depleted not only when we've already shifted into survival mode but also while we're juggling multiple stressors or dealing with a persistent source of fear that consumes a massive amount of energy—much like an app that continually drains our phone's battery.

A constant state of alert, for instance, uses a lot of energy. Yet paradoxically, having no hope—a defeatist mentality—can deplete resilience even more because it draws on a deeper, more pervasive psychological reserve. When we feel hopeless or believe we can't escape danger, our brain churns through negative loops: ruminating, anticipating the worst, and worrying about possible catastrophic outcomes that exist only in our head. This mental spiral can exhaust our emotional reserves as much as, or even more than, physical hypervigilance. Hope, on the other hand, is a powerful motivator—fueling effort and sustaining our ability to bounce back. Without it, even simple tasks can feel insurmountable, prolonging a cycle of inactivity and despair.

Our capacity to recover often hinges on how we perceive available support—whether we see it as scarce or accessible. When traumatization is running, we may unconsciously adopt a **scarcity mindset,** believing that safety, healing, or the possibility of recovery is either limited or entirely out of reach. This perceived "lack of" can keep us trapped in hypervigilance, helplessness, or resignation, making recovery feel impossible.

By beginning to recognize that help, hope, and growth do exist—that life can offer opportunities—we start to shift into an **abundance mindset**—a cognitive shift that signals safety to our nervous system and allows natural healing processes to resume. From there, we can access both our internal strengths and the support around us more effectively.

This shift toward abundance requires a willingness to consider that transformation, connection, and growth are more accessible than they may seem—and that change begins with how we choose to relate to what's available to us. Here is a summary of this model to help us begin shifting toward an abundance mindset.

	SCARCITY MINDSET	ABUNDANCE MINDSET
EMOTIONAL	Worry, fear, comparison, complains, victim mentality	Gratitude, acceptance, and optimism
RESOURCES	Feels limited/constrained, not enough to get around	Believes in sharing. Gives without expecting
BEHAVIOR	Seeks validation, clings to lack, usual protests	Focuses on growing & learning, embraces opportunities
CHALLENGES	Feels overwhelmed, avoids risks, stores and saves	Sees challenges as opportunities, stays open and hopeful
OVERALL	Operates from fear and dissatisfaction	Operates from abundance and possibility

Scarcity vs Abundance Model

SEE WHAT HAPPENS WHEN DREAD TAKES OVER

"Fear teaches the brain to expect pain—until hope and trust teach it to expect peace."

At the heart of trauma lies fear—the main force that activates our survival circuits. While fear was traditionally viewed as a hardwired emotion, we now understand it starts as a hardwired affective state—an automatic physiological reaction to potential threats that our brain then interprets as a signal to activate protective responses.

But let's not forget that as an emotion, its construction makes it deeply personal. It's shaped by your unique life experiences that scared you, cultural influences that told you what to fear, the information you've gathered about what's dangerous, and the specific context in which a threat arises. Constructed fear, then, combines your emotional responses and your instinctual actions, tailored to what you believe is necessary for survival. Hence, fear is both universal and highly individual—a dynamic emotional force that evolves. However, fear has also become a pervasive concept that appears to encompass a wide range of insecurities. From *"I'm afraid of dying"* to *"I'm afraid of being late."*

This lack of clear definition becomes especially problematic for individuals living in a traumatized state, where the experience of fear can be particularly intense. Fearful narratives build upon one another, layer after layer—powerlessness reinforcing indecision—until a persistent sense of fear becomes embedded in the system. What begins as the fear of a single triggering event accumulates and generalizes, making it increasingly difficult to perceive anything but danger, lack of safety, low confidence, and mistrust.

When fear has spread throughout the entire system, pinpointing its sources can be nearly impossible. Yet this very understanding—that fear is constructed and layered—also reveals why it can be deconstructed and reduced. With this in mind, let's explore the powerful force of fear, how it shapes our emotional world, and what we can do to reduce it.

Does trauma always have to involve fear, or are there other manifestations that don't involve fear/dread per se?

While other emotional states—such as shame, anger, hopelessness, or emotional numbness—are commonly present in individuals who have experienced traumatic events, fear plays the foundational role in the trauma phenomenon. Trauma is connected to survival, and surviving relates to emotions that signal danger or threat. Fear is the quintessential indicator that the body has recognized the need to safeguard itself. Other emotions often arise as reactions to the initial survival-based fear response, but they are not the initiators of the traumatization process itself.

Joseph LeDoux, a prominent neuroscientist, explains this dynamic by stating that *"Danger is ancient, but fear is a recent invention."* Multiple scientists have confirmed that trauma is fundamentally rooted in the perception of danger and the brain's survival-based physiological responses driven by the anticipation of threat. These responses give rise to the raw affective state that forms the basis on which meanings and reactions construct the emotion of fear. In this sense, fear can be considered the "seed" of the trauma phenomenon, serving as the foundation for protective mechanisms.

To clarify how fear is integral to trauma, let's examine the process when danger is perceived:

Perception of danger or threat: The brain detects something it interprets as threatening and anticipates possible scenarios—whether it's an immediate physical risk (e.g., an accident) or an emotional one (such as physical abuse).

Raw affective state activation: Hardwired survival mechanisms activate to protect the individual—prevention, mobilization, or immobilization—based on the need to find help, fight back, flee the site, or surrender to the "predator" (e.g., running from a house fire).

Brain override for survival: The brain prioritizes survival by overriding less urgent processes like emotional regulation, reasoning, and higher-order thinking to focus entirely on immediate threat response (e.g., inability to think clearly during panic or making rational decisions while fighting back or running away).

Fear's learned instructions: Drawing on previous experiences and accumulated information, the brain assigns meaning to the threat and determines what this fear requires—how to act in cases of danger, what to believe about themselves and others, and what survival strategies to employ (e.g., meaning: *"Men are dangerous"* with the instruction, *"Avoid men and be hostile towards them"* after an abusive relationship; or meaning: *"I can't trust my judgment"* with the instruction *"Become submissive and quiet"* after being manipulated).

Fear and hypervigilance: Once the brain adopts hypervigilance as its default safeguard, the initial fear no longer stays tied to the original trigger. The result is a widening net: sights, sounds, smells, or even thoughts that only faintly resemble the original danger now activate the same alarm (e.g., an upset man triggering panic in an abused person, or raised voices in a movie causing someone to dissociate after witnessing domestic violence). If hypervigilance persists, structural and chemical changes make the system increasingly quick to detect peril and slow to stand down. At this stage, the organism no longer merely reacts to danger; it organizes itself around it. Now the fear script includes all sorts of alarms, and previously non-threatening things become triggers.

Once fear is running the show, other emotions or mental states—such as shame, anger, or hopelessness—may surface, caused by biological factors (shared neural circuits), perceptual factors (the level of danger perceived and what they believe they deserve), and consequential factors (negative self-talk, rumination, victimization, or resentment). The individual might initially feel fear of rejection or harm, followed by shame of being weak and a failure. This self-perception adds another layer of stress, further prolonging the feeling of being unsafe and exacerbating survival mechanisms.

If fear keeps signaling that survival responses are still needed—whether because threats continue or because fear scripts grow unchecked—dysregulation sets in. Persistent hypervigilance and continuous waves of fear trap the person in a cycle of reactivity and heightened emotionality. This dysregulation is a stamp of trauma, where fear and its associated narratives dominate the person's mind, making it difficult to recover a sense of safety, reduce shame, or develop hope.

In short, fear begins as a lifesaving seed, but when the nervous system can't complete the cycle back to safety, that seed grows unchecked, rooting the entire organism in a wilderness where danger feels perpetual and peace seems biologically out of reach.

WHAT ARE THE BIG FEARS THAT CAN REALLY DAMAGE SOMEONE?

Fear often expands into a broad set of stories and negative beliefs about what might threaten each of us, tied to our unique contexts. We don't learn solely through emotional experiences. Cognitive processes also play a significant role, as does the information we absorb—first from caregivers, then from our environment, and later from sources like books, TV shows, or lately, podcasts.

We all fear differently, but there are specific things most of us fear. I see our fears as rooted in several interrelated, inherent safety needs, which can be categorized into four levels. Not having those needs met may scare us the most.

Physical needs: At the most primal level, humans fear anything that threatens basic survival—whether it's death, starvation, inability to reproduce, homelessness, illnesses or the agents that can cause them (animals, insects, psychopaths), or losing one's capacity for self-sufficiency. Even preverbal experiences can shape our foundational fears. *For example, if a baby experiences prolonged hunger, cold, or abandonment, these threats to survival get encoded before language develops, creating lasting vulnerabilities that the person may not even be able to articulate or understand.*

Emotional needs: On an emotional level, humans—like all mammals—need to feel a **sense of belonging** to feel secure. Generally, mammals cannot survive in isolation, and this psychosocial need feeds their fears of rejection, loneliness, and expulsion. Traits or characteristics that make us feel weak, incompetent, undesired, unaccepted, unlovable, unimportant, or inadequate can amplify these fears by threatening our sense of belonging. Shame can play a prominent role here, maintaining a state of fear by fueling the dread of being "found out" as inadequate or unworthy, even if no one else notices. Similarly, guilt can operate subtly, causing anxiety when individuals disapprove of their own actions and become extremely worried about being discovered, rejected, punished, or expelled.

Cognitive needs: At the cognitive level, humans may fear not being intelligent, talented, or "special" enough to succeed. In many cultures, success is treated almost as essential as survival, fostering fears of failure, judgment, or incompetence. Although this layer is primarily shaped by social factors rather than biological ones, it can still be equally harmful. Here, shame again plays a pivotal role, reinforcing the fear of being exposed as insufficient.

Spiritual needs: On a spiritual level, humans often feel a strong need to believe in concepts like forgiveness, salvation, or moral dualities (e.g., good vs. evil). These beliefs emerge from how we interpret abstract ideas about existence, higher powers, and the possibility of life after death. This realm can generate particularly intense fears—such as the fear of eternal condemnation or divine punishment—which are often magnified by cognitive insecurities and guilt. When spiritual fears combine with cognitive insecurities and shame, they significantly intensify the emotional burden, further solidifying the belief that one's fundamental essence is in jeopardy.

	Physical	Emotional	Cognitive	Spiritual
Worst Fears	Fear anything that threatens basic survival	Rejection, loneliness, and shame-driven inadequacy	Failure, judgment, and shame-driven incompetence	Eternal condemnation, loss of salvation, and shame-driven unworthiness
Most Important Needs	Protection, food & water, shelter, self-sufficiency	Belonging, acceptance, self-worth, freedom from guilt and shame	Competence, recognition, self-worth (cognitive confidence)	Salvation, worthiness, meaning (purpose), peace

Most Important Emotional Needs

Now, returning to the complete question about which fears can really damage someone: the most harmful fears are those that create self-reinforcing cycles across these safety levels simultaneously and become so pervasive they dominate our entire worldview. These include

- fears that isolate us—fear of rejection, abandonment, or being fundamentally unlovable,

- fears that paralyze us—fear of failure, judgment, or not being good enough,

- fears that make us feel helpless—fear of death, serious illness, or losing loved ones—and

- fears that attack our very identity—fear of being fundamentally flawed, evil, or condemned.

For example, a person who fears rejection may become so anxious in social situations that they withdraw or act defensively, inadvertently pushing others away and reinforcing their belief that they are destined to be alone.

In my clinical practice, I often ask clients about their worst fears, and the responses are remarkably consistent: fear of losing their children or parents, bugs or rats, serious illness, death, and violence. **If you recognize your own fears in this list, you're not alone—and you're certainly not weak.**

These fears make perfect sense when we understand them through the lens of our most basic safety needs. They represent threats to our physical survival, our emotional bonds, and our sense of security in the world. The key isn't to eliminate these natural fears but to prevent them from dominating our lives and becoming pervasive.

Understanding our fears helps us take greater control over how they evolve, rather than leaving them to chance or external influences. As children, we naturally absorb the fears presented by our environment. As adults, we have more power to reassess and reshape our relationship with these fears.

> **The Fear Mapping and Safety Anchoring Protocol.** To identify fear patterns, challenge fearful narratives, and reconnect with safety in the present moment. The objective of this exercise is to help you notice the fear sensations as signals while recognizing that you are safe now.
>
> Let's begin by mapping your fear: Find a quiet space. Identify the current fears you're experiencing—from minor concerns to major terrors. Make a list of them and write them down.
>
> Now, take several deep breaths, extending your exhale longer than your inhale. Keep yourself grounded by connecting with your environment and your body. The idea here is to prevent fear from overwhelming you and activating your system more than needed. You'll allow yourself to feel the fear while maintaining the awareness that you are not currently at risk.

Looking at each fear you wrote, starting with the mildest, close your eyes and focus on that fear. Notice if your body responds with sensations or only thoughts. Notice how intense that fear feels.

On a piece of paper, draw columns according to this template:

Fear Name or Description	Level of Disturbance (0-10) Cognitive / Sensations	Frequency (R, F, VF)	Shame/Guilt (Y/N)	Anchor

Write down that first fear you are noticing, and next, rate its intensity from 0 to 10 according to two different values: one for how bad you think it is (cognitive) and one for how severe it feels in your body (sensations). Notice if they are different. Add how frequently it appears in your daily life (**R**=rarely, **F**=frequently, **VF**=very frequently). Check Y/N whether that fear makes you feel shame or guilt. Do the same for each fear. (If at any point you feel that you are getting too disturbed, do a grounding exercise before or instead of continuing).

Now, beginning with those you marked as **VF,** ask yourself, *"Is this fear about something happening now or something I'm anticipating?" "How realistic is it to expect it to happen?" "What evidence supports this fear?" "What evidence contradicts this fear?" "What percentage of this fear is based on past experiences versus present reality?"*

Now, let's create some safety anchors: Identify and write down three "safety anchors"—concrete evidence from your present life that you are safe right now. Think of three things in your current life that reflect safety, stability, or support. These can be people, places, sensations, routines, or even inner strengths. Examples: A locked door and warm lighting in your home → *"I am in my own space, and no one can come in without my permission."* A friend who regularly checks in on you → *"I am not alone. I have people who care about me."* The rhythm of your breath or heartbeat → *"My body is steady. I'm alive and grounded."*

Each phrase you create for each anchor is to be repeated when fear arises. Practice saying these phrases while maintaining a relaxed breathing pattern.

This exercise helps disrupt the cyclical nature of fear by combining cognitive restructuring with physiological regulation. The mapping portion brings unconscious fears into awareness, reality testing challenges catastrophic thinking,

> sensory grounding returns attention to the present moment, and safety anchors build resources to counter fearful narratives.
>
> I recommend practicing this exercise regularly, not just when fear is intense, but to monitor your progress in reducing your reactions toward what you fear.

How does trauma disrupt our internal balance, and why does this matter for emotional pain and overall mental health?

Homeostasis—the term used to describe the body's ability to maintain internal balance—has become increasingly present in discussions about traumatization. Trauma indeed disrupts this essential function. The concept was introduced in 1926 by Walter Bradford Cannon—the same academic who introduced the "fight-or-flight" concept—to describe how our body continuously strives to remain stable despite external changes or challenges.

As part of survival, our body is constantly working to keep every organ and system stable. When balance is disturbed, various forms of illness can emerge, including mental health disorders. Without homeostasis, our system becomes dysregulated, and symptoms begin to appear not just emotionally but also cognitively and physically.

Think of homeostasis as your body's internal balancing act. Just as a tightrope walker continuously makes small adjustments to their posture and movements to stay upright, our body constantly regulates various systems to stay within healthy ranges. For example, our temperature must stay close to 98.6°F, blood pressure needs to remain within certain limits, blood sugar levels must be carefully controlled, and oxygen and carbon dioxide levels require precise regulation.

To maintain this equilibrium, the body relies on sophisticated feedback systems. "Negative feedback loops" work like a thermostat, bringing systems back to optimal levels when they drift too high, while "positive feedback loops" amplify necessary changes, such as those occurring during childbirth or blood clotting. Essentially, **we're well-equipped with the tools needed to restore balance and maintain health and stability.**

Homeostasis	Allostasis
Core body temperature	Stress response (HPA axis activation)
Blood pH	Energy allocation and metabolism
Blood glucose levels	Immune system regulation
Electrolyte and fluid balance	Cardiac output and blood distribution
Blood pressure	Thermoregulatory adjustments beyond baseline
Respiratory rate and oxygen/CO_2 levels	Sleep-wake cycling and circadian rhythms

Homeostasis vs Allostasis

Now think of this internal equilibrium not just as a balancing act for survival, but as an adaptive mechanism that keeps us prepared to face ever-changing situations. **This adaptive mechanism is called allostasis,** which describes how the body achieves stability through constant adjustments, anticipating and responding to new conditions rather than merely reacting after the fact. By constantly regulating temperature, blood pressure, and numerous other vital parameters, our bodies ensure we can respond flexibly to stressors—whether those involve physical exertion, emotional upset, or external threats—without tipping into dangerous extremes.

In the realm of emotional pain, internal equilibrium implies that our system strives to maintain an internal "emotional stability," much as it does for temperature or blood pressure. When we feel threatened, sad, or overwhelmed, internal feedback loops work to restore balance—stress hormones gradually subside once the threat passes, and physiological processes (like slowed breathing or muscle relaxation) naturally ease distress out of our awareness.

Consider how you feel after intense physical activity—tired, thirsty, and in need of rest. That's the body "asking" for what it needs to re-establish equilibrium and return to optimal functioning. Ideally, emotional stress should follow a similar arc: once the challenge has passed, the system should signal the need for soothing, reflection, or connection to restore emotional balance—just as we naturally seek comfort, understanding, or support after a difficult conversation or stressful day.

It's when we don't take the time to process and integrate the experience that emotional equilibrium gets disrupted and the rebalancing process stalls. Instead of resolving, states like anxiety, irritability, or sadness may linger and even intensify—eventually turning into emotional wounds if they're not acknowledged and addressed. Imagine ignoring your body's need for sleep for weeks after exhausting yourself—eventually, your immune system weakens, cognitive function declines, and physical health deteriorates. This scenario explains why some people rebound quickly after adversity, while others remain cycling through emotional suffering. They aren't failing or irremediably damaged; rather, their balancing mechanisms may be overloaded or misdirected and need to be recalibrated.

Why does this matter for trauma? When survival mechanisms remain activated for too long, they disrupt the body's natural rebalancing systems, leading to the persistent dysfunction.

Without internal equilibrium, natural calming mechanisms become less effective, and bodily systems—immune, digestive, and cardiovascular functions—begin to malfunction. Just as diabetes represents a breakdown in the body's ability to regulate blood sugar, trauma represents a breakdown in the body's ability to regulate stress responses and return to balance.

> **Breath Equilibrium Practice.** A simple exercise to **help your nervous system stay balanced** is through breath awareness. Balanced breathing helps regulate your autonomic nervous system.
>
> Several times a day, check whether your inhalation is as free and easy as your exhalation. If not, gently exaggerate the side that feels weaker for a few breaths. Continue until you notice both your inhaling and exhaling become equally comfortable—flowing naturally without effort or strain.

WHY DO SOME PEOPLE SEEM WIRED TO EXPECT FAILURE, AND WHAT'S FUELING THAT SELF-DEFEATING TRAP?

Defeat is an extremely important concept to explore if we want to prevent trauma or lasting emotional pain. As a mental state, defeat plays a pivotal role in why some individuals become traumatized while others do not. In my clinical experience, a defeatist mentality emerges when someone internalizes the belief that success is not possible—often rooted in fear of failure, past setbacks, or a fragile sense of self. I'm not talking about succeeding in business or gaining recognition, but rather about believing in one's ability to overcome challenges. This mindset triggers a cascade of emotional and cognitive reactions, such as helplessness, hopelessness, and a sensitivity to life's difficulties.

This state often reveals itself in subtle ways—like when someone responds to guidance with *"I'll try!"* That phrase already entertains the possibility of failure, hinting at a defeatist (or scarcity) mindset quietly operating beneath the surface.

As we've discussed, the brain functions as an anticipatory system—constantly using past experiences to predict what might happen and prepare for it. When a defeatist mentality takes hold, the brain begins to anticipate failure by default. In the progression of trauma responses, defeat marks the point where the system gets dysregulated and shifts to survival mode. This happens because the brain interprets anticipated failure as a threat to safety, security, or survival itself, triggering protective responses repeatedly. Time becomes distorted—the past bleeds into the present, creating a continuous threat experience where old defeats feel immediate and current. This explains why defeat is so central to trauma: it transforms the brain's protective anticipatory function into a trap that maintains chronic dysregulation, making recovery difficult until the defeatist cycle is interrupted.

Anticipates failure
Assumes inability
No motivation
No curiosity
No energy

Defeatist Mentality

Consider how this cycle works: someone with a fear of insects begins to anticipate encounters with them everywhere. This constant vigilance expands—first to other small creatures, then to concerns about contamination or disease they might carry. Each time they avoid or feel overwhelmed by these situations, their brain logs another "defeat"—another confirmation that they cannot handle these challenges. Eventually, the anticipation of fear itself becomes the threat, creating anxiety about anxiety and transforming daily life into a minefield of potential dangers where every avoided encounter reinforces their sense of helplessness.

These entrenched worries gradually crystallize into a core belief: *"I will inevitably be harmed, rejected, or fail."* When this becomes a persistent state, it triggers a profound shift in brain function. The brain shifts into energy conservation mode, reducing motivation and effort as a protective measure against further disappointment. Over time, this chronic state depletes emotional and physical resources, frequently leading to emotional numbness, dissociation, or physical manifestations such as chronic pain, adrenal fatigue, and migraines.

The origins of this mentality can vary widely—from external experiences like rejection or neglect to internal factors like chronic pain or relentless self-criticism. Sometimes, it emerges through a feedback loop, where external difficulties reinforce internal doubts, and those doubts magnify new setbacks. Whatever its origin, it keeps people trapped in inaction and resignation, often reinforcing a victim mentality that can trap the system in survival mode indefinitely.

> **An Anti-Defeatist Daily Practice.** Here's an exercise designed to help shift away from a defeatist mindset and begin to rebuild hope, motivation, and self-efficacy.
>
> At the beginning of your day, choose one small task that you've been avoiding because you think, *"What's the point?"* or *"I'll probably mess it up"*—like sending a follow-up email, taking a 10-minute walk, organizing "that" drawer, or trying a new response when you get a call from someone you have animosity towards. Keep it small enough to succeed but meaningful enough to matter.
>
> By the end of the day, ask yourself, *"Did I try?" "What helped me take action?" "What thoughts tried to stop me?"*
>
> Find one or more answers to those questions and write them down as a way to track your progress. Answers could sound like, *"I was tempted to skip the walk because I thought it was pointless, but I did it anyway. It didn't fix everything, but I felt more energized afterward."*
>
> Each time you hear thoughts like *"Why bother?"* or *"It won't work,"* answer with a lived mantra and allow it to land in your body: *"Effort builds capacity—even if results take time." "Trying is a form of success." "If I keep practicing, something will shift." "Defeat is not in failing—it's in not showing up. Today, I showed up."*
>
> At the end of the week, make a quick list of every task you attempted, whatever the outcome. Then ask yourself, *"What would this week look like if I hadn't tried at all?"*

> Notice your body's response—any lift in mood, energy, confidence, or clarity. Name your level of satisfaction; even subtle gains count. Keep practicing.

WHAT QUALIFIES AS A VICTIM MENTALITY? IS IT TRAUMA-RELATED?

We can define victim mentality as a psychological pattern in which individuals primarily see themselves through the lens of suffering and perceived injustice, shaping their self-view and reactions around continual mistreatment rather than personal agency. This is different from:

(a) the healthy experience of **feeling victimized** after genuine harm—an understandable, appropriate response—and

(b) **being a victim,** which describes a real circumstance rather than a mindset.

Victim mentality becomes problematic when it turns into a default lens: suffering remains central to how a person sees themselves and engages with the world, regardless of the present situation.

Consider a student who fails an important exam. For many, this might be just an academic setback—disappointing but manageable. However, for someone with a victim mentality, the narrative shifts from "I failed this test" to "I failed because the system is against people like me." This belief may lead them to study less for future exams *("Why bother?"),* avoid asking for help *("No one will care anyway"),* and withdraw from study groups *("They probably exclude people like me on purpose").*

Each choice, driven by this victim mindset, creates new problems—lower grades, isolation, missed learning opportunities—that ultimately cause more harm than the initial failure. The student's victim narrative becomes a self-fulfilling prophecy, generating real obstacles that seem to confirm their belief that they are indeed being victimized.

Although a defeatist mentality (focusing on one's own inadequacy) and a victim mentality (focusing on external blame) have different roots, they often reinforce each other. In our student example, a defeatist mindset might say, *"I'm just not smart enough to pass,"* while a victim mindset insists, *"The professor is unfair and wants me to fail."*

These beliefs work in tandem—feeling personally inadequate makes the student more likely to see others as antagonistic, and perceiving external hostility further entrenches their sense of personal failure.

Together, these mindsets convince the student that success is out of reach, leaving them feeling powerless to improve their situation—a recipe for ongoing dysregulation.

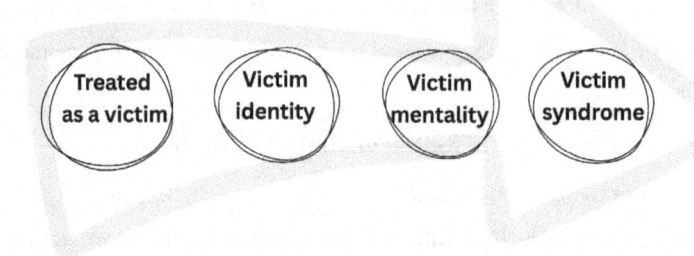

Treated as a victim → Victim identity → Victim mentality → Victim syndrome

Victim Mentality Continuum

This is where trauma becomes relevant: when this sense of helplessness keeps the nervous system constantly alert and distressed—watching for signs of "inevitable" failure or others' "certain" obstruction—it can affect the body similarly to being under genuine threat. A chronic victim mentality can indeed be deeply trauma-related, especially when the person's perceived powerlessness stems from truly damaging events. However, it can also develop in situations where no actual abuse occurred, particularly when everyday challenges like parental discipline or normal conflicts are interpreted through a trauma lens.

While accountability is important—abusers should face consequences for their actions—accountability alone rarely heals emotional wounds. Several authors have pointed out that the language of victimhood can be both validating and, at the same time, limiting. For instance, Gill Straker & Jacqui Winship recently wrote in *The Guardian*: *"The exclusive identification as a victim can overshadow more positive aspects of someone's identity, limiting their autonomy, enjoyment, and creativity."*

Being labeled a victim acknowledges that real harm occurred, but it doesn't automatically restore emotional well-being. In some cases, it can leave people feeling disempowered, reinforcing a belief that they are weak, helpless, or defined by what was done to them.

> **Assessing Real Victimization: The B-P-I-D Framework.** A victim is someone hurt, injured, or killed due to a crime, accident, or another person's actions. If you're wondering whether your experience counts as victimization, use the B-P-I-D heuristic to assess it:
>
> **Breach:** Was there a clear violation of your boundaries, rights, or consent? For example, was your safety, freedom, or property compromised? Does the event qualify as a crime (like assault or theft) or an accident (like a car crash)?
>
> **Power:** Was there an imbalance of power or resources you couldn't overcome at the time? Did the person or situation have control over what happened, leaving you feeling powerless?
>
> **Intent:** Was the harm deliberate, or was it accidental? Did you feel targeted, or did the event seem random?
>
> **Damage:** Did the event cause significant harm, such as physical injuries, medical issues, or financial loss? Has it measurably disrupted your life, like missing work, needing legal or medical help, or facing ongoing consequences? Were these events frequent, serious, and lasting?
>
> If you answer "yes" to two or more of these, the experience likely qualifies as victimization. Seeking external support (e.g., a friend, therapist, or legal help) may

be a wise step. If you have one or zero "yes" answers, you may have experienced ordinary adversity—painful, but easier to navigate with reframing or skill-building. This distinction can help you focus on healing what's truly deep without treating every hurt as a lasting wound.

Addressing this topic matters. Given the complexity of distinguishing between healthy responses to genuine harm and problematic victim mentality, I'm giving you another exercise here to learn how to interrupt the victim mentality.

The Victim Alternative Inquiry. Understanding the difference between being victimized and adopting a victim mentality is crucial, but sometimes we need to examine our own responses more closely. The following exercise helps you explore whether you're viewing situations through a victim lens when other perspectives might be more empowering and accurate. This isn't about dismissing real harm but about expanding how you see yourself and your capacity to respond.

Close your eyes for a moment and recall an instance in which you felt victimized. Stay there for a few seconds and notice any sensations or emotions that arise. Is there tension in your body? Do certain thoughts loop in your mind? Images? Feelings? Pause briefly.

Shift the frame.

Ask yourself, *"If I could not see myself **only** as a victim here, how else could I view this situation?" "What would I believe about myself instead?"* Possibilities: learner, boundary-setter, resilient survivor, advocate, strategic planner. Sense even a flicker of expansion—maybe your chest loosens or your posture straightens.

Stay there for around 30 seconds, and return deliberately to the victim stance. Then back to the alternative. Note changes in breath, muscle tone, and narrative. Which lens leaves you with more agency and accuracy?

Write one sentence for each lens:

Victim sentence: *"I was powerless when ___."*

Agency sentence: *"I can/will ___ to protect or restore myself."*

Keeping both sentences honors reality and possibility.

> This exercise isn't about denying real harm but about expanding the lens through which you see yourself—helping you move from powerlessness to possibility.
>
> Practice it often, and you'll start noticing the difference.

For those who recognize they've developed chronic victim mentality patterns, breaking free requires consistent, intentional practice. Victim mentality often becomes automatic—a mental habit that interprets situations through the lens of powerlessness before we're even aware it's happening. The following structured exercise provides a daily framework for interrupting these patterns and rebuilding a sense of personal agency. Regular practice helps rewire ingrained thought patterns and develops the mental flexibility needed to respond rather than react from a victim stance.

> **Intention, Reframe, Action, and Affirmation to interrupt a victim mentality (IRAA).** Here is an exercise for individuals who have developed a victim mentality—a state where one chronically sees oneself as powerless, wronged, or stuck. It guides you to shift your internal narrative from helplessness to agency. I recommend doing this at the end of each day.
>
> > **I** — Let's **set the intention** to shift perception from *"things happen to me"* to *"I influence what happens next,"* even if it's only in small ways. Then, ask yourself *"In what situations did I feel like a victim today?"* *"What made me feel powerless or wronged?"* *"Was I actually victimized, or did I feel like it as my habitual response?"* An example of these situations can be *"My coworker ignored my input in the meeting. I felt dismissed and unimportant, and my mind went into generalizing how my opinion doesn't count, nobody likes me, and how they want to make me feel small."*
> >
> > **R** — If you notice any of those patterns, **reframe the experience** by asking yourself *"Is there another way to interpret this?"* *"Even if*

I didn't cause this, how did I respond?" "What response could help me feel more in control or grounded next time?" An example of reframing could sound like *"Maybe they were distracted or under pressure. I stayed silent, which made me feel more invisible. Next time, I can calmly repeat my point or follow up afterward."*

A — Think of one small, constructive **action** you can take to reclaim agency. Examples include speaking up when something feels unfair, setting a boundary with someone who drains your energy, or doing one thing you've been postponing due to helplessness—even something small like organizing your inbox or taking a walk outside.

A — Finally, choose one empowering **affirmation** to repeat several times (while tapping the top of your head) to finish the exercise. Examples include *"I am not my past. I shape my future," "I choose my response, even when I can't choose the situation," "Each step I take gives me more clarity and strength," "I'm not a victim, and I won't allow anyone to victimize me."*

This exercise assumes that victim mentality is maintained by repetitive inner dialogues of injustice, helplessness, and blame.

By practicing these simple steps, you can develop self-observation (meta-awareness), promote cognitive flexibility, and build emotional resilience by focusing on response rather than reaction.

WHAT TURNS A BAD EXPERIENCE INTO ACTUAL TRAUMA?

Sometimes, the best way to understand trauma is through a simple analogy. Let's take the COVID-19 pandemic as an example. Do you believe COVID-19 killed thousands of people? Most would say yes—but technically, it wasn't the virus alone. It was how each person's body responded to its invasion. Having the SARS-CoV-2 virus in our system doesn't always cause COVID-19. Some people who contract the virus remain asymptomatic, while in other cases, the virus triggers an immune system overreaction, causing severe inflammation that leads to tissue damage and organ dysfunction. What causes death in severe cases isn't the virus itself but the body's effort to protect the system.

This concept helps us understand psychological trauma. Much like COVID-19 isn't the virus but the illness caused by it, trauma isn't the event but the psychological and biological reaction and the aftermath. Just as some individuals can carry the SARS-CoV-2 virus without getting sick, some people can experience traumatic events without developing lasting psychological distress.

When a traumatic event triggers an exaggerated response that destabilizes the nervous system, significant damage can occur—similar to an immune system overreaction. The nervous system, attempting to protect us, reallocates resources to survival functions, diverting energy from other processes even when this shift creates its own problems.

The brain shifts significant energy to prioritize survival. When a threat is detected, it activates automatic, reflexive responses that operate like a fire sprinkler system, flooding every zone at once. These immediate responses prioritize speed over precision because in genuine danger, a quick reaction offers better survival odds than a perfect response that arrives too late.

However, these rapid solutions come with costs. While lightning-fast and requiring minimal energy initially, they bypass sophisticated processing systems—the reflective, analytical functions capable of nuanced decision-making, emotional regulation, and accurate memory formation. These systems consume more energy and time but are designed for accuracy and sustainable outcomes. Importantly, they don't automatically engage once danger passes but require conscious activation through deliberate actions like pausing or breathing.

When automatic survival systems keep working without allowing us to think things through, important functions can be affected, causing problems with memory, emotions, and clear thinking. The persistence of these responses becomes tied to our internal meaning-making processes—how we perceive safety versus threat.

Psychological trauma results from the lingering effects of our responses to the event, sustained by internal factors: negative core beliefs, distorted perceptions of danger, helplessness, rigid emotional scripts, unresolved shame, rumination, and chronic feelings of vulnerability. These factors continuously signal to the nervous system that a threat is still present, prolonging the crisis state.

In complex trauma, these changes build slowly, in small increments. Each time the stress response activates to deal with a perceived threat, the nervous system makes tiny adjustments to preserve equilibrium. These accumulate until the system can no longer adapt without serious consequences. This is how conditions like C-PTSD and Developmental Trauma Disorder emerge.

Leave the Past Where it Belongs

"Integrating your pain becomes the foundation for something greater."

A common question in the minds of many is *"What does healing from trauma look like?"* Some people get disappointed to learn that it's not a dramatic, overnight transformation. It's more like a quiet return to wholeness, or, if you prefer a less ambiguous term, to normalcy. Resolving trauma is a gradual rebuilding of the emotional foundation that may have once been cracked or fractured. Becoming whole again requires patience, courage, and a dose of self-compassion, acceptance, and hope.

But what does this gradual process actually look like? Think of it like building strength and endurance at the gym. You don't walk in one day and leave transformed. You show up consistently, even when it's hard. Some days you feel progress; other days, it's just about staying committed. Over time, with repetition and care, the system and your worked muscles grow stronger.

Reestablishing your system after trauma works the same way. It involves practicing emotional regulation, setting boundaries, reconnecting with your body and the sense of who you are, and challenging the beliefs that trauma left behind—all developed through consistent, patient effort.

Is it bad to center your life around your trauma?

When the relationship you establish with a traumatic event becomes so central that everything else in your life begins to revolve around it, we may say that you have adopted a "trauma centrality" viewpoint. This is another concept that helps explain why some individuals are deeply affected by experiences—regardless of their apparent severity—while others with seemingly similar experiences are less impacted for less time.

Trauma centrality refers to the degree to which a traumatic event becomes the dominant focus of an individual's personal narrative, identity, and self-perception. It occurs when someone over-identifies with the experience, allowing it to become their primary defining characteristic. This mindset is a major impediment to recovery, but knowing about it may help dissolve it.

Think of someone who introduces themselves through their trauma story—*"I'm the one who survived that car accident"*—as if their identity begins and ends there. They might constantly revisit the experience in conversations—*"Nobody knows what I've been through"*—or use it to explain every current difficulty—*"This is why I can't drive"* or *"I'll never be able to do that because of what happened to me."* Even decisions and life goals may be filtered through that lens—*"I'm unable to live there because of my trauma."*

When this level of trauma centrality takes hold, the event assumes disproportionate weight, overshadowing previous beliefs, experiences, and aspects of identity. This pattern reinforces perceptions of yourself as damaged and permanently altered, keeping your system in crisis mode by fueling negative schemas, chronic rumination, avoidance, and persistent self-blame.

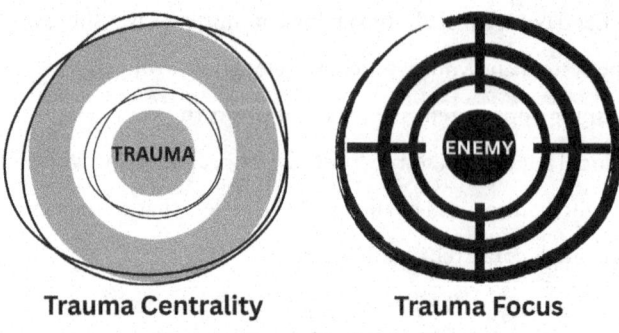

Trauma Centrality   **Trauma Focus**

Trauma Centrality Mental State

Beneath the surface, there's often a pervasive sense of defeat, coupled with the belief that others are adversaries, intent on hurting or rejecting you. The emotional injury becomes the lens through which you interpret the past, experience the present, and anticipate the future. This perspective can obscure your strengths, inner resources, and capacity for resilience.

Resolution can't happen when your entire focus remains fixated on the traumatic event. That's why any healing journey needs to begin by identifying this pattern and learning to integrate the experience as one part of a larger, more complete life story.

> **Identity Reclamation Practice.** Let me offer you an exercise designed to help shift your perspective from being focused on feeling victimized to becoming empowered.
>
> Start by reflecting on how you currently define yourself. In a journal, or quietly in your mind, complete the sentence: *"I am someone who..."*
>
> Let yourself answer freely. Notice whether the traumatic event—or the identity formed around it—dominates your response.
>
> Now, imagine your life as a story with many chapters, and ask yourself, *"What are the main chapters in my life?"* *"What parts of me existed before that traumatic event?"* *"What parts have emerged since?"*

> Place the traumatic event in one chapter—not as the title, not as the whole book, but as one meaningful and difficult part of the story. Then, gently shift your focus—expand the spotlight away from the traumatic event and toward the full story of your life. Who were you before the pain? Who are you becoming now?
>
> Consider this metaphor to elaborate on your narration: Imagine you had fractured your leg but continued limping long after it healed. You begin calling yourself *"the cripple."* Now imagine the strain that ongoing limp might create—the damage that continues, not because of the fracture itself, but because of the pattern it left behind.
>
> Now think about what it means to continue organizing your identity around traumatic events, even after you've done meaningful healing work. Notice how your body responds to that thought. Does it bring tension? Restriction? Does it feel like it limits your growth or how you see yourself?
>
> Take a deep breath and let go of judgment. Then bring your attention to the words of Carl Jung: *"I am not what happened to me; I am what I choose to become."* Let that line settle in your body and become a seed for your future narratives.
>
> Now, think about what you choose to become—as if that were the title of a new memoir. Complete these two lines: *"I choose to become..."* and *"My life as a book will be called..."*
>
> Return to these phrases regularly. Let them ground you in your power to become—not in what happened, but in what is possible now.

AM I ACTUALLY HEALING, OR AM I JUST GETTING USED TO FEELING BROKEN?

Resolving emotional injuries isn't easy—and when those injuries developed over years of distress, healing can feel elusive. Some people remain convinced it's impossible, while others learn to distinguish between being injured and having recovered from the damage.

Let me share something painful but real as an example: *My son recently broke his wrist; it looked awful. He had to have surgery right away to reconstruct the shattered* bones. *A few months later, he regained full mobility and functionality. However, if you examine his X-rays, you will notice screws and a plate replacing the healthy tissue and bone that were present before. The injury is repaired, and the wrist is no longer fractured, but I imagine he'll occasionally experience discomfort because of the extreme interventions required to restore functionality. His wrist will never revert to what it was, but the injury is resolved, and the symptoms of a shattered wrist are gone.*

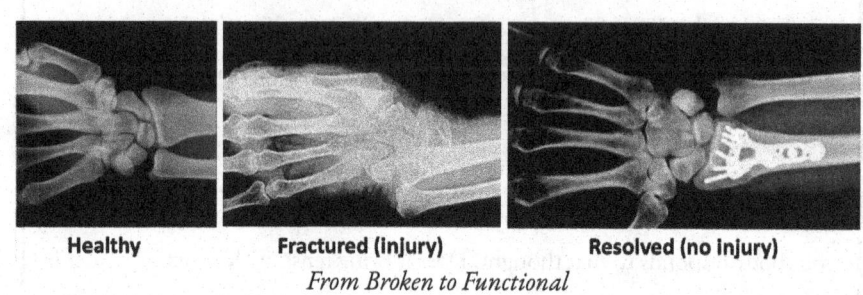

Healthy   **Fractured (injury)**   **Resolved (no injury)**

From Broken to Functional

This example illustrates an important principle about psychological healing. Rather than using a diagnosis or clinging to the trauma label, it's more helpful to look for signs of recovered functionality. Instead of expecting absolute resolution, you can appreciate the system's natural flexibility and balance.

Evidence of psychological trauma resolution shows up in quiet but powerful ways: becoming more in tune with your emotions, responding rather than reacting, feeling steadier in the face of stress, considering the needs of others under a different light, and reconnecting to your core—even in the presence of what once hurt you. It means finding ease and confidence where there was fear and presence where there was avoidance. Ultimately, resolution is about changing your relationship to what happened—finding meaning in it and gently reclaiming the parts of yourself that got lost along the way.

How do you cope with fear and not panic?

Experiencing panic can be very distressing and often indicates that our nervous system has become overwhelmed by perceived threats—whether real or imagined. Panic attacks can affect anyone, regardless of their resilience or resources. They often occur when our threat-detection system becomes hypersensitive or when stress accumulates beyond our current capacity to process it. Let's differentiate between fear and panic.

Fear is your system's way of alerting you to potential danger. Panic goes beyond emotion; it's a reaction that arises when the fear response overwhelms your capacity to process what's happening effectively.

Think of it like a car's engine light. When it first comes on, you can check what's wrong and address it—this is like fear giving you useful information. But if you ignore the warning and keep driving, the engine might overheat and you could lose control—this is like panic overwhelming your system.

This is what happens in your body: Fear activates a stress response to help you stay alert or triggers more extreme survival reactions if it escalates. The key difference is that fear allows your mind to still assess the situation and signal safety, thereby preventing over-activation.

Panic occurs when your system becomes flooded with stress hormones and your thinking brain goes offline, leaving you at the mercy of survival reflexes. Although it may seem like you're reasoning, your cognition becomes clouded rather than strategic.

Fear of the symptoms themselves—say you notice your heart racing and think, *"I'm having a heart attack"*—adds a second layer of alarm. That thought pumps out more adrenaline, which makes the heart pound even harder, confirming the worst-case story your brain just told. Each jolt of sensation sparks fresh worry, and each burst of worry intensifies the sensations, spiraling into a full panic. In other words, "fear of fear" becomes fuel for the feeling, locking you in a loop where fear keeps manufacturing more fear.

Fear Interruption Protocol. Let's do something practical about handling fear and stopping panic from appearing.

Think about something you normally find scary. Allow your body to connect with whatever comes when you keep the image of what you fear clearly in your mind. When you notice that first wave of sensations—perhaps a quickened heartbeat or a jolt of adrenaline—**pause and acknowledge it.**

The pause and thoughts like *"I think I'm extremely nervous"* or *"I'm really scared and I don't like the feeling"* are intended to help keep your cognition online so it can assist you in regulating the reaction and maintaining awareness of the emotional process you're experiencing.

> By reminding yourself that the sensations and bodily responses are simply information meant to protect you, you strengthen your reflective capacity and shift your focus back to the present moment.
>
> Then you can take one slow breath and briefly scan your surroundings, telling yourself, *"I'm here right now, and it seems I'm not in imminent danger."* Bring your hands to your face and rub your cheeks very softly, repeating, *"I'm here, and I'm feeling connected to myself."*
>
> If you catch your thoughts spiraling—like *"I can't handle this"* or *"I'm losing control"*—label them as fear-based reactions rather than immediate facts and keep focusing on your breath. With each exhale, let a bit of the tension release, reassuring your system that you're safe in this moment. *"I'm breathing out some of the fear that I'm experiencing, and I notice how my body feels a little calmer."*
>
> The goal isn't to eliminate fear altogether but to develop awareness, build tolerance, and maintain enough regulation so you can use fear's message without letting it overwhelm you. Practice daily, or whenever you notice fear coming up. Remember that to reprogram your brain, you have to create new habits to replace the unhealthy ones, and habits only develop with a lot of repetitions. The one you want to create here is "pause and assess before panicking."

Will Trauma Always Be Part of My Life?

As a trauma therapist, I'm genuinely optimistic about healing—and for good reason. I've not only witnessed it countless times with my clients, but I've experienced it myself. I have, like my clients, shed the weight of profound emotional injuries I once thought would never leave.

How is healing possible? Your brain has an incredible natural ability to heal when given the right environment and support, especially when you actively participate in your recovery. To understand if trauma can truly be left behind, you need to get clear on how traumatization affects different aspects of your being—distortions in your perception, emotions, regulation, dissociative tendencies, or disturbing memories—what healing actually looks like in each area, and what practical steps you can take to make that healing happen.

Think of trauma like discovering structural issues in a house after an earthquake that prompt necessary renovations. Healing from trauma is like renovating the house to be strong, secure, and livable again—reinforcing the foundation so you feel stable, upgrading the systems so your emotions regulate properly, and improving the structure so you can navigate life more effectively. With proper renovation, the house can be better prepared against future earthquakes.

How does someone resolve emotional trauma?

Resolving emotional trauma depends on what specifically needs to be addressed. For many people, it's about regaining a sense of safety, confidence, agency, and the capacity to regulate fear and the overreactions it causes. Mostly, it involves learning to understand and reshape your automatic responses to sensory information that triggers reactions that have kept you in a state of despair and defeat.

Unlike emotional wounds, which may heal naturally over time or with reflection, self-care, and support, trauma requires more intentional intervention because the system has made alterations to its functioning. Trauma is not only emotional; it's physiological.

Another key aspect is understanding your emotional patterns. Often, what appears to be one emotion (like anger) may actually mask another (like fear). *For example, a person who feels angry in social settings might be grappling with unprocessed fear rooted in past experiences of rejection or ridicule.*

Additionally, many traumatized individuals develop rigid rules to stay safe—like *"Never trust anyone"* or *"Always be on guard."* While these rules once served a protective function, they can end up blocking healthy interactions. Resolving trauma means gradually learning more flexible ways of relating: *"I can be cautious while still allowing myself to trust safe people."*

Consider that the strategies that your system developed to overcome threats are like an internal alarm system that's become oversensitive—imagine a smoke detector that goes off every time you toast bread, or a car alarm triggered by a gentle breeze. The system now can't tell the difference between a burned piece of toast and an actual fire. Resolving trauma means recalibrating this system so it can distinguish between real threats and false alarms. This recalibration happens gradually, through repeated experiences of safety that teach your nervous system to update its threat assessment. You still need it for genuine dangers, but the system requires fine-tuning of its sensitivity. Instead of letting automatic reactions control you when your internal alarms go off, you learn to consciously choose how to respond.

In short, you know healing is taking place when your body feels more like home than a threat, the past becomes a story you can share instead of a storm you're still enduring, your emotional responses align with current situations rather than past dangers, and you can envision a future that excites rather than frightens you.

Chapter Four

DISCONNECTION

HOW TO RECOGNIZE THE IMPACT OF CRITICISM, BETRAYAL, REJECTION, AND NEGLECT

"We crave connection, yet those we love most can wound us deepest."

There's an ironic paradox at the heart of being human: we long for connection, yet our deepest pain often comes from those very relationships. When you open ourselves to others—whether a friend, a partner, or a family member—you hope for acceptance, empathy, and understanding. Sometimes, that vulnerability is met with warmth and care. But other times, it's met with disregard, contempt, mockery, rejection, or abandonment—leaving wounds that linger in ways you never expected and never learned to address. Sometimes the wound comes not from what someone does to you, but from what they fail to do—the attention, care, or recognition you needed but never received. The depth of the wound doesn't depend on the type of it, but on how meaningful the relationship was and how unprepared you were for the hurt, as well as how long you left it to fester, waiting passively for someone else to bring the remedy.

We often describe these wounds in physical terms—"hard feelings" or a "broken heart"—and brain science confirms this is more than metaphor. Emotional wounds activate many of the same brain circuits as physical injuries, which explains why betrayal and rejection can literally hurt in your body. There's that familiar sinking sensation when someone you love delivers an unexpected blow—a spouse making a cruel remark or a supportive colleague blindsiding you with unfair criticism. These emotional injuries deserve attention in their own right.

Unlike trauma that threatens your physical safety, disconnection wounds rarely endanger your survival—yet they can shake the foundations of your emotional world. They happen not in dark alleys with strangers but around kitchen tables and through text messages from people you once believed cared enough not to hurt you. When left unprocessed, these everyday betrayals can disrupt your days and dim your sense of connection to others. The question isn't whether these wounds hurt—it's how deeply they've penetrated and what kind of interventions they actually need.

Make Sense of Heartbreak, Insecurities, and Other Ego Threats

"Most emotional wounds live in the space between what we wanted, we needed, and what we received."

Understanding emotional wounds on their own terms increases the chances of effective resolution. While emotional pain is registered by some of the same brain regions that process trauma, it does not trigger the intense survival responses associated with life-threatening experiences. For instance, discovering a friend's betrayal might cause intense heartache and sleepless nights, but it doesn't activate the same fight-or-flight responses as facing eviction. Instead, emotional wounds primarily affect how we process relationships: how we form memories about people we trust, how we interpret others' intentions, and how we manage our emotional responses when relationships feel uncertain. Additionally, they influence our emotional scripts, which in turn affect how we will experience our emotions in the future.

Most research on emotional wounds has focused on specific types of hurt—"betrayal trauma" exists in one research area, "social rejection" in another, and "fear of abandonment" in yet another. Even worse, most emotional wounds are often categorized as trauma in popular understanding, which obscures the crucial distinctions between survival-based responses and relational pain. Understanding emotional wounds as expressions of our relational needs, yet distinct from trauma, can facilitate the development of more effective healing approaches and help us resolve most of our relational pain.

What makes some hurts turn into wounds while others don't?

Some hurts fade, while others become wounds indeed. Emotional wounds come from broken promises, exposed lies, dismissive comments, and cruel criticisms that make us want to disappear, cut ties, and doubt stories we once believed— *"Did they ever love me?" "I never thought they could hurt me like that."* Although these blows don't threaten physical safety, they can shake our trust, sense of worth, and willingness to connect.

Such wounds share three elements. First, they occur within relationships we value. Second, they challenge our agency and belonging. Third, they linger—long after the moment passes, the memory still feels raw. What turns a hurt into a wound is this lasting impact on emotional functioning and whether their effects become schemas—internal truths based on assumptions and hurts. Our brain struggles to integrate the experience, remaining in pain until we can make sense of what happened and learn how to handle similar situations differently in the future.

Emotional wounds are frequently tied to the specific individual who inflicted the harm and our uncertainty about their motivations. In the worst case—and especially if the wound stays open too long—our brain may generate protective patterns that extend beyond the initial upset, generalizing our responses to similar situations. Someone who was deeply betrayed might never forgive the person who betrayed them but may also develop a heightened sensitivity to dishonesty, reacting strongly even to minor infractions from others because the brain has learned to anticipate threats to trust.

I have identified several key characteristics that define emotional wounds:

First, emotional wounds revolve around violations of core human needs—such as security, belonging, recognition, or meaning. The depth of the wound typically depends on how fundamental the affected need is to our overall well-being. *For instance, if you discover that a group won't welcome you (you weren't invited to their party), it can cause an emotional wound tied specifically to that group. However, if you fear isolation, you may interpret the experience as "being forever expelled," which can escalate your experience and lead to a generalized expectation of rejection from everyone.*

Second, emotional wounds often lead to protective adaptations—changes in our thoughts, feelings, and behaviors designed to prevent similar hurt in the future—for example, becoming more cautious about sharing personal information after being gossiped about. However, when they remain unresolved or become overly rigid, protective adaptations can turn maladaptive, resulting in heightened vigilance, distrust, or avoidance.

Unresolved emotional wounds can accumulate over time. Each time we get emotionally wounded and fail to resolve it, we add metaphorical bricks to a wall meant to protect us. These bricks are made of beliefs we form to stay safe, like *"I'm better off alone"* or *"Showing emotion makes me weak."* Eventually, these protective structures don't just keep harm out—they also keep connection out. We become guarded, emotionally withdrawn, and isolated.

In contrast, when emotional wounds are acknowledged and worked through, they don't harden into walls. Instead, they become resources—tools that help us adapt, stay connected, and respond to others with clarity and strength. *For instance, someone who has processed a betrayal might develop better boundaries and the ability to recognize trustworthy people, while someone who has worked through rejection might become more compassionate toward others who feel excluded.*

Third, emotional wounds can become deeply embedded in our memory, triggering automatic reactions. We might snap at a friend who casually comments on our cooking because we were once harshly criticized in a way that left a "wounded" spot around food and hosting. Although others may see the remark as harmless, it hits a nerve tied to those earlier, unresolved hurts.

My descriptions may sound a lot similar to the ones about trauma that abound in social media, but the brain handles these wound memories differently than traumatic ones. Because they aren't assigned top-level priority for survival, the system retains better equilibrium, and perception remains less distorted. The schemas linked to emotional wounds tend to be less generalized—*"I can't trust my friend X,"* rather than *"I can't trust anyone."* They are still charged with emotions, which is why many individuals confuse them with traumatic material, but they remain within the system's capacity to process them.

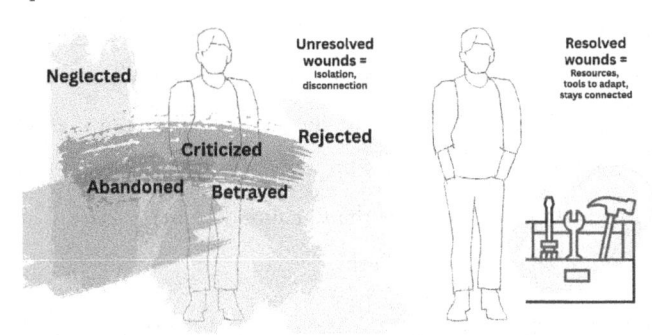

Unresolved vs Resolved Emotional Wounds

Finally, emotional wounds often arise in relationships where we've invested significant trust and closeness—making them highly impactful despite seeming minor to outside observers. You might feel deeply hurt if a close friend dismisses your concerns, even though others view the hurt as trivial. Because you've opened up to that friend, the casual dismissal cuts far deeper than it would coming from someone less important, due to surprise (disconnect between what you thought you knew about this person) and expectations (unspoken agreements that your feelings were to be treated with care).

WHAT FACTORS MAKE EMOTIONAL PAIN STICK AROUND?

We get emotionally wounded when something meaningful gets ruptured—a relationship (a friendship), a sense of identity (who we thought we were or how others see us), or a core emotional need (being understood or accepted). What turns pain into a wound is often not the incident, but how alone we feel in it and whether there is an opportunity for repair. This includes both what happens to us and how we relate to it. *For example, if the private information your friend shared with others causes you to lose something important, it may feel irreparable. If it was harmless gossip, it could be resolved with an apology.* Remember that we can also intervene—and attend to ourselves—internally. That's why it's helpful to identify the aspects we do have influence over. For your friend's betrayal, you can ask for a direct acknowledgment of the pain it caused and set new boundaries—deciding what you will and won't share in the future. You can also remind yourself that their lapse reflects their choices, not your worth.

One area that's often overlooked is the role of **expectations.** Emotional wounding is closely tied to the expectations we carry about relationships and people. These expectations often determine the emotional weight of an experience. The higher—and sometimes less realistic—our expectations are, the more intense our disappointment and the greater the likelihood of being hurt. This formula could help you understand how it works:

DISAPPOINTMENT = EXPECTATIONS − REALITY

SATISFACTION = REALITY − EXPECTATIONS

Disappointment formula

If reality closely matches our expectations, disappointment will be close to zero. But if our expectations significantly exceed reality, disappointment will be high. On the other hand, when reality exceeds our expectations, we experience satisfaction.

Imagine meeting someone who seems flirtatious every time you're together, leading you to build up expectations. You might start envisioning a future with this person and fantasizing about a life together. If they don't follow through, the disappointment can be profound and leave you feeling wounded. You might think you're hurt because they "rejected" you, but in reality, it's also the unmet expectation—the failure to receive what you believed was already yours—that creates the deepest disruption.

Our expectations don't form at random—they grow out of our deepest needs. We look for loyalty because it safeguards our sense of security, seek attention because it tells us we matter, and crave appreciation because it confirms our worth. These expectations are shaped by past experience, culture, family patterns, core schemas, and personal values. We carry this set of assumptions without checking notes with others or reviewing them with new relationships. We just assume mothers love unconditionally, friends keep secrets, and partners stay loyal if they love us. That's why two people can face the same event and react in completely different ways—the gaps between their private expectations and shared reality are unique to their histories. When those gaps widen, it's the unmet need beneath the expectation that feels wounded, not merely a loss of predictability.

Understanding the formula for disappointment doesn't mean we must eliminate expectations. We all carry them; living without any would be impossible—and unhealthy. Instead, the formula invites us to craft **conscious, flexible expectations** that honor our legitimate needs while acknowledging reality. Resolving emotional wounds often requires working both sides of the equation: softening unrealistic assumptions and building relationships and environments where reasonable ones can actually be met.

Beyond expectations, several factors decide whether emotional pain fades or turns into a lasting wound. **Isolation** magnifies hurt—pain left unshared tends to fester. **Lack of acknowledgment,** from ourselves or others, keeps emotions unresolved. **Rumination,** the mental replay of a slight, etches the wound deeper rather than letting it close. **Repeated offenses** in the same emotional area (a second betrayal) can open partially healed "tissue." Finally, environments that block processing—ongoing conflict, unsafe settings, or pressure to "just move on"—block recovery. When pain lacks the conditions necessary for resolution, it transforms from a temporary hurt into a lasting wound.

WHAT ARE THE WORST THINGS THAT CAN BREAK SOMEONE'S HEART?

There are moments that don't just make us sad; they crack something fundamental in our sense of how the world should work and test our capacity to adapt. I group these painful realities into external hurts (things that happen to us) and internal hurts **(those that arise from our own meaning-making).** Many wounds begin outside us—a betrayal, a harsh remark, a sudden loss—while others, or the after-effects of those first blows, grow inside us as self-blame, chronic insecurity, or identity collapse. The split matters because our agency (or lack of) lives in the internal realm: although we can't undo the original event, we can change the stories and strategies that keep the pain alive. This means we can develop agency over the internal states and alter their course. This table lists both:

MOSTLY EXTERNAL	MOSTLY INTERNAL
Rejection	Rejection Sensitivity
Betrayal, Broken Promises, Deception	Self-Blame and Misplaced Guilt
Cruelty, Criticism, and Character Attacks	Lack of Confidence and Chronic Insecurity
Neglect, Abandonment, Withdrawal of Affection	Loneliness
Loss	Grief
Unwanted Confessions, Painful Disclosures	Social Exclusion
Emotional, Physical, Verbal Abuse	Identity Crises and Existential Loss

Most Significant Heartbreaking Circumstances

Notice I use the word "mostly" in the header because external blows often turn into internal wounds: abandonment can morph into insecurity, betrayal can breed self-blame, and loss can evolve into an identity crisis. Now, let's look at how each of these experiences can add to our emotional pain.

REJECTION: Few experiences challenge our sense of worth as directly as rejection. Whether it comes from a romantic partner, a parent, a peer group, a job application, or even a creative endeavor, rejection strikes at the core of our desire to be seen, valued, and included. It carries the implicit message *"You are not wanted here,"* and the pain of that message often extends far beyond the moment it was delivered.

What makes rejection uniquely wounding is that it often leaves us with no explanation—or worse, offers vague or confusing ones. Ambiguity gets internalized as a reflection of personal deficiency, especially for children: *"I wasn't enough," "I'm too much,"* or *"I must be fundamentally flawed."* In this way, rejection doesn't just hurt—it can alter how we see ourselves. We may start to abandon our needs preemptively, silence our voice, or stop trying altogether to avoid further dismissal.

From an evolutionary perspective, this makes sense. Humans are wired for connection and belonging—being cast out from a group once meant a real threat to survival. That's why rejection activates not only emotional pain but also physical pain pathways in the brain, signaling the need to address the threat to our social bonds. This intense alarm system explains why rejection generates such extreme responses: we either withdraw completely to avoid further rejection or overextend ourselves in hopes of earning acceptance back.

This may also explain why rejection can escalate to pathological levels (traumatic). When rejection becomes constant, a person may develop **"rejection sensitivity"**—a type of hypervigilance focused specifically on detecting signs of rejection—which becomes truly debilitating. In severe cases, this tendency can progress to "rejection-sensitive dysphoria"—a sensitivity so intense that it causes extreme reactions, including emotional outbursts, withdrawal, paranoia, and even self-harm.

What can complicate resolving a rejection wound is that many people don't see it as a legitimate emotional injury. We're told, *"Brush it off—don't take it personally,"* so the grief gets skipped and leaves residue that later shows up as fear of intimacy, people-pleasing, perfectionism, or even suicidal ideation. Yet rejection is rarely a final verdict on our worth; it's usually a reflection of the other person's timing, fears, or unresolved issues too. It may feel deeply personal, but most often it isn't. Verdicts can be appealed, and no single judgment should define us.

To resolve rejection, we must begin by reclaiming our sense of worth—not by proving ourselves to others, but by recognizing that our value doesn't depend on disapproval. Rejection often says more about the rejector's circumstances than about ourselves. It also helps to honestly examine whether we're making efforts to connect authentically or expecting others to adapt entirely to us. It helps to grieve what we hoped for, acknowledge the pain it caused, and then gently question the story we began telling ourselves in its wake: *"Am I ugly, or simply not their type?" "Am I truly flawed, or is this about their preferences, timing, or biases?" "Could I have been more flexible so they felt comfortable?" "What's my part in it?"* True recovery isn't about never feeling hurt again; it's about maintaining the courage to show up as ourselves—even after hearing *"No!"*

BETRAYAL, BROKEN PROMISES, AND DECEPTION: Realizing that someone close has shattered our trust is a tough wound to confront. Betrayal, broken promises, and deception strike deeply through infidelity, persistent lies, or meaningful vows left unkept. Beyond the initial sting, these experiences undermine our sense of safety in relationships and make us question our own judgment about whom we can trust. The closer the bond—such as with a spouse or best friend—the more gut-wrenching the betrayal, dismantling the core belief that those we love will protect our well-being. Pain, anger, and lingering disappointment often flood in. We can also wound ourselves when we realize we've caused similar pain to others—discovering we've betrayed someone's trust or broken a promise can create shame wounds that are just as difficult to heal.

Trust wounds have a slippery trap we need to watch for. When trust breaks, we often invalidate the entire history we shared with the person who hurt us. *Picture a wife who discovers infidelity: she may conclude she was never truly loved and that her "whole life has been a lie."* This sweeping rewrite—though sometimes a temporary protective reflex—only magnifies the pain. Ironically, the mind does this to create a coherent story for an otherwise disorienting contradiction: that someone can both love us and betray us. The emotional overwhelm pushes us into black-and-white thinking and seeds doubts about our judgment, worth, and desirability. When we catch ourselves there, we need to notice what we're feeling and gently remind ourselves that clarity will return once the immediate "bleeding" stops.

Betrayal wounds are not caused solely by others' actions; they also spring from the gap between what we took for granted and what actually happened. Rather than viewing betrayal only as something done to us, we might begin to understand it as a collision between expectation and reality. This collision can involve unspoken agreements that weren't mutual (you assumed loyalty or exclusivity that the other person never intended), having different values or definitions (one person sees honesty as full transparency, while the other sees lying as avoiding harming others), or realizing that others may see the situation through entirely different lenses (they may interpret the same event through their own fears, history, or needs), whether consciously or not. Sometimes it takes years to realize that people close to us operate from a different set of values or that they may lack the capacity to foresee consequences or recognize our pain.

It's not about excusing harmful behavior; it's about acknowledging a simple truth: if it's hard to fully know ourselves, it's even harder to fully know someone else. That's why healing begins by turning inward. We address the wound with the awareness that **our needs deserve care now,** instead of endlessly waiting for the other person to make amends. The relationship may be broken, but our task is to rebuild our own strength so we're not dependent on someone else before we can feel whole.

Consider this example: *M has been best friends with S for years. When M confides their marital problems to S, they assume their conversation is completely private—this feels so obvious that it doesn't need stating. Later, M discovers S mentioned these details to a mutual friend who was "concerned." M feels deeply betrayed, their trust shattered. From one perspective, S violated an implicit trust.*

But looking deeper, M realizes they never explicitly asked for confidentiality, and S genuinely believed they were helping by seeking support from someone who cares about both of them. While M's pain is real and S's actions had consequences, resolution begins when M takes care of their needs first: acknowledging the hurt without minimizing it, processing their feelings of betrayal and vulnerability, deciding what boundaries they need going forward, and determining whether they want to repair the friendship or step back from it—all without waiting for S to validate their pain or make it right. After that, M can recognize that their unspoken expectation of absolute confidentiality collided with

S's different understanding of how friendship works during difficult times, regardless of whether S acknowledges the harm caused.

REVENGE: Whether we find ourselves the target of someone's vengeful actions or consumed by our own desire for retaliation, revenge represents the experience that captures the complete inversion of human connection. Where love once lived, there is now a deliberate intention to cause pain.

Most people get hurt when they discover that someone else resents them or has been holding grudges because they may be oblivious to having caused pain. What they can't imagine is that this person may be planning silently how to hurt them back. It's heartbreaking.

Being targeted for revenge carries a unique form of betrayal that goes beyond rejection or abandonment. It's not simply that someone no longer wants us—it's that they actively want to see us suffer. This realization can shatter our fundamental assumptions about relationships and human nature. The cognitive dissonance alone can be overwhelming.

What makes revenge particularly devastating is its calculated nature. Unlike anger, which can be hot and immediate, revenge is often cold and planned. Revenge has a deliberate quality; it rarely feels like an emotional outburst we can forgive—it feels like a verdict on our worth as a human being.

When we're caught in the revenge cycle—either as target or perpetrator—we often lose sight of our core selves. The person seeking revenge may abandon their values and compromise their integrity in pursuit of settling old scores. We can wound ourselves deeply through our own vengeful actions—realizing we've become someone we don't recognize, someone capable of deliberately causing pain, can create lasting shame or fragmentation that's often harder to heal than the original injury. Meanwhile, the target of revenge may become hypervigilant, lose trust in others, and adopt a worldview that perceives relationships as fundamentally dangerous.

What complicates healing from revenge is that it often feels justified. Someone genuinely hurt us, violated our trust, or damaged our lives. The desire for them to face consequences feels not only natural but also morally right. Yet true resolution rarely comes through retaliation. Revenge creates cycles that can span years or even generations, and "getting even" doesn't bring the peace we expected—it only reveals how much of ourselves we've lost in the process.

CRUELTY, CRITICISM, AND CHARACTER ATTACKS: Bullying, slander, and public humiliation can feel like personal assaults on our identity. Whether it's a single devastating put-down or sustained cruelty from peers or authority figures, these experiences often lead to internalized shame that undermines self-esteem and personal agency. When lies or damaging rumors spread, the impact deepens—tearing apart our sense of belonging and forcing us into a constant watchful state. Depending on the severity, frequency, and intent, such experiences can cause long-lasting harm or even escalate into trauma—a destabilization of the system that occurs when they actually threaten our safety, livelihood, or social survival.

LONELINESS, NEGLECT, ABANDONMENT, AND WITHDRAWAL OF AFFECTION: Humans have a fundamental need for connection. When emotional support is absent or inconsistent—even in an "always-plugged-in" world—the isolation can feel brutal. Chronic invisibility often leads us to conclude we are unimportant or unloved. Emotional neglect isn't always deliberate; caregivers may be distracted, overwhelmed, or unaware, yet the impact is the same: a dull, persistent ache, a fading hope of being seen, and the haunting belief we must forever remain outsiders. Loneliness can become one of those silent pains that brings tears the moment we think about it.

Once formed, these wounds can go deep, affecting our attachment systems and creating patterns that make future relationships challenging. We may develop a heightened sensitivity to dismissal cues, withdraw preemptively to avoid potential hurt, or become excessively accommodating to secure relationships. If the pain jeopardizes our biological need for social connection—a drive as fundamental to human survival as food or shelter—the wound can activate survival mechanisms.

LOSS AND GRIEF: Losing a loved one through death, estrangement, or a painful breakup wounds us deeply and can leave an ache that may never truly disappear, even if it doesn't make us feel insecure or at risk. Over time, we may learn to carry this grief—often by moving toward acceptance—but it can still resurface unexpectedly, especially during milestones, anniversaries, or life transitions. In those moments, we're reminded of how permanent certain absences can feel.

While loss can sometimes feel like trauma in its intensity, it is more accurate to see it as an adaptive form of pain—one that reflects the value of what (or who) we once had. This distinction matters: grief, while deeply painful, is a sign of our capacity for love, attachment, and meaning-making. The ache we feel is a reflection of the depth of the bond we had, which gives significance to the absence.

Don't pressure yourself to "get over" a loss too quickly or expect the pain to vanish. Grief doesn't follow a strict timeline, and healing doesn't mean forgetting. It may continue to hurt for a long time, but holding onto the idea that we can carry the essence of the person within us—not just in memory, but in how we live, love, and grow—can offer comfort and help transform sorrow into a quiet form of presence. This perspective aligns with what grief counselor Debbie Augenthaler observes in *You Are Not Alone: A Heartfelt Guide to Grief, Healing, and Hope*. *"There are many gifts that come with loss, including spiritual awakenings and discovering the connected bond of eternal love. We often develop a deeper capacity for compassion and an appreciation for the blessings that come from the challenging journey of grief, leading us to healing, transformation, and a new kind of joy."*

UNWANTED CONFESSIONS AND PAINFUL DISCLOSURES: This kind of pain isn't talked about enough—and yet it's just as important. Sometimes, the most heartbreaking moments come not from what's withheld, but from what's carelessly revealed. When someone close to us unburdens themselves by confessing transgressions, secrets, or "demons" that directly affect our lives, they may be seeking relief from their own guilt—while inadvertently transferring the emotional weight onto us. These revelations—whether about infidelity, past betrayals, or long-hidden truths—can rupture our sense of shared reality and force us to integrate painful knowledge we never asked to carry.

Similarly, discovering through others what has been said behind our backs or learning uncomfortable secrets about friends can create a form of emotional contamination. Once heard, these revelations can't be unheard, often shifting how we perceive relationships we once valued. The wound stems not only from the content of what's learned but also from the unwanted responsibility of deciding what to do with that knowledge: whether to confront, stay silent, or quietly withdraw.

What makes these disclosures so wounding is their one-sided nature. We're taught to value honesty—but the truth can be devastating when shared at the wrong time, in the wrong way, or for the wrong reasons. The confessor may feel relieved after disclosing, while the recipient is left grappling with shock, confusion, and hurt. When confessions serve mainly to unburden the speaker rather than to respect the listener, they can feel especially selfish and inconsiderate.

These situations manifest in various ways: *Consider a partner who, seeking to unburden their conscience, confesses they've been flirting online with coworkers for months—not physically cheating, but deliberately seeking validation. Although the partner may feel relieved after disclosing, it leaves them with irrevocable images and a shattered trust. Or consider a friend who reveals that your mutual friend's recent promotion came after they sabotaged a colleague—information you never sought that now poisons your perception of someone you respected. This knowledge now burdens you, compelling you to either remain silent in complicity or jeopardize relationships by confronting it. Perhaps most difficult is when a family member shares graphic details of their suicidal ideation—not while seeking help, but in emotional offloading. Their disclosure leaves you feeling responsible for their well-being without the training to properly support them, creating a burden of worry you're ill-equipped to carry, not to mention the excruciating pain of knowing how much they are suffering.*

IDENTITY CRISES, SOCIAL EXCLUSION, AND EXISTENTIAL LOSS: Sometimes, a wound is not caused by a single event but rather by the collapse of one's worldview or sense of purpose—such as a sudden loss of direction, a major life transition, or a spiritual crisis. When our core identity feels destabilized, we may experience profound anxiety. This is particularly true when uncertainty about who we are arises from discrimination, racism, invalidation, or misrecognition—either by others toward us or toward the community we identify with (like being repeatedly told your career passion is "unrealistic" or having your cultural identity dismissed as "not really authentic"). These circumstances can prompt questions like *"Who am I now?"* This internal disorientation can be just as distressing as any external betrayal.

Unlike wounds caused by specific events, identity crises require a different kind of care to be resolved. The best way may be engaging in the difficult process of reconstructing meaning, reassessing your sense of self, and addressing the cracks in your identity.

Resolution often begins with acknowledging the disorientation rather than rushing to fill the void with premature answers. *Consider someone who loses their career after decades, a person whose faith community rejects their sexual orientation, or someone whose chronic illness forces them to reimagine their capabilities—in each case, sitting with the uncertainty becomes the first step toward rebuilding.*

EMOTIONAL, PHYSICAL, AND VERBAL ABUSE: Any form of abuse undermines our fundamental sense of safety and self-worth. Whether it's chronic verbal belittling, threats of physical harm, or emotional manipulation, abuse creates profound wounds that often reach traumatic levels—a topic we'll explore thoroughly in Chapter Five. What makes abuse particularly heartbreaking is that it violates our basic expectation that those close to us won't deliberately harm us. Many people struggle to acknowledge abusive interactions, perhaps telling themselves, *"It wasn't that bad"* or *"They didn't mean it"* to avoid the overwhelming reality that someone they trusted intentionally hurt them.

To conclude, the categories of what can break someone's heart that I just described aren't always mutually exclusive; they often intersect and compound one another's effects. A person enduring betrayal might also face public humiliation and deep self-blame; someone experiencing rejection might simultaneously struggle with a loss of identity. These experiences can escalate and create a sense of threat—feeling betrayed and fearing future harm, being slandered and losing one's job or reputation—which in turn can activate the brain's survival circuits, potentially transforming emotional wounds into something more serious and lasting—even trauma.

WHAT SITUATIONS BRING OUT EVERYONE'S WORST INSECURITIES?

We don't need rocket science to understand that we feel insecure after something that broke our heart. We can also notice how insecurity feels similar to fear even when they are not the same. While fear is an acute survival signal *("Get out of here now!")*, insecurity is a slower-burn appraisal *("Am I safe, lovable, or competent?").* They feel similar because both tighten your chest and flood you with unease, but fear points to an external threat in the moment, whereas insecurity grows from internal doubts that color how you see future situations. Insecurity is not stress either, even when many confuse them. **Stress is a state, while insecurity is a story**. Still, insecurity and stress can feed each other—chronic stress can erode confidence, and deep insecurity can make daily hassles feel more stressful.

When lack of confidence becomes habitual—when a sense of inadequacy or perceived lack of physical, emotional, or social resources is carried almost constantly—insecurity becomes much harder to explain, identify as wounding, and, let alone, resolve. Unlike more straightforward emotions like joy or anger, insecurity doesn't just affect how we feel—it shapes how we think, behave, and ultimately, who we become, since it modifies our personality.

Insecurity is as if we're wearing distorting glasses that change how we see everything while simultaneously projecting those distortions outward for others to see. It manifests as anxious self-doubt or a fragile sense of self, often accompanied by internal narratives like *"I'm not good enough," "Nobody likes me,"* or *"I wish I was someone else."* Over time, these feelings can lead us to avoid risks, withdraw from relationships, or act in ways that don't feel true to ourselves.

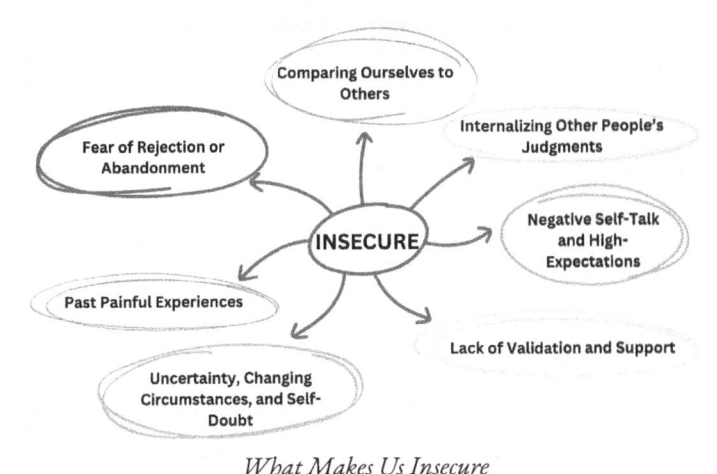

What Makes Us Insecure

Here are some of the most common factors that fuel insecurity—and why their impact can be so debilitating. As you read, you may identify with many and notice that **what's actually uncommon is to feel consistently confident.** Knowing this can help us trust ourselves—not by denying our insecurities, but by understanding and working with them, knowing we're not alone. Nearly everyone—even those who appear supremely confident—harbors doubts about some aspect of themselves.

Our insecurities, similar to our emotions, are trying to help us notice we need to make adjustments rather than pointing to a flaw. *Think of insecurity as an overly cautious GPS that constantly reroutes you away from any potential traffic, construction, or detours. We don't need to turn it off completely, just update its settings to be less anxious—by treating ourselves with kindness, seeking realistic feedback, and choosing supportive environments over competitive ones.*

When insecurity first shows up, it's usually a quick flash—brief self-doubt after a rejection, failure, or tough comparison. If we notice it, assign an acceptable meaning, and move forward, the feeling fades on its own. But when that doubt gets ignored—or keeps getting hit again and again—it can grow into chronic self-doubt: constant negative self-talk and avoiding things that start controlling our daily choices. Life becomes about staying away from the next hurt rather than going after what we want.

If this constant pattern gets strong enough to mess with our sense of safety or belonging—like social rejection feeling life-threatening or self-doubt causing panic attacks—it turns into an emotional wound that disrupts our mood, behavior, and relationships. This may be the most important obstacle to developing self-love or self-compassion because the wound creates a hostile internal environment where criticism feels safer than kindness. When we're caught in these patterns, self-love can feel dangerous—as if being gentle with ourselves might make us unprepared, weak, impostors, or vulnerable to more hurt. The wounded part of us believes that harsh self-judgment is protective, keeping us alert to potential failures or rejections. But this constant internal criticism becomes the very voice that prevents us from offering ourselves the understanding and care we need to heal. In the worst cases, when the wound convinces our nervous system it has to stay in crisis mode to survive, we've crossed the line into trauma.

Understanding this progression reminds us that the best time to do something is early—when insecurity is still just a quick feeling—by checking if our doubts are realistic and getting support before they turn into something deeper and harder to heal.

> **Insecurity Escalation = Temporary Insecurity → Chronic Self-Doubt → Emotional Wound → Trauma**

COMPARISONS TO OTHERS: Envy or self-doubt, especially when seeing someone else's achievements, appearance, or lifestyle—perhaps magnified by social media—can profoundly affect our confidence. Consider how even the most admired celebrities undergo plastic surgery and use filters, creating impossible standards that no one—including themselves—can naturally achieve. Constantly measuring ourselves against curated snapshots of others' lives creates insecurity about whether we can measure up. These comparisons are particularly damaging because they're often based on incomplete information (you see their new car but not their credit card debt, their wedding photos but not their arguments, their fitness selfie but not their struggles with body image)—we compare our behind-the-scenes reality to others' highlight reels, their finished products to our works-in-progress, and their public personas to our private struggles. What makes this pattern so insidious is how automatic it becomes; we might scroll through social media and absorb dozens of comparisons without conscious awareness, each one subtly reinforcing the message that we're falling short. Failure to process and reflect on these feelings and to stop developing acceptance and confidence in our strengths instead of fixating on our perceived lacks can leave us deeply insecure.

FEAR OF REJECTION OR ABANDONMENT: Although this fear is often pathologized and linked to borderline personality disorder (BPD), it is fundamentally human. Because humans are social mammals who rely on connection, the worry about rejection by peers, friends, or romantic partners (such as being ghosted by someone you dated or excluded from your friend's group) is central to our emotional system. Even slight feelings of exclusion can be distressing because isolation has historically posed a survival threat to our ancestors. When our sense of belonging feels endangered, insecurity naturally follows—normally transient. However, when the fear becomes intense and constant—or when abandonment feels like a perpetual threat (constantly worrying that people will leave once they really know you)—this insecurity can escalate to traumatizing levels rather than remaining temporary. This fear is closely connected to the type of attachment we established in childhood, which may require resolution in adulthood to prevent overwhelming insecurity.

INTERNALIZING OTHER PEOPLE'S JUDGMENTS: Absorbing negative feedback or criticisms—especially from authority figures or those we admire and trust—and using them as the basis for our self-concept can quietly undermine our sense of self. Consistent exposure to such judgments may eventually convince us they're true, eroding our confidence in our own worth and abilities (like a teacher's comment that you're *"not a math person"* becoming a lifelong belief about your intelligence, or a parent's criticism about you being *"too sensitive"* making you doubt your emotional responses). Sometimes it was our parents who, out of their intention to bring out the best in us, left us feeling incapable, insufficient, and far from the ideal they had in mind. Or their own insecurities are transmitted to us. Sooner or later, that internalized wound needs to be resolved—perhaps through developing empathy for their "good intentions," perhaps through self-acceptance.

> **Return to Sender Exercise.** Use this short routine whenever an outside judgment starts to burrow in.
>
> Close your eyes and recall a recent negative judgment that stuck with you—maybe a parent's remark, a boss's comment, or a friend's offhand dig. Notice the exact words or tone.
>
> Picture the words sitting in front of you like a package that was delivered to the wrong address.
>
> Ask yourself, *"Is there solid proof I'm actually what they said, or is this just their momentary judgment?"*
>
> List one or two facts that contradict the criticism—past successes, supportive feedback, or personal strengths. Let them sink into your system to connect with the positive feeling of knowing that nobody owns the truth about you. Remember that you are able to connect to your qualities or achievements even if you are the only one that appreciates them.

Then, visualize yourself handing the package back, or imagine it drifting away on a small boat. Silently say, *"That's not mine; it doesn't belong to me,"* and *"That's their opinion, not my identity."* Feel the space that opens when you no longer carry someone else's label.

Finish by stating an alternative belief: *"I'm learning and improving,"* *"I'm capable,"* or simply, *"I'm better than they think."* Breathe in that statement once or twice to anchor it. Let that truth settle—not just in your mind, but throughout your whole being. Give it space to take root, gently replacing the old narrative with something more honest and supportive.

The more often you *"return the package,"* the less power those borrowed words will have over your self-concept.

NEGATIVE SELF-TALK AND HIGH EXPECTATIONS: Setting unrealistically high standards—and then criticizing ourselves harshly for not meeting them—is obviously draining. When our inner dialogue is filled with self-criticism—telling yourself *"I'm such an idiot"* after a minor mistake or *"I should be further along by now"* when comparing your progress to others—we reinforce feelings of inadequacy, creating a cycle that's difficult to break. This pattern could be the result of self-directed anger or from growing up with caregivers who frequently scolded, belittled, or set unattainable expectations.

Internalized Anger and Negativity

Children often internalize those criticisms as absolute truth. It may also be the aftermath of being bullied, shamed, or verbally abused—or the echo of a society that idealizes achievement and flawlessness. Whatever the origin, this pattern is like living in a boxing ring, taking hits day and night—and who could possibly feel confident while being treated like a worn-out punching bag?

LACK OF VALIDATION AND SUPPORT: Feeling overlooked, unheard, or consistently undervalued by the people who matter—parents, partners, friends, or mentors—slowly wears down self-esteem. When encouragement and honest feedback are scarce, we start doubting our own abilities and even our right to take up space (like never receiving praise for your efforts at work or having family members who only point out what you're doing wrong). Seeking approval in everything we do is also debilitating—when every choice, from what you wear to what you eat, depends on someone else's thumbs-up. Living on borrowed approval can become a habit that keeps us insecure and vigilant.

One practical safeguard is to be intentional about the voices you allow in: seek friends who celebrate your efforts, mentors who offer constructive guidance, and media or books that inspire rather than diminish your confidence. Regular exposure to affirming relationships and uplifting content acts like emotional nutrition—counteracting the deficit created when key figures in your life fail to validate or support you.

UNCERTAINTY, CHANGING CIRCUMSTANCES, AND SELF-DOUBT: Losing a job, moving to a new place, or navigating major life transitions (divorce or serious illness) can create unsettling levels of uncertainty, raising questions like *"Will I succeed?"* or *"Am I safe here?"* These doubts often spark insecurity, making an already difficult situation feel overwhelming. Self-doubt compounds this effect—much like negative self-talk—especially when we assume we won't be able to meet the challenges these changes bring.

Remember that self-doubt is a natural part of being human—it's baked into the very machinery that once kept our ancestors alive and still pushes us to learn and adapt today. It takes a lifetime to know ourselves, and we're not objective enough to understand our value, qualities, or even flaws because it's hard to ignore the feedback we receive and because perception gets distorted easily. This dilemma becomes especially challenging when what we hear today can be the opposite of what we hear from someone else tomorrow. Persistent self-doubt, when combined with actual setbacks, can lead to more serious emotional struggles. To help with this, practice grounding yourself in what you know to be true about your character and capabilities, regardless of external feedback. Your internal dialogue can be like a coach who encourages you rather than an enemy.

PAST PAINFUL EXPERIENCES: Obviously, having suffered from bullying, abuse, betrayal, or any situation that qualifies as traumatic chips away at self-confidence and has the potential to reshape how we see ourselves, leaving us with lingering doubts about our safety. One of the highest costs of trauma is the drainage of internal resources, including self-esteem, sense of self, and agency. Chapters Five and Six deepen this understanding.

Each of the factors described that weaken our confidence touches on core human needs: belonging, acceptance, stability, and recognition. When we sense that any of these needs might go unmet, we instinctively become more guarded and self-critical. Children may have the tendency to believe they are the problem, while adults often develop sophisticated defensive strategies—avoiding vulnerability, controlling situations, or numbing themselves to avoid the pain of unmet needs. Some of those needs are evident, but there are others that are hard to recognize, like the need to feel in control, or to be right, or to win, or "needs" that may be more connected to internal fragilities than to genuine well-being.

One way to begin untangling insecurity is through the humility to acknowledge our limitations. We won't be everyone's favorite person. We won't always be seen, understood, or chosen. And we won't possess every quality or skill we admire in others. But what we can do is learn to make the most of what we *do* have—cultivating our gifts, embracing our imperfections, and building confidence not on perfection, but on self-respect and growth.

> **Mirror of Strengths Exercise.** Practice this to help you shift your focus from your perceived inadequacies to your inner resources and personal strengths.
>
> Think of a time in your life when you faced a challenge—something emotionally, mentally, or physically difficult. It doesn't have to be dramatic, just something that truly tested you and made you feel insecure but that you were able to overcome.

> Ask yourself, *"What did I do that helped me get through it?" "What qualities did I show (patience, creativity, persistence, kindness)?" "Did I reach out for help, stay calm, speak up, or adjust?"*
>
> Bring to mind **at least three strengths** that showed up in that moment, even if they felt small or imperfect. These might include resilience (you kept going despite setbacks), resourcefulness (you found creative solutions or asked for help), courage (you faced the situation even when afraid), compassion (you treated yourself or others with kindness), adaptability (you adjusted when things didn't go as planned), determination (you didn't give up), wisdom (you learned from the experience), or emotional regulation (you managed your feelings without being overwhelmed by them).
>
> Now, reframe the memory briefly: *"I may not have felt strong at the time, but looking back, I can see that I showed [insert strengths]. That part of me is still here."*
>
> If you'd like, close your eyes for a moment and breathe into the feeling of having those strengths within you. Let your body remember what it felt like to be capable, even in the face of difficulty, and what it feels like right now to connect with that strength in you. Stay with that feeling for a minute or two, allowing it to reach every inch of your body, inside and out.

What's the real relationship between ego and feeling insecure?

Yes, that "thing" we call ego is tied to our insecurities in a significant way. We may not understand the ego well, but understanding its connection with our suffering can help us diminish the weight of our insecurities and reshape how we relate to ourselves.

The challenge with discussing the ego is that it has no single, tidy definition, and it isn't housed in one spot of the brain, so researchers study its functions instead. It's pieced together over time from sensation, memory, and social feedback—self-protection is one of its jobs, but it's not its only reason for being.

In neuroscience, what earlier psychology called the ego is usually viewed as an emergent function—activity spread across several brain networks involved in self-awareness, executive control, and flexible behavior. Under that lens, its job is to coordinate what happens inside us with what we do outside, acting as a bridge between our older survival circuits and our newer, reflective cortex. By weaving together instincts, emotions, memories, and perceptions, it sustains a coherent sense of self—one able to relate to others and adapt to social worlds shaped by status, competition, and quick judgments.

Picture the ego as the house manager of your inner world. Its job is to keep the household (your sense of self) standing, tidy, and presentable. Whenever a storm rolls in—criticism, rejection, fear—the ego rushes to board up the windows with defenses: Denial, minimization, or rationalization act like plywood sheets, blocking out painful facts that feel too harsh to face. Projection or blame works like a drainage system, directing unwanted emotions towards others, ensuring the interior remains "dry and clean." All those hurried repairs reveal the insecurities hidden beneath the paint. The ego isn't the source of those insecurities; it's the caretaker who notices every wobble in the structure and decides which quick fix will keep everything from collapsing—at least for now.

So when we say the ego "hosts" our defenses and insecurities, we mean that it detects threats to our self-image *("Am I safe?" "Am I valued?")*, deploys protective strategies to keep those threats from shattering the picture we and others hold of ourselves, and stores the blueprints—our private insecurities of not being enough, of being unlovable or powerless—that guide which defenses pop up first.

Eastern philosophies often describe the ego as an illusion, a transient construct that emerges through identification with thoughts, roles, and sensations. In Buddhism, the ego is understood as the mind's attempt to create a fixed identity in a world characterized by constant change. This effort to impose permanence on what is inherently impermanent leads to suffering—because we cling to a self that doesn't truly exist in any stable form.

These perspectives converge with neuroscience in one crucial insight: the ego is constructed, shaped, and maintained by experience, memory, vulnerability, and attention. While neuroscience doesn't call the ego self-illusory, it shows that our self-model is a predictive, flexible simulation built from brain activity influenced by our relationships, social environment, and bodily states. This means that the ego can be shaped by fear, comparison, and conditional worth and can also be reshaped—not through self-annihilation, but through disidentification from rigid or harmful self-concepts.

One of the ego's core functions is to manage our sense of how we are perceived by others. This is why it plays such a central role in insecurity. The ego helps construct our self-narrative by drawing from past experiences, external feedback, and internalized expectations. We all need an ego because it helps us assess how to fit in. Insecurity takes root only when that narrative grows rigid or leans too heavily on other people's opinions.

In trying to meet perceived expectations and avoid being seen as we fear we are, we begin building layers of protection—smokescreens designed to make us appear as we assume others want us to be. This creates chronic vigilance: constantly scanning for cues, adjusting behavior, and seeking approval while losing touch with our core self—the one that hosts our values and authenticity. The more we "perform" identities we haven't consciously chosen—identities that develop from assuming we should be better—the shakier our foundation becomes. This instability feeds persistent insecurity because, deep down, we sense that the version being evaluated isn't entirely us. That's why I often refer to this fake ego as the "hollow self": it lacks substance, existing primarily as a projection of how we want to be seen, rather than who we truly are.

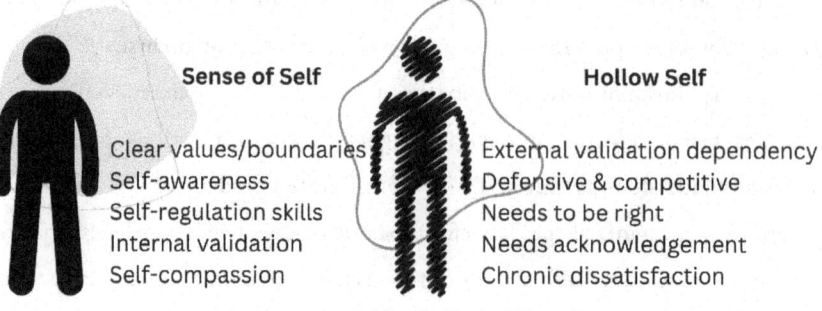

Sense of Self
Clear values/boundaries
Self-awareness
Self-regulation skills
Internal validation
Self-compassion

Hollow Self
External validation dependency
Defensive & competitive
Needs to be right
Needs acknowledgement
Chronic dissatisfaction

Strong Self vs Hollow-Self

Consider Maya, for example. She scrolls through social media and sees endless images of flawless bodies and curated lives. Though she knows these images are filtered and posed, she still finds herself dressing to match trends she doesn't like, sitting at the edge of the chair to shrink herself, and hesitating to voice opinions that might not be popular. Every time she doesn't get noticed or validated, she dislikes herself a little more—she's just not sure who she is outside of who she'd like to be, and she feels like she's failing most of the time. Her ego, caught in a loop of comparison and approval-seeking, slowly builds an identity that looks polished on the outside but feels hollow within.

Resolving insecurity isn't about puffing up a grandiose self-image—the ego's favorite trick—but about loosening our fusion with limiting beliefs, inherited roles, unnecessary defenses, and distorted expectations. A practical way to do this is to cultivate an "observing-self"—a quiet inner witness that can spot the ego in action.

> **Training the "Observing-Self" to Defuse Insecurity Exercise.** You can practice this exercise to shift from ego-driven reactions (inflation or collapse) to clear, choice-based responses.
>
> **Daily practice:** Pick a routine transition—walking to lunch, brushing teeth—and notice your thought process. When you're idle—not focused on a task—what do you think about how others perceive you? Do you replay past events where someone made you feel bad about what you said? Or maybe you imagine scenes where you become famous and well-recognized. Observe your thought process without judgment. This will help you develop the habit of observing your thoughts rather than letting them run wild.
>
> **Remembering social situations:** Bring to mind a situation where you noticed yourself becoming defensive. Notice how it felt in your body as you review the memory. Did you feel they were looking down on you, or when someone argued with you, did you feel disapproved of? Try to identify what triggered that defensive reaction and what thoughts are connected to it. For now, just keep observing. The idea is to develop this observing capacity.
>
> **In real time:** When you feel a spike of defensiveness, self-doubt, or the urge to impress, label it by telling yourself, *"Ego alert—wanting to prove myself,"* or *"Ego collapse—shrinking."* Name the feeling in the body: heat, tension, rush, or hollowness. Breathe once before you speak or act. That single breath is your mini-pause for awareness and choice.
>
> **Later reflection:** Once at home, you may try to process the needs that the ego is trying to get met. Ask yourself, *"What danger does this reaction think it's*

solving?" "Which old wound or story is it protecting?" No need to fix—just name it: fear of rejection, shame of not being enough, need to be appreciated, etc.

As you keep practicing observing your defensive responses and noticing how they feel, record what types of situations are most triggering. Next time, create a split-second pause between the trigger and your response. This practice will help you develop your observing-self.

IDENTIFY WOUNDS THAT CAUSE NUMBNESS OR NEEDINESS

"Not being seen doesn't hurt all at once. It hurts slowly, in the spaces where love should have lived."

The way neglect makes us feel disconnected from others and even from ourselves can cause injuries that bleed silently. The invisible wounds left by being ignored don't just affect children; they can be experienced at any age when we reach for connection and find a void instead. The pain of being unseen, unheard, or deemed unworthy of attention leaves a dent in our psyche that can redirect the entire course of our emotional lives, especially during periods when we're most vulnerable or dependent on others for emotional or practical support.

As human beings, we share fundamental emotional needs: to be seen, understood, and cared for; to feel a sense of belonging, safety, and purpose; to experience independence and reliability; and to enjoy connection and stability. When these needs go unmet, emotional fulfillment may easily slip out of reach, and the effects can be hurtful, disappointing, or crippling. This is why neglect can be damaging, particularly in childhood, where it can disrupt healthy development.

For the person who feels neglected, their emotional life may feel built on what's missing, creating a mindset of scarcity. That scarcity lens becomes the opening scene in every later emotional script: new experiences, even positive ones, get filtered through *"I don't count,"* so each storyline—friendships, work, love—unfolds on a stage already painted with absence. In this section, we'll look at the depth of the damage neglect can cause and how it can shape our emotional perspective. We will also see how a need turns into neediness the moment we feel compelled to prove, demand, or chase it instead of simply expressing it. When the request for care shifts from *"see me"* to *"reassure me, complete me,"* the original need can tip into a survival plea.

WHAT HAPPENS WHEN YOUR FEELINGS WERE IGNORED AS A CHILD?

Emotional neglect is one of those sad experiences that often goes unnoticed. Both the absence of emotional support and the impact of that absence can be subtle and hard to identify, not only by observers but also by the neglected. It occurs when our fundamental needs for connection and care are consistently unmet—when those close to us fail to perceive, understand, or respond to what we need emotionally. Unlike more visible forms of mistreatment, emotional neglect is defined by what's missing: no validation, no attention, no appreciation, no nurturing, no love—all essential for healthy development, emotional stability, and a sense of self-worth.

Our sense of self begins to form through an interaction that functions like a mirror—it develops largely by seeing ourselves reflected in our caregivers' responses when we're children. When a parent notices their child is sad and says, *"I see you're feeling down today,"* they're helping that child recognize, name, and value their emotional experience. But when emotional needs are consistently ignored or misread, it's like looking into a mirror that reflects a blurry or distorted image—or no image at all. Over time, this lack of reflection can make it hard for the child to develop a solid sense of self or trust their feelings.

For instance, a child who cries for comfort but repeatedly meets silence will gradually internalize the message that their feelings don't matter. Or consider a spouse who prepares dinner night after night, only to eat alone without receiving a call to explain the absence—they develop not only resentment but also a profound sense of being fundamentally on their own in the relationship. This absence leads to individuals feeling invisible, unsupported, and emotionally abandoned.

Emotional neglect in childhood may not always be traumatizing in the clinical sense, but it affects the developing sense of self and can impair healthy emotional and cognitive development. You'll find more detailed descriptions of how arrested development affects us in Chapter Five.

Neglect is paradoxical. Even when it doesn't feel threatening, being ignored or dismissed is painful—and the outcomes reveal the remarkable, yet costly, adaptability of the human psyche. Many people who experience neglect grow up unsure of how to recognize or tend to their own emotional needs. The outcomes vary widely:

Compulsive caregiving: Some become intensely focused on meeting everyone else's needs, seeking acknowledgment of their worth or effort that may never arrive, which can become debilitating. When validation is withheld, it can trigger feelings of injustice and amplify emotional hunger. But when validation is received, some people successfully transform this initially unhealthy pattern into a genuine source of identity and self-worth, developing authentic confidence in their caring abilities.

Adaptive validation-seeking: Some neglected individuals actively seek validation as a goal and use it to soothe deep fears of abandonment, creating temporary relief that could become problematic if it leads to constant external dependence. However, when balanced with self-awareness, this can evolve into healthy relationship-building skills and the ability to create supportive communities.

Wounded generosity: Others develop remarkable generosity, finding meaningful community roles—though this may come from people-pleasing rather than genuine choice. While this can lead to exhaustion and resentment when motives remain unconscious, it can also evolve into genuine comfort in benefiting others and authentic altruistic leadership.

Self-reliant isolation: Some cultivate strong self-reliance and agency, appearing to overcome scarcity mindsets in fulfilling ways. However, if this mindset is not consciously examined, it can lead to problematic isolation or difficulty in accepting help when it is genuinely needed. When developed consciously, this self-reliance can become a genuine strength that allows for both independence and healthy interdependence.

What unites these responses is that they all represent the psyche's attempt to better adapt despite emotional deprivation. Still, even apparently successful adaptations often carry hidden costs—emotional numbness, difficulty with intimacy, or chronic hypervigilance—that may only become apparent when relationships deepen, stress increases, or when they get combined with other types of wounds.

NEGLECT OUTCOMES → Neglect themselves and their needs → Dedicate to service professions as worth → Develop self-reliance and agency → Focus on the needs of others → Self-healing when validated / Resentful if not validated

Neglect Outcomes

This variation may be rooted in how the child's system responds to neglect. Some become scared of being alone and activate survival mechanisms; others manage the pain by dissociating—a protective strategy that allows them to keep growing, even if disconnected. I'm referring to adaptive dissociation—a mental shortcut that protects the mind from overwhelm—that you may find pathologized everywhere. Many children resource themselves by daydreaming, creating imaginary friends, or getting absorbed in specific activities like drawing. Ordinary play sits on a healthy end of that spectrum; it tips into "maladaptive daydreaming" only when the fantasy world crowds out real-life functioning. This disconnection may require conscious work to reverse in adulthood when deeper emotional connection becomes important.

Emotional neglect is more common than most realize, and it isn't just about physical absence. It can be embedded in cultural or religious beliefs that label self-care as "selfish," discouraging us from acknowledging our own needs. In societies where family enmeshment is idealized, individuals are expected to sacrifice personal needs for family or community. This, too, is emotional neglect when those norms chronically invalidate the child's or adult's legitimate emotional needs—as in teaching that members are to be responsible for other people's happiness, but not their own. When combined with actual neglect, it becomes natural to struggle with low self-worth, which quietly breeds resentment and suppressed anger. These invisible wounds can leave individuals either overly exposed emotionally or disconnected from genuine support—caught in cycles that protect them from pain but also keep them from healing.

When does neglect cross the line into trauma territory?

The idea that neglect is inherently traumatic has become widespread—largely because it's often paired with abuse and framed in the imposing tone that now dominates many discussions about adversity children encounter. I've been careful to separate neglect from abuse because I've observed that they impact the nervous and emotional systems in different ways—a distinction that's often overlooked. To better understand how deeply neglect can wound, I break it into two distinct forms: one is a non-threatening absence of attention, and the other is a lack of heartfelt care so extensive that it endangers a person's core sense of self or livelihood.

Non-threatening neglect might look like emotional distance or occasional inattentiveness, yet the person's basic needs—like food, shelter, supervision, and some emotional contact—still get met. The provider might be absent, distracted, or overwhelmed due to work schedules, multiple children, health issues, or emotional strain. The child or dependent adult remains physically safe and doesn't experience constant fear. The child learns to adapt—perhaps by playing alone or seeking comfort from siblings—without feeling threatened. While lacking emotional warmth wounds our sense of worth and creates loneliness, it doesn't spark the intense, fear-driven state that derails normal development. In short, the neglected person may feel alone or unseen and carry an emotional wound but not feel unsafe—so this kind of neglect isn't traumatizing.

Threatening neglect is different—it compromises a person's sense of safety and survival. It might involve not having enough food, supervision, or protection to feel secure, or emotional dismissal combined with punishment or rejection. No one steps in to shield them from real danger. This ranges from emotionally unavailable caregivers overwhelmed by their own struggles to more severe situations where adults fail to protect children from serious harm, such as ignoring signs of sexual abuse, illness, or developmental delays. However, instead of hypervigilance, the system may decide to shut down, disengaging to escape the pain of feeling worthless—and the terrifying realization that no one will protect them. The nervous system flips between hypo- and hyper-arousal, but numbing may be more dominant. Picture a baby not fed regularly, young children left alone for hours in unsafe environments, an elderly person's illness ignored, a parentified child assuming adult responsibilities, or a bedridden adult abandoned. This kind of neglect isn't just painful—it becomes traumatizing.

WHY AM I SO TERRIFIED OF PEOPLE LEAVING ME?

Neglect is closely tied to feelings of abandonment. As we discussed in the previous section on insecurity triggers, fear of abandonment is fundamentally human—a natural, adaptive response shared by all mammals who rely on groups for survival. When cut off from the pack, mammals become easy prey with no one to fight alongside them.

But humans are particularly fragile. We need someone to meet our basic survival needs from birth, or we die. Losing connection with our main caregiver—whether through absence, emotional distance, or coldness—can trigger our brain to react as if *"something dangerous is coming."* This sparks not just fear of abandonment but panic too. Babies who lose their parents feel raw, intense distress. Since they can't process loss like adults, their system anticipates not having basic needs met: food, love, safety, and steady care. Fear then settles in as their baseline, affecting the child's psyche and putting their body into constant alertness.

Abandonment fear can also develop in the opposite scenario—when connection becomes too intense. In enmeshed families, individuals become so tangled up that personal needs and identity get lost or ignored, blocking real emotional freedom. Losing the group feels like losing themselves, creating abandonment issues through over-connection rather than individual neglect.

Since we covered the evolutionary basis and normalcy of abandonment fears earlier, let's focus here on how childhood neglect specifically creates these fears. The key difference is that neglect-based abandonment fear often stems from never having secure attachment in the first place, rather than losing it. When caregivers are consistently unavailable—physically or emotionally—children develop a chronic sense that connection is unreliable and that they must constantly work to maintain relationships or risk being left alone.

> **Building Your Circle of Belonging.** Here is an exercise designed to help you begin reducing the fear of abandonment by strengthening your connection to your inner self, your qualities, and the web of support around you. When we feel the panic of disconnection, it's often because our nervous system is reliving an ancient fear: being left alone and unprotected. This exercise invites you to build a visual and emotional anchor—a personalized space where you belong, even when others feel distant. The more you repeat it, the more your system learns that you are not alone and never truly without connection.
>
> Let's start by sitting comfortably. If you like, place one hand on your heart and one on your belly. Take three slow, deep breaths all the way down to your diaphragm. Let your body feel your presence—just that.
>
> Now, bring to mind a recent moment where you felt afraid of being abandoned—emotionally or physically. Allow your body to react. Just notice the sensations without needing to change or judge them.
>
> Now, visualize a large circle in front of you or within you. This circle represents your personal space and your connection to everything around you. In the center of the circle, place a representation of yourself. This can be an image of you, a symbol, or an abstract figure that captures your essence.
>
> Gradually, begin adding symbols that represent your personal qualities and inner strengths around your central self. For example, a sun for your warmth, a tree for your resilience, a star for your hopes, a shell for your protectiveness, and a flame for your passion. Take your time to feel what each symbol means to you. These form your **inner ring of qualities.**

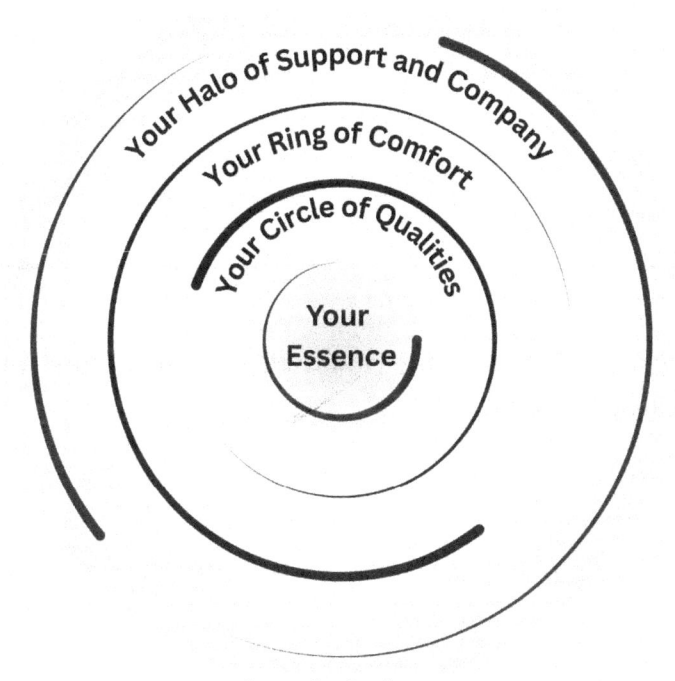

The Circle of Belonging

Now, begin placing whatever brings you comfort in life—your favorite place, music, a food that nourishes you, a color, or a spiritual symbol. Please take your time adding elements. Let this **ring of comfort** surround your strengths and essence.

Next, visualize the people who support, teach, or care for you—past or present, near or far. These can include friends, family, mentors, therapists, neighbors, and even inspiring public figures like actors or movie characters. Place them around your inner symbols, each in their own space. Let yourself feel how each of them contributes to your **halo of support and company**—a circle of safety, connection, and recognition.

Now, repeat silently several times: *"I'm not alone. Even if someone steps away, I have plenty inside of me."* Pause and feel what shifts in your body as you say these words while visualizing your circle. You can also add other affirmations, such as *"I may fear being left, but I no longer leave myself."* Say these words gently, even if part of you doesn't fully believe them yet. The brain learns through repetition—especially with safety-focused phrases like these.

> Repeat this visualization and mantras daily, especially during moments of disconnection or relational distress. You can evolve the circle over time, adding or removing figures and symbols as your life and inner world grow. The goal is not to "banish" fear of being alone, but to offer it a place within a larger container of support and wholeness.

WHAT PROBLEMS DO EMOTIONALLY NEGLECTED KIDS HAVE WHEN THEY GROW UP?

In part, it's hard to gauge the true impact of emotional neglect because, unlike physical neglect, it leaves no visible marks. Children rarely realize they're being emotionally neglected, and they seldom adopt the victim identity that can sometimes accompany overt abuse.

You may have noticed throughout this book that I resist the widespread tendency in psychology to over-pathologize everyday experience. When the topic of emotionally neglected children arises, the common response is often a litany of severe psychological problems—accompanied by dire predictions. While it's probable to get wounded, I prefer to emphasize what's often overlooked: many people who experienced neglect do gradually heal as they mature.

That said, neglect creates genuine challenges for many. Those who learn to disappear, take up less space, or suppress their needs may chronically activate dissociative mechanisms. Over time, such behaviors can result in emotional disengagement, reduced self-awareness, and mild delays in development. Issues can flare up intermittently, feeling most acute during moments of heightened need or vulnerability—a championship game when no one cheers, birthdays forgotten or dismissed as unimportant.

However, the natural wisdom of the human psyche drives them to seek supportive relationships, pursue personal goals, and discover their own worth. Without someone to teach them essential life skills or provide emotional nurturing, many neglected individuals develop remarkable self-reliance and independence. As adults, they often thrive professionally and become dependable partners and friends, guided by discipline, intrinsic motivation, and a strong sense of personal agency.

Some may argue these resilient individuals are the exception, but it's hard to know—we lack comprehensive data on outcomes. Serious cases of neglect, where a person finds no clear path to healing, are more visible and thus easier to recognize, but not the others.

WHY DO I PUSH PEOPLE AWAY EVEN WHEN I WANT THEM CLOSE?

Push-pull behavior often stems from early attachment experiences, so let's explore the answer from that perspective. Secure attachment is built through at least one reliable caregiver who offers a consistent sense of safety and emotional connection. Babies are biologically wired for this—even a single dependable figure can fulfill that core need. While we're born fragile, we're also remarkably adaptable, so infants will bond with whoever is present, even if that connection results in insecure attachment patterns. These early adaptations often carry into adulthood, especially when we've learned that people may not consistently show up when we need them. Fortunately, attachment styles are not static. They can begin to shift the moment a truly dependable person enters our life. I'm one of those therapists who firmly believes that secure bonds can be built at any stage of life—because healing doesn't require a perfect past, just a present experience of willingness, safety, consistency, and genuine connection.

Still, when neglect is combined with rejection, abandonment, or chaos during early development, it's undeniable that the impact can be more profound. Trust and bonding may not form properly, often leading to disorganized attachment—the only form of attachment considered pathological. This style is marked by conflicting impulses: unpredictable longing for closeness mixed with avoidance and *"I'll reject you first"*—a neurobiological imprint of unmet needs.

In my clinical experience, neglect often gives rise to a particular relational pattern: a persistent sense of neediness that remains, whether it's openly expressed or carefully concealed. This unresolved hunger for connection tends to create strain in relationships. Some individuals present as fiercely independent. Others appear overtly dependent while quietly resenting their own emotional needs. This ambivalence toward closeness—a biological drive for connection mixed with fear and even contempt for vulnerability—creates either a painful back-and-forth or rigid detachment, both of which are emotionally exhausting for the person and their partners. This explains why someone might push people away even while desperately wanting connection: the nervous system has learned that closeness often leads to pain, so creating distance first feels like the safer option, even when it conflicts with the deepest craving to be acknowledged and valued.

Is it normal to feel disconnected from yourself after emotional neglect?

Feeling disconnected from ourselves after emotional neglect is not only normal—it's the byproduct of adaptation or survival. Threatening neglect traps a child in a chronic state of fear and helplessness, leaving them feeling fundamentally unprotected and in pain, and to avoid it, the brain disconnects or slows down some of the circuits of awareness.

This effort of the brain to seek relief numbs emotional distress, detaches from unbearable feelings, compartmentalizes perceptions of the neglectful caregiver, or disengages from the inhospitable environment. For some, this manifests as several different characteristics that range from a reduced ability to recognize or express emotion, a "flat" affect, and a high tolerance for physical pain to periods of feeling distant and disconnected—like watching life from the outside. Many children learn to isolate painful memories from everyday awareness, creating compartments in the mind that can persist well into adulthood. Because dissociation can slice off emotions, memories, or needs in different combinations, the work often starts by mapping which parts of experience each person lost touch with.

How do you tell if you're genuinely nice, a people pleaser, or just desperate for approval?

Confusion in relational dynamics often leads to people-pleasing being labeled as a flaw rooted in neglect. Personally, I find that view overly simplistic and often incorrect.

Perhaps because the therapeutic profession includes many individuals who could fit that label, I've had the opportunity to observe a more nuanced reality.

I've found important distinctions between those who have a natural tendency toward generosity and care and those who please others to gain love, approval, or safety. These differences are subtle but meaningful. To better understand them, we can explore three core motivations that often underlie people-pleasing behavior.

Giving Love: Altruism—the selfless concern for others' well-being—is both innate and adaptive. Found throughout the animal kingdom, particularly in species with complex social structures, altruism is a natural tendency that brings profound emotional satisfaction. Neurobiologically, altruistic behavior activates regulatory circuits that release feel-good hormones like dopamine and other bonding neurochemicals, providing a natural, healing effect.

Many people discover this fulfillment early in life and gradually incorporate giving into their identity—not intentionally as healing but because of its beneficial effects. *I remember a client who learned from his grandmother to buy extra groceries to give away. As an adult, whenever he could, he would purchase gift cards or pay for the groceries of people who were struggling financially. He remembered how some judged this as a people-pleasing impulse, without realizing that it actually lifted his spirits and reconnected him with his grandmother's kindness.*

Needing Love: Our fundamental need for attachment, validation, and belonging can manifest as people-pleasing behavior. This is common among those who experienced emotional neglect, where consistent absence of attention creates a deep hunger for connection. These individuals may go to great lengths to get the love they need, often disregarding themselves completely to satisfy others. While this might extend to extreme submissiveness or self-denial, it often represents a learned strategy for gaining the emotional acknowledgment missing in early life. Pleasing others becomes a habitual way to avoid further abandonment, hoping to finally receive the care they missed.

This isn't necessarily pathological—genuine niceness, even when motivated by need, can create positive feelings and regulate the nervous system. If someone suffers from not feeling valuable, giving to others can make them feel useful and worthy. However, when driven by desperation, it can create internal conflict, stress, resentment, and disappointment, potentially leading to a "false self"—where someone becomes so focused on being what others want that they lose touch with their authentic feelings and desires. It also creates the risk of being unaware when someone takes advantage of this vulnerability.

Seeking Safety: The most complex form of people-pleasing is rooted in survival mechanisms, often developed in response to neglect combined with other adversity. Some researchers describe this as the "Please and Appease" response—a pattern that merges the instinct to stay socially connected with the need to manage perceived threat. Individuals remain relationally engaged on the surface while simultaneously suppressing emotions and desires to avoid conflict or rejection. They appear connected but are often internally shut down and angry—silencing their needs to feel safe.

As you can see, people-pleasing can emerge as one of our most adaptive survival strategies, a genuine expression of compassion and generosity, or a complex mix of both.

What Drives Your Impulse to Give? A Quiz. Here's a short quiz designed to help you identify your dominant motivations for helping or pleasing others in a clear and non-pathologizing way.

Are you pleasing, giving, or seeking safety?

Answer each statement below with: **O** = Often true **S** = Sometimes true **R** = Rarely or never true

Section 1

___ I feel joy and energy after helping others.

___ When I help, I'm not thinking about what I'll get in return.

___ Kindness feels like a natural part of who I am.

___ I don't feel guilty or anxious when I say "no" if I need to.

___ I enjoy supporting others, even when no one notices or praises me.

Section 2

___ I feel anxious or guilty when I say no to someone.

___ I often agree to things just to avoid disapproval or rejection.

___ I sometimes feel invisible unless I'm being helpful.

___ I hope that by being kind, others will love or accept me.

___ I feel drained after helping others, but I keep doing it anyway.

Section 3

___ I stay quiet or agreeable around difficult people to avoid conflict.

___ I act nice or overly accommodating to keep others calm.

___ I learned early in life that my needs might cause problems.

___ I often suppress my emotions so I don't upset others.

___ I sometimes feel like I have to earn my right to exist by pleasing people.

Scoring: Tally your O/S/R responses in each section. The section with the most **O** responses reflects your dominant motivation. A balanced score across sections suggests mixed motivations, which is common and valid. As a general rule, if you scored

- **Mostly O's in Section 1 – Giving Love:** Your kindness is likely rooted in a natural tendency to care and connect. You give from a grounded place and maintain healthy boundaries.

- **Mostly O's in Section 2 – Needing Love:** You may be giving in hopes of receiving connection, approval, or validation. Such generosity doesn't make you flawed—it's often a response to emotional neglect or unmet needs from early life.

- **Mostly O's in Section 3 – Seeking Safety:** Your kindness may function as a self-protective strategy. You may have learned to please others by staying safe or avoiding emotional harm. Such behavior suggests deep early adaptations that can be addressed with compassion and care.

Examine Growing Brains and Their Fractures

"Development doesn't pause for pain. It grows around it—sometimes like scaffolding, sometimes like poison ivy."

When our young brains and personalities are still forming, interruptions can have consequences more serious than we may realize or notice right away. Our minds and bodies develop much like a house under construction: harm to the foundation compromises everything built on top of it, while disruptions during construction shape the structure differently than damage that occurs after it's complete. When adversity is accompanied by constant stress or intense fear during these critical developmental windows, it doesn't just leave emotional wounds—it can rewire the core systems that shape how we think, feel, and relate.

This section explores what happens when emotional pain intersects with development, altering not just our experience of the world but the very architecture of how we process it. We'll look at how the stages of development are often overlooked or mislabeled—and how distress effects can quietly shape core elements like personality, behavior, and emotional regulation. Rather than focusing solely on what happened, we'll investigate when it happened—because when it comes to development, timing shapes the impact much more than the happenings themselves.

What Happens to a Child's Brain When They're Emotionally Hurt?

When children experience emotional suffering that feels threatening—like physical intimidation or witnessing violence—it activates stress responses and, in some cases, full survival circuits, directly impacting brain development. But what happens when there's no immediate threat? Even in non-threatening situations—as in emotional neglect—psychological pain from dismissiveness or disapproval can still significantly influence how the brain matures. These chronic experiences of relational suffering—rejection, exclusion, criticism, punishment, or invalidation—repeatedly activate pain circuits.

In hurtful situations where there is no threat, the brain's adaptation mode engages long before survival alarms activate. Emotional pain is essentially a signal: *"Pay attention and learn how to adjust."* The problem is that young children lack the developmental capacity to decipher what's expected or to regulate themselves, so the lesson can't land. This is why most children don't learn to "obey" as quickly as parents would like until they develop better self-regulation skills, usually around ages 4 to 6.

To understand what happens to the child's brain in these situations, we must consider age, frequency, and duration. Preschoolers rarely replay painful scenes the way adults ruminate because their autobiographical memory and self-story are still forming. Only about 10-15% of children brood for hours or bring up the same slight months later—often those with high anxiety or insecure attachment patterns. Most childhood upsets dissolve within minutes because young brains reset rapidly once comfort or distraction appears. Emotional pain lingers when the same hurt repeats over and over and involves a primary caregiver who doesn't repair it. *For example, a child who gets scolded for not finishing their food from early childhood through adolescence by a parent too busy to notice when the child does comply.*

When ongoing conflict inflicts constant emotional pain, it draws the child's attention inward, pulling energy away from curiosity and connection and trapping the mind in confusion, doubt, and insecurity. If the conflicts involve safety, the child experiences not only pain but also fear. Chronic activation consumes much of the brain's energy, diverting critical resources away from key developmental processes like learning, integration, and self-concept formation.

Over time, how a child relates to themselves and others gets shaped by whether they experience only pain or also fear for their survival. Some children become hypervigilant or overly reactive; others retreat into emotional disengagement. In the absence of guidance, the system improvises—defaulting to strategies that prioritize survival over growth. What might be mistaken for a "difficult temperament" is often unresolved emotional struggles the child cannot yet integrate.

This matters especially because early childhood (roughly ages 0–7) is when the brain wires foundational circuits for curiosity, emotional regulation, learning, and social connection. This sensitive period requires not only physical safety but also space for investigation, consistent emotional presence, attunement, and enriching stimulation. While repeated, high-stakes insecurity can derail development through chronic stress responses, the cumulative weight of loneliness and invalidation can be equally damaging.

When emotional pain happens pervasively throughout childhood, it can impair neural development. Neurons that would otherwise form adaptive networks may be pruned away or left underactive. Overall brain volumes may remain smaller than in children raised in emotionally supportive environments. Such conditions can result in an underdeveloped prefrontal cortex, making tasks like focusing, learning, and impulse control significantly more difficult.

Yet not all children exposed to emotional pain are derailed by it. Children are remarkably adaptive by design. Many preserve their core strengths through imagination, connection with siblings or peers, or brief but meaningful interactions with supportive adults. Some are naturally more resilient, helped by temperament, genetic factors, or a nervous system that recovers quickly after stress. Others find emotional "bubbles of safety": a teacher who listens, a neighbor who smiles, a pet, a routine, or a creative outlet.

When children find these safety spaces, their system learns to buffer pain in small but powerful ways. Even if a primary caregiver is emotionally inconsistent, the child may still experience enough attunement—from that caregiver's better moments or other sources—to build a basic template of connection. These children may carry vulnerabilities, but they also develop strengths—often becoming unusually perceptive, resourceful, or sensitive to others' needs. Importantly, their brains continue developing, frequently finding alternative neural pathways that allow for resolution, integration, and growth later in life. This is the brain's preferred direction: toward adaptation, restoration, and connection whenever possible.

CAN SOMEONE GO THROUGH A TERRIBLE CHILDHOOD AND TURN OUT TOTALLY FINE?

Since our system is always working to stay healthy, and thanks to decades of resilience research, I can say yes—there is a possibility that someone who went through adverse circumstances in childhood could grow up with few or even no lasting issues. How could that be? The fuller story is that resilience usually reflects a web of inner strengths and outside supports rather than natural wisdom alone.

Let's begin by acknowledging that the term "severe childhood trauma" is highly subjective. Much like beauty is in the eye of the beholder, threat is in the eye of the perceiver. What one person experiences as terrifying, another might interpret differently—based on temperament, perception, context, or the scripts they carry about fear. *For some, having guns in the house is dangerous, while for others, learning to use them early was taught as a sport or protection.*

A child who grows up in a home that others might label as chaotic can personally experience moments of fun, connection, or meaning.

Just recently, a client told me her grandmother drank every night. I asked whether that had been stressful for her, and she smiled and said, "The opposite! I couldn't wait for her to get drunk—she was hilarious! That was the best part of the day." What others might classify as neglect or dysfunction didn't register that way in her experience.

That's not to say high stress and threat don't matter—but perception, temperament, resources, and resilience all shape how traumatic circumstances are metabolized. Some children have natural tolerance, while others benefit from buffering factors like emotionally attuned relatives, teachers, friends, or internal coping resources like imagination, sense of humor, and playfulness. These factors can serve as "protective scaffolding," allowing development to continue relatively unimpeded even in adverse conditions.

However, if the question asked about "developmental trauma" instead, I might hesitate to give such an optimistic answer. Developmental trauma refers to repeated or ongoing adversity during the years when a child's brain and nervous system are still forming—typically from birth through late adolescence. This means the accumulation of stressors—like chronic abuse, exposure to violence, emotional abandonment, or living with a caregiver who is consistently frightening and emotionally unavailable. In such cases, the consequences are often long-lasting. The child's system must reorganize to survive, and the adaptations made during these sensitive periods can become wired into the brain's architecture, affecting many functions.

Still, even developmental trauma needs to be assessed correctly. Consider timing:

- **From birth to age five,** the brain undergoes rapid development. Chronic stress during this phase can disrupt motor skills, language acquisition, emotional regulation, and attachment.

- **Stress around ages 9 to 12** may more significantly impact peer relationships, moral reasoning, or self-esteem.

- **In adolescence,** traumatization may derail identity formation and autonomy development.

A short period of adversity during an otherwise stable childhood doesn't cause lasting harm if the child returns to a supportive environment. By contrast, prolonged exposure without repair can ripple through multiple developmental stages and create deeper, more pervasive effects.

Can You Tell If You Have Developmental Trauma, or Is It Invisible to You?

If we are talking about developmental trauma as a condition, we're referring to Developmental Trauma Disorder (DTD). DTD was proposed as a diagnosis distinct from PTSD or C-PTSD to capture what occurs to a child's brain and personality when their system suffers from severe stress during formative years, including attachment injuries when caregivers aren't responsive to the baby's needs.

Unfortunately, this diagnosis has not been officially accepted into diagnostic manuals, limiting its use primarily to research contexts. It still offers a useful tool to understand the effects that can emerge early in a child's development. Most people with DTD aren't aware they have it—in fact, most people who suffered traumatization during their developmental years cannot recognize their symptoms. It requires significant help or education about what to look for.

One reason is that dysregulation often gets chalked up to someone's "personality" rather than recognized as a survival response to ongoing threat, especially if the symptoms started early, when they're confused with temperament or inherited traits. Family members might say things like *"She's always been anxious"* or *"He's just naturally withdrawn,"* without recognizing these patterns as adaptations to chronic stress. The child grows up believing these responses are simply who they are, rather than understanding they developed these traits as protective strategies. This misattribution becomes deeply ingrained—the person may spend years trying to "fix their personality" instead of addressing the effects of long traumatization.

Another factor is that the chronic stress that leads to DTD typically causes small, incremental changes in the brain and nervous system, often under the radar. These changes produce subtle symptoms that feel like quirks rather than red flags of trauma responses. Some symptoms themselves push people to avoid facing or acknowledging distress, especially if they've become emotionally numb or convinced they're not worth attention.

Many symptoms are negative symptoms—the reduction or absence of normal functions like difficulty experiencing pleasure, reduced curiosity, or inability to feel excitement about future plans—or physical ones such as chronic pain, sleep disturbances, or frequent infections, which are rarely identified as trauma-related.

For instance, someone might have trouble feeling joy, connecting with others, or accessing childhood memories—like being unable to remember much before age 10, feeling disconnected during happy moments, or struggling to form close friendships—but these gaps feel normal to them. They might also experience chronic headaches, digestive issues, or unexplained fatigue that seem unrelated to their emotional history.

Complicating things further, the situations leading to DTD can be hard to identify—someone might grow up blaming themselves for inciting a parent's fury instead of seeing the emotional abuse. Also, long-term traumatization may become so normalized that the child learns to cope with it. Then, when one significant threat occurs, all the accumulated symptoms suddenly become visible—but that moment can come decades later. All of this makes it easy to go through life unaware that a trauma-related disorder is at play.

Transition From Silent to Whole

"Your willingness to heal transforms warning signs into guidance systems."

Whether you're dealing with overwhelming emotions, unresolved wounds, active trauma, or managing the aftermath of any of them, your participation in your mental health is essential. There is always a way forward. Think about the scars you carry from childhood. Everyone has them—maybe from a fall while biking, a cut while cooking, or a more serious injury from surgery. Some scars are barely noticeable (from scratches or even fractures), while others remain sensitive and cause shame (like visible marks from self-harm, surgical scars from traumatic injuries, or disfiguring wounds from accidents), and some can create dysfunction themselves (like contractures that restrict joint movement, internal scarring that affects breathing, or nerve damage that causes chronic pain). They remind you of their presence in certain weather or during specific movements. Even with proper medical care, these marks often stay with you. It all depends on the location of the scar, the depth of the original wound, and the story you attach to it.

Psychological scars work similarly. They don't always cause pain, but they serve as reminders—protecting us from similar hurts. But their presence doesn't mean you're damaged or that they have to control your life. What makes emotional wounds and trauma complex is feeling like *"We've been here before. Let's make sure we don't miss the warning signs this time,"* and not knowing how to change the direction of those unhealthy instructions.

Repeated emotional injuries can erode trust and safety, especially if you haven't resolved the previous ones. When wounds remain open, the brain prepares for the worst, making your conscious participation even more important in developing hope and finding safety. Proper healing is key. If you treat emotional wounds with the same care you would a physical injury, you develop a new relationship with these experiences. Even when facing similar situations, your processed and integrated understanding helps you respond with wisdom rather than reactivity. That's the whole point of healing: becoming better at reading situations so you can respond more adaptively.

WHAT'S THE POINT OF FORGIVING SOMEONE WHO ISN'T EVEN SORRY ABOUT HURTING ME?

The point of forgiving isn't to benefit those who hurt you or excuse their behavior. Forgiveness is often framed as a moral obligation, but its true power lies in freeing you from unresolved pain. Rather than waiting for someone to acknowledge their wrongdoing—which may never happen—viewing forgiveness as **an internal act** becomes empowering. Importantly, forgiveness doesn't require reconciliation or renewed vulnerability. You don't even need to tell the person you've forgiven them. The act is for you, not them—it's about releasing their emotional hold over you while maintaining protective boundaries.

A helpful way to define it: *forgiveness is the willingness to release negative feelings toward someone who hurt you without compromising your protection, needs, or well-being.*

Under this healing framework, forgiveness means refusing to let someone else's actions pollute your heart—valuing your own well-being enough to stop carrying their poison. Research confirms that forgiveness reduces stress hormones, lowers blood pressure, eases anxiety, and improves sleep. Refusing to let go, conversely, is a burden that damages both mental and physical health.

Remember that forgiveness isn't a one-time decision but a journey, especially for deep hurts. You might need to "forgive again" when memories resurface—this doesn't invalidate your process but acknowledges how our minds heal from significant wounds. By forgiving, you break the cycle that keeps you tethered to past pain. That said, if anger motivates healthy boundary-setting, that's valid too. Both feelings can coexist. The key is preventing unforgiveness from defining you long-term. When approached as self-care, forgiveness restores your capacity for joy and authenticity.

> **Releasing the Weight of the Wound Exercise.** Here is a reflective process to reduce the emotional grip of past hurt—whether or not you're ready to forgive today. This exercise isn't about forcing forgiveness. It's about checking in with the pain and creating space for release—on your terms, at your pace.
>
> Close your eyes and take a quiet moment. Bring to mind the situation or person who hurt you. Instead of focusing on what they did, focus on what the hurt means to you.
>
> Ask yourself, *"What meaning did I assign to this hurt?"* (*"This proves I'm unworthy"*), *"What was I expecting from this person before—and what do I expect now?"* (*"I expected an apology; now I just want to stop feeling angry"*), *"What story do I tell myself about this pain? About myself, them, or the world?"* (*"It meant I wasn't worthy of respect, or it showed they are cruel"*).
>
> Take your time. You can write your answers down or simply observe them quietly in your mind.
>
> Give voice to the wound—gently and honestly. Next, investigate the impact by asking, *"How has holding onto this pain been affecting me?"* *"Sleepless nights, constant resentment, self-doubt, difficulty trusting?"* *"Where do I feel this tension in my body?"* *"What has it cost me—in energy, relationships, health, or peace of mind?"*
>
> You can visualize or write these answers as well. This is not about blaming yourself—it's about understanding the burden you've been carrying.
>
> Now externalize the pain.
>
> Imagine this emotional burden—shame, rage, sadness, betrayal—as an object you've been carrying. Let it take a shape. Is it a heavy stone? A rusted chain? A foggy weight around your chest? Whatever form it takes, hold that image clearly.
>
> Now ask, *"Is this mine to carry forever?"* *"What part of this pain belongs to me—and what part came from someone else's immaturity, fear, or limitations?"*

> Take a few deep breaths. As you exhale, imagine returning the weight that doesn't belong to you. Visualize setting it down. Or cutting the chain. Or watching it dissolve.
>
> Say silently or aloud: *"I release this pain to protect my peace. This no longer weighs heavy on me."*
>
> Take a deep breath and exhale slowly. Then say, *"I am choosing to prioritize my healing and well-being. Releasing this doesn't excuse what happened—it frees me to move forward."*
>
> To end, let's reconnect with your needs.
>
> Shift your attention inward and ask, *"What do I need now that I didn't get then?"* (compassion, validation, safety.) *"What would support my healing—not just in thought, but in action?"* (setting boundaries, journaling, seeking supportive connections). *"What boundary, affirmation, or insight helps me feel protected today?"* (*"I'll no longer explain myself to people who don't listen,"* or *"I'll only invest in relationships that nourish me."*)
>
> By anchoring forgiveness in your needs, boundaries, and readiness, this practice honors emotional pain without bypassing it. You are not erasing the wound—you are tending to it in a way that restores your clarity and power. Forgiveness, when it comes, is not a surrender to what was done but a return to yourself—free from someone else's harm.

WHAT WOULD YOU PUT IN AN EMOTIONAL FIRST AID KIT?

Imagine you're walking down a busy street when suddenly you step on something, twist your ankle, and tumble to the ground in full view of dozens of strangers. In that moment, a flood of emotions washes over you—confusion, alarm, embarrassment, anger, pain, doubt, and sadness colliding all at once. Before you can even process what's happening, people surround you with concerned faces, asking, "Are you okay?" and "Do you need help?" Some extend their hands, ready to help you up. In this split second, with your body hurting and emotions swirling, what's the best way to respond? Should you jump up quickly to minimize embarrassment? Accept help? Assess your injury first. Or do something else entirely? The natural impulse might be to jump up immediately, "prove" you're fine, or feel so lost and confused that you ask for an ambulance.

Our typical responses focus on getting back to "normal" as quickly as possible, without considering what our system truly needs. **This rush to move on is often what transforms a painful moment into a lasting injury.**

One of the most important insights about traumatic situations and emotional wounds you can take from this book is that **the care you give yourself right after a challenging, hurtful, or threatening incident is key to whether you'll suffer a lasting injury or not.**

After experiencing something deeply scary or upsetting, create space and give your brain and nervous system time to regain presence—to reorient, refocus, reconnect with the environment, and restore your ability to think clearly. In all shocking, unexpected, or hurtful situations, reflexes—along with protective and emergency mechanisms—activate, temporarily impairing or disengaging many other functions. That's why it's so important to pause and recover some of these capacities before reacting or opting for anything else.

Before deciding what to do, you need to regain the ability to make decisions and assessments. Before even moving your body, you need to mentally scan it to assess for serious injury—not just what you can see, but **what you can feel.** Before accepting or seeking help, you need to discern what kind of help is required. Before reporting your pain, you need to distinguish whether it's coming from your emotions, the physical injury, or confusion itself.

A small incident like the one I described mirrors responses to larger traumatic events. Using this scenario, let's consider what an **"emotional injuries first aid kit"** should include. Think of these tools like the bandages, antiseptic wipes, and gauze you'd find in a physical first aid kit—but for your mind and emotions. An emotional first aid kit should contain techniques to pause reactions, ground yourself, process feelings, seek appropriate support, practice self-compassion, and integrate the experience. Let me break down each component:

Emotional Injuries First Aid Kit

Stop the Bleeding. In the heat of the moment, our first instinct is often to spring into action or react out of embarrassment, fear, anger, or whatever emotion is most present. In a physical injury, you'd start by applying pressure to stop the bleeding. Emotionally, this translates to pausing the swirl of reactions. Give yourself a moment and "clear the space" by not prioritizing those around you, their opinions, or even their immediate offers of help. You need the space for yourself first. Try practical pause techniques: count slowly to ten, take several slow, deep breaths, or silently repeat a calming phrase like *"Take a moment"* or *"I can respond, not react."* If appropriate, physically step away from the situation—even briefly. If you were in a conflict, you might excuse yourself to the bathroom before responding; if you were in an accident, you might ask for a place to sit before engaging with others. This signals to your body and brain that it's safe to switch off the emergency alarm, at least long enough to regain clarity.

Come back to your senses. When dealing with a physical wound, you might apply a splint or keep weight off an injured ankle. Emotionally, "stabilizing" means grounding yourself—feel your feet on the ground, wiggle your toes, notice your surroundings, and take a moment to deliberately feel each breath. Grounding techniques prevent you from accidentally "re-injuring" yourself emotionally by rushing ahead too quickly. This helps anchor you back to the present moment and supports your nervous system in settling down. Before deciding on any next step, check in with yourself: *"How am I doing physically, emotionally, and mentally?"*

Clean the wound by identifying and acknowledging your feelings. Just as you'd rinse dirt and debris from a cut, the next step is to notice and acknowledge your emotions—shame, fear, anger, sadness—without judging them or yourself. Simply name them as they arise: *"I feel scared," "I feel exposed," "I feel frustrated."* By recognizing them, you're clearing away the emotional "gunk" so it doesn't fester below the surface.

Apply a bandage by offering yourself immediate support. After getting a cut, you'd reach for a bandage. Emotionally, this means considering what immediate support you need. Do you need to call a friend, write in a journal, or step away from the situation? Give yourself permission to do whatever helps you feel safe and soothed, without prioritizing what others expect from you. This might be the moment to let tears flow, acknowledge your pain, or reach out for comfort.

Decide what kind of help you need. There's a time to stand on your own and a time to accept help. Once you've paused, grounded yourself, and checked in, you'll have a clearer sense of whether you need reassurance, a friend's presence, professional help, practical assistance, silence, or simply time alone. When you're emotionally rattled, it's easy to either jump at the first offer of help or reject it entirely. Instead, slow down and discern what would actually serve you best. Acknowledge it and decide how to proceed.

Protect yourself from infection. Most of us become our worst critics: *"How could I let this happen?"* or *"I'm so clumsy."* That's equivalent to rubbing dirt into the cut and developing an infection. Give yourself a break by offering yourself compassion. Imagine speaking to a dear friend who just tripped. You'd be gentle, understanding, and supportive, right? Offer yourself that same grace. A small internal reminder, like *"It's okay to take a moment,"* *"This is embarrassing, but I'm not perfect,"* or *"I wasn't expecting this, but these things happen,"* can go a long way.

Reflect and integrate. Once the immediate crisis subsides and you've made the necessary decisions to care for yourself, it's time to learn from the experience. Maybe you realize you need more support than you thought, or perhaps you discovered a new emotional trigger you weren't aware of. Take some time to reflect on what happened and how you responded. Making meaning from the experience significantly helps prevent lasting emotional wounds. This is how you transform stumbles—physical or emotional—into stepping stones for growth. *"This was tough, but I'm impressed by how well I handled it,"* or *"This hurts, but I know it will eventually pass."*

Notice that in the kit there is no mention of how to deal with the event or the person that hurt you. That's probably what we do wrong most of the time. We focus on the external circumstances and forget about ourselves. We get trapped in the danger, the offense, the aggressor, the reasons, and the doubts, but we don't check on the wound, give ourselves the priority we deserve, or the comfort we crave.

Maintenance Through the COMPASS Practice. I invite you to make it a routine to check in with yourself, especially in the days or weeks after an emotionally challenging situation. A helpful way to remember this ongoing care is through the word **COMPASS,** which can guide your emotional maintenance.

> **Calm yourself (pause and create space)**
> **Orient to present (ground and return to your senses)**
> **Mention your feelings (acknowledge/name your emotions)**
> **Prioritize your needs (consider your needs first)**
> **Ask for appropriate help (help)**
> **Show self-kindness (practice self-compassion)**
> **Summarize lessons & be aware (learn/grow from the experience)**
>
> *Emotional First-aid Kit COMPASS*

Just like you'd monitor a sprained ankle instead of dwelling on the road you fell on, the shoes you wore, or the people who saw you, give emotional bumps and bruises the same attention and care. Rather than focusing on what the other person is doing or why they acted as they did, focus on how to help yourself heal.

These steps aren't rigid rules but gentle guidelines to help you respond thoughtfully to life's emotional and physical stumbles. When you pause, ground yourself, and show a little self-compassion, you're far less likely to carry an injury—emotional or otherwise—into the future.

WHAT DO YOU DO WHEN YOU REALIZE YOU WERE EMOTIONALLY NEGLECTED?

There's a distinct advantage in asking how to resolve the wounds from emotional neglect rather than thinking only in terms of "healing trauma." When you clearly understand what you're trying to resolve, your efforts tend to be more effective. I often see people trying to heal trauma without knowing exactly what to target—circling around painful memories without a clear picture of what truly needs attention. With emotional neglect, the task is often to build what was never there to begin with—like enriching barren soil so something can finally take root and grow.

The first hurdle is recognizing that emotional neglect occurred—and understanding how deeply an internal sense of *"I don't matter"* may have taken root. Emotional neglect can be recognized by what didn't happen: the emotional attunement, validation, care, and nurturing that were absent. Some people can identify that it was just their family that didn't value them. Others internalize it more deeply, becoming convinced they truly lack worth, don't deserve love, or will never be chosen.

Since neglect can be hard to recognize, be patient and practice honest, sensitive reflection toward yourself. That way, the outline of what was missing slowly emerges. Ask yourself, *"Have I kept myself small?"* *"Do I believe I have inherent value?"* *"How do I feel about my own dignity?"* These questions can help uncover what was once invisible and open a path toward resolution.

Resolving neglect usually revolves around six overlapping practices:

1) Learning to notice and name emotions you once ignored.

2) Becoming aware of your own needs and wants.

3) Allowing yourself to feel worthy of those needs.

4) Forming new, healthier patterns of emotional connection.

5) Trusting that your feelings matter and treating them with compassion—instead of dismissing hurt as "being too sensitive" or anger as "overreacting," you learn to honor your emotional responses as valid information about your experience.

6) Taking up space—literally and figuratively standing taller, speaking up in conversations, expressing your opinions, noticing and valuing your presence in rooms, and refusing to apologize for simply existing.

Taking Up Space Exercise. Let's practice overcoming the pain of having been neglected.

Close your eyes or lower your gaze and turn your attention inward. Quietly ask yourself, *"What am I feeling right now?"* Name whatever feeling arises, even if it's vague: numb, tense, or hopeful.

Then ask, *"What do I need or want in this moment?"*—perhaps a glass of water, a stretch, or a bit of reassurance.

Whisper to yourself, *"I'm allowed to have that need."*

> Now let your body grow taller: uncurl your shoulders, widen your stance, or gently extend your arms. Feel the space you occupy and affirm, *"My presence belongs here," "It feels good to expand," and "I matter!"*
>
> Imagine inviting someone into this expanded mental space and briefly sharing the feeling or need you identified. Notice how you feel as you expand in another's presence.
>
> Through this practice—naming feelings, honoring needs, taking up space, and opening to connection—you reinforce your inherent worthiness.
>
> Repeat the exercise whenever you catch yourself shrinking or apologizing for simply being.

Resolving neglect may also require "reparenting" yourself—offering the validation and care that were missing early on. Reparenting goes beyond finding safe relationships or a therapist who models attunement; it means *honoring your own emotions* and building self-nurturing habits that meet unmet needs. Let yourself arrive a few minutes late without over-apologizing, give your body rest when it's drained, or pass on a social event when your system needs quiet—and learn to say no without shame. Speak to yourself in a kinder tone, cook meals that truly nourish, and ask, *"What do I need right now?"*—then actually deliver it.

This inner work often involves identifying specific neglected aspects of your emotional development and deliberately attending to them. For instance, if your accomplishments were never celebrated, you might create personal ceremonies to acknowledge your achievements and honor your accomplishments. This works best when paired with sharing wins with a trusted person—social reinforcement cements new self-worth circuits. It also means attending to day-to-day needs the way a supportive caregiver would: setting consistent routines, speaking to yourself with warmth rather than criticism, and creating environments—physical and social—that make you feel protected and seen. If your feelings were dismissed, you might practice writing about yourself in the third person—your qualities, your behavior, and your achievements.

During these practices, attend to your body's sensations and acknowledge any emotions that arise. This transforms them from mere self-help techniques into profound acts of neurobiological rewiring—creating new patterns of self-relation that gradually bring your system to a more integrated experience.

Reparenting is about building trust with yourself in small, consistent ways—showing up with the care you once needed but didn't receive. Over time, those acts accumulate, reinforcing the sense that your needs matter, your feelings are valid, and your presence in the world is worth protecting and celebrating.

What Do You Do When Guilt and Shame Won't Leave You Alone?

Understanding and overcoming shame and guilt begins with recognizing how differently these emotions function in our lives. If you recall from Chapter Two, shame is a natural emotion with protective and adaptive characteristics. It evolved as a social survival mechanism—a visceral response to potential rejection or failure to meet group norms. At the same time, it can also serve a useful function by drawing our attention to behaviors or traits that misalign with our values, prompting us to grow and reconnect with our best selves.

However, many individuals experience shame as a destructive force, formed through a subjective evaluation that something is fundamentally wrong or unacceptable about who they are. It goes beyond feeling bad about a mistake; shame has the power to make us feel that *"we are"* the mistake.

This emotion can become embedded in several ways. When we have a fragile identity or low self-esteem, we're more likely to internalize criticism. Shame can also be contagious—transferred from parents with unresolved shame, projected onto us by abusive partners, or shaped by environments where we felt we had to hide our authentic selves to gain acceptance. *For instance, in an environment where being ostentatious is valued, someone can be ashamed of being discreet, even if modesty was taught as a value at home.* Many adults carry shame that doesn't belong to them—absorbed in childhood from witnessing shame-based behavior, experiencing attachment ruptures, or inheriting collective shame from a community.

As I suggested in Chapter Two, there are always opportunities to rewrite the script you carry about any emotion—to give it a new meaning and begin a different relationship with its presence. This is especially true for shame, whose script is often among the most disempowering.

Make it a practice to ask yourself, *"Is this feeling truly based on my actions, or am I carrying someone else's projections? A religious belief I've internalized? A harsh judgment I don't deserve?"*

What makes shame particularly difficult to experience and resolve is how often it remains hidden, surfacing instead as chronic low self-worth or patterns of punishing ourselves or others. When you bury authentic parts of yourself to gain acceptance, you may inadvertently create more shame through the inauthenticity that hiding requires. But when you begin to see shame as adaptive protection, you can start to unpack its deeper message and move toward a more compassionate understanding of yourself.

Both shame and guilt are emotions—and that means you can apply what you learned in Chapter Two about how to regulate and process them.

> **Engage in a Dialogue with Shame Exercise.** Shame thrives in secrecy and self-judgment, so the key is to externalize, normalize, and metabolize it with compassion. Here's a powerful exercise that can assist you in the process. I recommend doing your reflection in writing or aloud.
>
> **Externalize the shame.** Imagine shame as a part of you (not all of you) or even as an external "character." Give it a name, symbol, gender, or an image ("The Critic," "The Shadow," or "a short lady from another planet").
>
> Now, **normalize the feeling** by asking these questions: *"What are you trying to protect me from?"* (Often, shame masks fear of rejection or failure.) *"What do you need me to know?" "When did you first show up in my life?"* (Link it to past experiences—childhood punishment, societal messages.)
>
> Next, try to separate shame from truth. Write down shame's "script" following the instructions of Deconstructing an Emotion from Chapter Two. Once you are done and understand it better, counter the same with:
>
> - Evidence: *"I've been loved by X, Y, or Z."*
>
> - Self-compassion: *"I'm human, and my past doesn't define my worth."*
>
> - Consider this perspective: *"Would I judge a loved one for this?"*

> With the understanding you're gaining from your answers and reflections, let's move into **reparenting the shamed part.**
>
> The first step is to try to meet their needs. If shame says, *"You'll be rejected if they see the real you,"* respond, *"Thank you for trying to keep me safe. Still, I'm learning that vulnerability creates real connection. I've got us now."*
>
> Visualize ways to give them comfort: imagine holding this shamed part or sending them love. Stay with them until you notice the shamed part relaxing and feeling supported. If the part needs something else from you, listen and find ways to reassure them that you care.
>
> If you are able to stay in contact with the shame part, establish a dialog and write down the thoughts and needs you hear from this part. Keep the dialogue going until you and the shamed part feel comfortable with each other and begin integrating.

Guilt can function almost like a form of "healthy shame"—it points to what you did and nudges you to make amends, without condemning your whole self. Unlike shame, which says, *"I am bad,"* guilt says, *"I did something bad and need to do something about it."* Rather than pushing you to hide, guilt often propels you to take responsibility, repair relationships, and act in alignment with your values.

> **From Guilt to Growth: The Five-Step Accountability Practice.** Try this practice to help yourself process guilt and transform it into growth.
>
> We start this exercise with the obvious. Take responsibility for specific actions you have felt guilty about without condemning your entire self. For example, if you feel guilty for neglecting a relationship, plan to reach out to reconnect or have an honest conversation.
>
> **Make amends wherever possible, apologizing sincerely and changing behavior.** Remember that apologizing is not just saying *"I'm sorry"* without meaning it, and it's different from explaining why you did it. Apologizing means becoming accountable and recognizing the hurt you inflicted on the other person. The message gives the impression—and hope—that it won't happen again and that the person can regain trust. For example, if you missed your child's important

school event because of work, a true apology might sound like, *"I'm sorry I wasn't there for your presentation. I know how much it meant to you, and I can see that my absence hurt you. Your achievements matter to me, and I want to show up for you."*

Practice proactivity by acting differently in similar future situations, even with other people. Create specific plans for how you'll respond when facing comparable circumstances in the future. For instance, if you feel guilty about losing your temper, develop calming techniques to use when you notice early signs of frustration. Such an approach transforms guilt from a burden into a catalyst for positive change.

Use introspection and humility to understand what led to the actions you regret. Explore the circumstances, thoughts, and feelings that contributed to your behavior without using them as excuses. This self-awareness helps identify patterns and triggers, allowing you to intervene earlier in the cycle and make different choices before regrettable actions occur.

Accept forgiveness from others and, most importantly, from yourself. Recognize that holding onto guilt after you've taken responsibility and made amends serves no constructive purpose. Create a personal forgiveness ritual if needed—write a letter to yourself, perform a symbolic act, or simply state aloud that you're releasing the guilt while retaining the lesson.

Remember that while unhealthy shame defines us by our weaknesses or things beyond our control, completely denying it isn't healthy either. Shame can serve as a social regulator, helping you respect group norms and approach new relationships with appropriate caution. What matters is learning to tolerate its strong emotional charge without letting it define who you are. Healing is a journey, not an event. Be patient with yourself as you learn to distinguish between who you are and what you've done—embracing responsibility without surrendering your inherent worth.

Chapter Five

UNLOVE

HOW TO RECOGNIZE THE IMPACTS OF HEARTBREAK, MANIPULATION, AND ABUSE

"The heart that opens wide is the same heart that bleeds profusely."

We crave connection because it promises love, intimacy, and acceptance—yet the same longing can expose us to exploitation when others take advantage of our emotional needs and openness. While Chapter Four explored the wounds of emotional absence and neglect, this chapter examines what happens when people are present but unloving or predatory—using our desire or need for connection to manipulate, control, or harm us.

Connection feels like being seen and understood, built on empathy, trust, and reciprocal recognition. But when someone recognizes our vulnerabilities not to nurture but to exploit them, our available heart becomes a liability. The very openness that makes deep connection possible also makes us susceptible to those who would abuse our trust, gaslight our reality, or feed off our emotional generosity.

Before we can recognize these dangerous dynamics, we must connect with ourselves: track our thoughts, sensations, and needs, and notice how inner attunement steadies emotion and clarifies identity. Otherwise we risk mistaking *"someone wants what I offer"* for *"someone values who I am"*—a confusion that abusive people deliberately cultivate. Closing our heart, we stop listening to ourselves and abandon self-love.

From subtle manipulation to overt narcissistic abuse, we'll examine how relationship injuries occur when generous hearts meet malicious intentions or self-absorbed minds. These dynamics can leave us susceptible to repeated victimization, often outside our awareness. To truly understand these injuries, we'll explore the darker side of bonding, where closeness becomes harmful and connection becomes a trap, and consider how we might reclaim the secure ground of healthy relationships. When love becomes a weapon, we must learn to distinguish between wounds that require boundaries and injuries that demand complete separation—the depth determines whether we heal in the relationship or away from it.

SEE HOW ABUSE SHOWS UP AND SHAPES US

"The most damaging wounds are often the ones we're told don't count."

Abuse is often recognized as a primary factor in the development of complex trauma. Complex PTSD, first introduced in the 1980s by Judith Herman, is frequently linked to experiences such as domestic violence, sexual abuse, and torture. While these forms of abuse remain central—and are extensively discussed in books and clinical literature—what's still missing are formal, nuanced conversations about other forms of abuse, such as systemic oppression and emotional manipulation.

The rise of terms like "gaslighting" in popular culture has increased public awareness of emotionally abusive behaviors, but it has also led to sensationalism, misrepresentation, and even a kind of romanticization of abusive dynamics. My hope is to explore common questions about what defines traumatic abuse, bringing clarity to the wide range of ways abuse can hurt.

WHAT TYPE OF ABUSE CAN BE PSYCHOLOGICALLY DAMAGING?

The question itself reflects a common misconception—that some abuse might be less damaging than others. In reality, all abuse causes psychological harm because it involves one person using power, manipulation, or control to exploit another. What varies isn't whether damage occurs, but rather its depth and complexity. While unintentional harmful behavior can certainly wound, deliberate abuse creates deeper, more complex harm because it involves the calculated exploitation of trust, emotional openness, or dependence.

Abuse can take many forms, some less obvious than others. Physical abuse leads to disconnection from bodily sensations, numbing, and sometimes aggression. Sexual abuse creates deep wounds around self-worth, body image, shame, guilt, sexuality, and attachment. Emotional abuse damages self-esteem and identity. Financial abuse erodes trust and security. Recent research indicates that physical abuse tends to manifest through behavioral issues and physical symptoms, while emotional abuse is more commonly associated with anxiety, depression, and intrusive thoughts.

We can also think of abuse like radiation exposure—even if you don't see immediate effects, you wouldn't doubt its harmfulness. We know the damage happens at a cellular level; some show skin burns (raw trauma), while others carry bone marrow damage (hidden wounds and long-term effects).

The impact varies among individuals based on several factors: the level of exposure and duration, the type and severity of abuse, the ability to recognize the abuse, personal resilience, the availability of support systems, and pre-existing beliefs about self-worth. As I mentioned in Chapter Four, abuse is one of the most significant heartbreaking circumstances, and here I'll focus on how it not only breaks our heart but can also cause prolonged traumatization.

A crucial factor in assessing the consequences of abuse is whether the individual recognizes they're being abused. Someone unaware of the abuse—or who doesn't label it as such—may silently suffer for years without seeking help or questioning the dynamic. Awareness, on the other hand, often allows a person to begin protecting themselves, even if doing so is difficult or risky.

Beliefs about self-worth also shape the emotional toll. Someone who internalizes the abuse with thoughts like *"I deserve this"* or *"I may not get anything better than this"* may experience less conflict in the short term. They don't resist, don't escalate the situation, and may even appear emotionally regulated on the outside. But this acceptance comes at a cost: over time, the belief erodes their sense of self, leading to deeper, more lasting injuries like chronic shame, helplessness, or identity confusion.

Conversely, someone who thinks, *"I don't deserve this,"* may respond with resistance—arguing, setting boundaries, or even considering leaving. This often brings more intense stress in the short term: fear of retaliation, anxiety, and the exhaustion of constantly fighting. But in the long run, they tend to fare better. Their sense of self remains less damaged, and they are more likely to escape the cycle of abuse with clarity about what happened.

Quicksand offers a powerful analogy for understanding these dynamics. The person who goes still and accepts the situation may appear calm and composed. In the short term, there's less visible struggle—they're not making waves, not triggering more aggression. But slowly, silently, they sink deeper. The cost of staying quiet and compliant is that they become more trapped and incapable of climbing out. In contrast, the person who fights back—who thrashes, calls for help, and reaches for something solid—might create chaos at first. It looks messier and takes a toll on the body and mind. But that movement, that refusal to sink, increases their chances of finding solid ground. The struggle may be painful in the moment, but it keeps them connected to the instinct to survive and the possibility of freedom. In summary:

**Submission to the abuse =
less effort now, more damage later**

**Resistance to the abuse =
more effort now, but more agency and less long-term damage**

The impact of abuse might not be immediately visible, but it affects fundamental aspects of psychological and emotional functioning. The sooner abuse is recognized and addressed, the better the chance of preventing long-term psychological injury.

IS IT AN EXAGGERATION TO SAY EMOTIONAL ABUSE TRAUMATIZED ME?

No, it is absolutely not an exaggeration to say emotional abuse can traumatize you. Emotional abuse occurs when one person distorts, manipulates, confuses, influences, or dominates another's thoughts and behavior—usually for their own benefit—while disregarding the needs of the abused. So many abusers claim they weren't aware their behavior was abusive. But whether they acknowledge it or not, most abusers know they hold an advantageous position—either because the other person depends on them or shows vulnerabilities that can be exploited.

I explained in Chapter Three why living with a victim mentality can be damaging. Here, I want to emphasize something equally important: **victimization is real and not only a mental state.** When someone uses intimidation, coercion, manipulation, harassment, objectification, gaslighting, yelling, swearing, lying, or obsessive jealousy, they create mental distress, confusion, fear, and insecurity. These behaviors steal agency and confidence, reliably activating survival circuits and often overwhelming the nervous system's ability to stay regulated. Over time, such conduct results in lasting dysregulation and symptoms consistent with complex trauma—especially when the abuse is chronic and rooted in close relationships.

What makes this especially insidious is how emotional abuse can become normalized within a relationship. The behaviors may lose their shock value over time, becoming woven into daily dynamics with no awareness of the damage being inflicted—either because the abused has become numb to it or because they accept it as unavoidable.

Imagine a family where the mother routinely yells, curses, mocks, and belittles the father or one of the children. Over time, this dynamic may feel so "normal" that others in the household begin to join in—even without conscious intent or a defined role in the abuse. The result is a persistent sense of helplessness and internalized messages about worthlessness, gradually eroding self-esteem, trust, and the ability to regulate emotions or sustain healthy connections.

Emotional abuse often overlaps with other types of abuse, like sexual abuse, which frequently relies on manipulation, coercion, or threats to enforce compliance—intensifying its psychological impact. Abuse can also involve covert grooming with profound developmental consequences. Some adults who abuse minors may use pseudo-affection to manipulate, causing the child to associate abuse and objectification with love or closeness. This creates a transactional understanding of relationships from a very early age, disrupting essential developmental processes related to boundaries, self-worth, consent, and identity.

But let's also acknowledge the other side: we have agency, and in many cases, we may have what it takes to stop the abuse, to name it, to resist it, or to leave it. If someone doesn't yet have the strength, safety, or resources to act, it doesn't mean they are powerless or must endure it in silence. There are external supports available—therapy, crisis hotlines, legal aid, financial assistance, support groups, and safe housing options. Internal resources can also be cultivated: boundary recognition, self-validation skills, safety planning, wellness practices, and self-compassion.

ABUSE

What we Know: all types of abuse are damaging

What's Common: most abused people carry emotional wounds and many of them, also trauma.

Possible Consequences: If internalized *("I deserve it!")*, short-term protection, log term cost (trauma). If resisted, short-term cost (fights, disharmony), long term stability (freedom, independence, agency).

Damage: from altered emotionality to constant toxic stress to mild dissociation, to complete disconnection from emotions or awareness

Level of Dysfunction: from unresolved emotional wounds to hypervigilance, instability, dysregulation, and complex trauma symptoms.

Information about emotional abuse is now widely available through globalization and social media, making it less invisible than before. When individuals recognize abuse early and access support systems before distress becomes overwhelming—or before they risk becoming abusive themselves—they can buffer against slipping into persistent survival-mode responses, potentially preventing abuse from hardening into a lasting trauma condition.

I remember a client who was in a very abusive relationship without the means to leave. It took us three years to implement a comprehensive plan: returning to school, graduating, securing a job, finding housing, and finally announcing that the relationship was over. Sometimes liberation doesn't happen overnight, but it is possible with persistence and the right support.

> **A Self-Reflection Quiz: Am I Experiencing Emotional Abuse?** Let me share a quiz (not a diagnostic tool) as a guide to help you reflect on how safe, respected, and emotionally supported you feel in a relationship—whether it's with a partner, parent, friend, or other close connection.
>
> For each question, answer **Yes (Y), Sometimes (S), Rarely (R), or No (N).**
>
> **Verbal and Emotional Climate**
>
> __ Does this person frequently criticize, belittle, or mock you—either privately or in front of others?
>
> __ Do you feel like you're in a minefield, constantly afraid of how they might react?
>
> __ Are your feelings often dismissed or minimized (e.g., *"You need help," "That's not a big deal"*)?
>
> __ Do they use sarcasm or "jokes" that hurt you, then accuse you of overreacting?
>
> **Control and Autonomy**
>
> __ Do they try to control what you do, who you see, or how you spend your time?
>
> __ Do they become angry or distant when you express independent thoughts or decisions?
>
> __ Do you feel like you're not allowed to say "no" without consequences?

__ Have you made changes to your appearance, habits, or behavior mainly to avoid their disapproval?

Guilt, Manipulation, and Gaslighting

__ Do they make you feel guilty for having needs or setting boundaries?

__ Have they ever denied things you clearly remember happening, making you doubt your memory?

__ Do they twist situations to make themselves the victim, even when they've hurt you?

__ Do you find yourself constantly apologizing—even when you're not sure why?

Impact on You

__ Have you stopped sharing your true thoughts or feelings around this person out of fear or exhaustion?

__ Do you feel drained, anxious, or "less like yourself" after interactions with them?

__ Do you second-guess your worth, your decisions, or your ability to trust your own perceptions?

__ Do you feel more isolated from others since the relationship began?

Reflecting on Your Answers

If you answered Yes or Sometimes to <u>most</u> of these questions, it may be a sign that you're in a relationship with **emotionally abusive dynamics.** If you marked just a few with a Y or R, you may consult a professional to see if there are signs you should start considering. In those cases, individual and couples or family therapy can help avoid abusive dynamics when there is no intention to hurt or control.

Emotional abuse is not always loud or obvious. It often builds gradually and can be **deeply confusing**, especially when mixed with moments of care or affection. But abusive dynamics are also a thing that can be prevented. Emotional safety is a basic human need—not a luxury. You deserve to feel safe, respected, and supported in your relationships.

Do people who verbally abuse you actually mean the horrible things they say? Or just connected to their anger and trauma?

To answer, we need to consider several factors. People who verbally abuse often don't literally mean what they say in the moment, but their intent to hurt can be very real. *I remember a client describing how his sister, in a fit of rage, screamed, "You're disgusting!" When they later asked if she truly believed that, she admitted, "No, I was just furious and wanted to say something that would hurt you."*

Anger—especially rage—clouds thinking. It's hardwired in our fight response, signaling crossed boundaries or unmet needs. When intensely angry, our reasoning brain gets less energy while emotional structures ramp up, distorting reality and making it hard to grasp other viewpoints.

Verbal abuse may also be a manifestation of learned anger patterns or part of the emotion's script. If the person is traumatized—with poor emotional regulation and survival mode as default—those scripts can fuel exaggerated emotionality, seeing others as threats to be eliminated.

After calming down, many people might regret their words, justify the outbursts, or ignore them entirely. Those who justify themselves keep ruminating on right versus wrong, stoking internal conflict and preventing adaptive growth. Their ego defenses go up to protect their fragility. This practice rewrites the scripts toward more negativity and extreme justification.

These distinctions can help us assess whether verbal abusers truly mean what they say. Fleeting anger might not reflect genuine intent, but persistent verbal attacks often come from habitual urges to dominate or offload personal turmoil. It's not about the meaning of the words but the intention behind them. Verbal attacks often suggest unresolved wounds as well as traits like low empathy and poor accountability. These patterns can dominate a person, leading them to adopt abusive behavior as if it were a personality trait.

Regardless of intent, the impact on the abused is distressing—and harms the abuser too. They may fuse anger and abusive practices with their identity, feeling temporarily empowered, while also secretly wrestling with guilt and shame. These buried feelings sever self-awareness and can breed chronic emotional pain. In essence, abusers aren't happy people; their harmful behavior ultimately backfires on them too.

WHAT'S IT CALLED WHEN PEOPLE GET PLEASURE FROM HURTING OTHERS? WHAT ARE THE POSSIBLE CAUSES OF THIS BEHAVIOR?

The technical term for finding pleasure in others' suffering is "sadism," named after the Marquis de Sade, an 18th-century French writer whose works reveled in cruelty and domination. This isn't just a personality quirk—it's a drive that can manifest in emotional abuse, where inflicting pain becomes its own reward. It may mask deeper turmoil or serve as a way to reclaim a sense of control. I prefer to describe it as "mental darkness"—highlighting poor reflective qualities and the absence of higher-order experiences like compassion, empathy, and connection that typically guide human interactions.

We all carry the capacity for challenging emotions—flashes of envy or anger are part of being human. We are also capable of having dark and troubling thoughts and impulses, which doesn't make us "bad people" because our evolutionary programming includes competitive and self-protective instincts. But taking consistent pleasure in another's distress (from schadenfreude or, at the extreme, everyday sadism) is frequently linked to reduced empathic responding and weaker emotion-regulation circuits. It represents disconnection from one's capacity for compassion and moral compass.

Neurobiologically, our capacity for empathy involves brain regions like the prefrontal cortex, medial prefrontal cortex, and anterior insula. When underactive or poorly integrated, a person may disconnect from higher-order experiences (love, compassion) and be governed instead by primal mechanisms like dominance and self-preservation.

Trauma may play a significant role here. For some people who lived in nonstop fear as children, dampening empathy wasn't a choice—disconnecting was the brain's way to get through the day. Muting vulnerability may have been the only way to keep moving in a hostile setting, and that's when aggressive dominance feels oddly soothing, likely because each small victory fed dopamine into a starved reward system. That doesn't mean every sadistic streak traces back to trauma, but early, chronic fear can set the stage. The mind disconnects from its own pain, learns to dismiss others' pain just as quickly, and discovers that causing hurt can deliver a grim kind of relief—especially in competitive moments where "win or be hurt" feels like the only rule.

Cultural forces can reinforce this impulse, too. Because empathy is calibrated to group identity, a community that defines certain people as "outsiders" or threats can make their suffering feel acceptable—even gratifying—to its members. The pleasure isn't automatic or universal, but it grows more likely when shared stories, rituals, or media frame another group as dangerous, inferior, or fair game.

When someone is operating largely from the brain's most primitive survival circuits, the prefrontal cortex shows reduced engagement, so they register neither the full weight of another person's pain nor the future consequences of their own actions.

How does abuse show up in someone's behavior?

I once heard about a professor holding up a glass of water and asking the class, "Can you describe this water?" Before anyone could answer, they poured it into a jar and said, "Now, can you describe it the same way?" Then they drank some, smiled, and added, "And now?"

The point of this story is that people, like water, take the shape of countless experiences and contexts. Trying to pin them to one label or box overlooks the infinite ways we exist and shift. Strictly speaking, since abuse involves behaviors that intentionally harm or manipulate another person, it causes damage, and damage manifests one way or another. It often leads to negative consequences for the abused—uncertainty, fear, and emotional pain—as their respect, consideration, or well-being is disregarded, regardless of the cost.

Yet every individual carries a unique set of conditions that shape their responses, creating differences in how situations affect them. How we react to abuse varies widely, influenced by factors like personality traits, the severity and duration of abuse, available support systems, and whether we've had therapeutic intervention or educated ourselves on healthy strategies—information is a powerful resource! At one end of the spectrum, some who've experienced abuse show remarkable tolerance and resilience. Certain individuals even respond with compassion, set firm boundaries, and resolve the issue before it inflicts lasting harm, preventing significant behavioral or emotional changes. At the other extreme, some people collapse emotionally—feeling lost, unlovable, or defeated by actions that others might consider minor or harmless. Still others become abusive themselves, with anger becoming part of their regular strategies from then on.

High Resilience	Copes/Reacts	Significant Impact
Sets firm boundaries	Support systems influence outcome	Persistent suffering
Responds with understanding	Access to resources	Identity-defining
Resolves issues fast	Impacted by abuse severity	Distorted worldviews
Prevents lasting harm	May maintain hypervigilance	Dysregulation/dissociation
Maintains self-worth	Interpretation of abuse varies	Significant life impact
	Emotional wounds	Trauma disorder (C-PTSD)

The Spectrum of Responses to Abuse

Take microaggressions, for example—subtle, often unintentional comments or actions perceived as discriminatory or demeaning, now recognized as a form of abuse. Microaggressions often come from those privileged enough to escape oppression or discrimination, serving—whether consciously or not—as tactics to marginalize or belittle individuals from disadvantaged groups. Examples include remarks questioning someone's abilities ("Are you sure you can do that?"), intelligence ("You speak so well for someone like you"), or worth based on race ("You're pretty for a [race]"), gender ("That's impressive for a woman"), sexual orientation ("So who's the 'man' in your relationship?"), or identity ("Don't worry, your disability isn't obvious"). Though these might seem trivial to those who deliver them, they come from a place of advantage, which fits the definition of abuse to recipients, as they signal a lack of acceptance, ongoing denigration, or oppression.

Common responses might then include anger, defeat, intolerance, anxiety about future encounters, rejection sensitivity, avoidance, phobias, and various expressions of insecurity, disempowerment, and pain.

Abuse is not always straightforward or unidirectional—it blends the abuser's actions and intent with how the recipient interprets and responds. *For instance, if a boss tells a subordinate to dress more professionally, one might see it as abusive, prompting behavioral shifts. Another might view it as constructive feedback or mentoring, even appreciating the attention to detail.*

When abuse is blatant, however, most people experiencing it show similar behavioral changes that deeply affect their personal and social lives. The most common include:

- heightened alertness to potential threats (hypervigilance);

- avoidance of triggers tied to the abuse;

- persistent emotional distress—sadness, anger, or fear;

- trust issues that make it hard to form or sustain relationships;

- substance use to numb the pain.

These struggles can lead to difficulties with communication, intimacy, and setting healthy boundaries. As you may notice, these are essentially the same descriptions of how trauma affects us.

I HAVE C-PTSD FROM CHILDHOOD SEXUAL TRAUMA, WHICH RESURFACED AS AN ADULT. I'M FEELING A LOT OF SHAME. WHAT DO YOU FEEL SHAME ABOUT?

Sexual abuse is a difficult and sensitive topic that many struggle to discuss or grasp. Why is shame such a common response to sexual trauma? After years of working with sexually abused individuals and teaching on the subject, I've observed that shame is almost always present, originating from two complex physiological realities that are rarely openly addressed:

Dissonance in the Response: Our bodies can react to physical stimulation independently of our emotional state or desires—a response often seen in grooming situations or sexual misconduct that lacks overt aggression. The nervous system processes touch or stimulation mechanically, even when it overlaps with fear or pain. This biological fact can spark deep confusion for the abused, especially children, who may feel physical sensations they don't comprehend—sensations they sometimes even enjoy. Young children might also receive positive attention or what feels like "special treatment" from their abuser, only realizing years later the profound violation that took place. Shame often surfaces when awareness develops, and the brain struggles to reconcile these conflicting and dissonant experiences.

Misattribution of Arousal: During sexual assault, the body may activate physiological reactions to minimize physical harm, including involuntary arousal or even orgasm. These responses can breed devastating shame for those who misinterpret them as "participation" or "enjoyment" during the assault. Consider how the body's automatic protective mechanisms work—protecting itself from physical injuries while the mind dissociates from the shocking, undesired, or aggressive act.

Additionally, if you carried shame from other childhood experiences, your system likely learned to hide and feel undeserving of support. This creates internal scripts that prevent you from engaging in activities others might judge as "bad." When this early shame combines with the complex emotions of being used solely for someone else's pleasure while your feelings were disregarded, it creates painful internal conflict. You may simultaneously feel the need to speak your truth while fearing the consequences of doing so or find yourself torn between fully processing your emotions and shutting them down to protect yourself from further pain.

Every person's experience and healing path is unique. Some may feel profoundly traumatized by inappropriate sexual encounters, while others may process them differently. There is no "right" way to feel about being disrespected or sexually abused. What matters most is having the space to explore your emotions without judgment or pressure to conform to others' expectations of how you "should" respond.

Shame is a natural reaction to such a profound violation—an unauthorized and invasive act—but it does not reflect any truth about your worth or your responsibility. The fault lies entirely with the person who caused harm, not with the one who was harmed.

> **The Shame Reframe Practice.** Let me offer an exercise to meet the shame of sexual abuse with truth and compassion. This is a quiet moment to acknowledge the shame without letting it speak for who you are. Let's start with grounding by sitting or lying down in a safe, comfortable space. Place one hand over your heart or stomach—or wherever you feel the heaviness of shame most often lives. Take three slow, steady breaths and say softly:

"My body did what it needed to do to protect me." "My mind did what it needed to survive."

Let this truth settle. Let it run through your blood. Let this truth become part of your skin.

Now let's name and validate the confusion. In your journal—or just quietly in your mind—complete the sentence: *"I feel ashamed because..."* Now ask, *"Whose behavior caused the harm?" "Did my body's response mean consent or control?" "What if my shame is a sign of my sensitivity, not my guilt?" "How's ignorance connected to consent?"* You don't need perfect answers. Just let the questions interrupt the old script, and repeat: *"My body did what it needed to do to protect me." "My mind did what it needed to survive."*

Now repeat the counter-message to the shame: *"My body responded automatically. That doesn't mean I participated." "What happened to me was an assault, no matter how my body reacted." "This shame belongs to the one who violated, not to me."* You can write one of these on a small card or save it in your phone—whatever brings it closer when shame resurfaces.

THIS SHAME DOESN'T BELONG TO ME!

Finally, make space for safety. Think of someone—real or imagined—who would look at you with understanding. Picture them saying, *"I see your pain. I believe you. You didn't deserve this."* If that feels hard to imagine, let yourself say these words, even if only as a whisper.

This practice is not about erasing shame overnight—it's about giving you the space to change the meaning of your pain. Shame thrives on secrecy and false responsibility. Speaking truth to it—even gently—reclaims your voice, your body, and your worth.

Uncover the Effect of Mind Games and Other Narcissistic Impulses

> *"Narcissistic harm is a theft of clarity—it turns love into confusion and loyalty into self-doubt."*

Narcissistic abuse represents such a distinct and damaging pattern of behavior that it requires its own focused exploration. Narcissistic abuse isn't just emotional harm—it's a quiet storm of manipulation, deception, and cruelty that wounds in ways other forms of abuse often don't. Rooted in a lack of empathy and a drive for control, it distorts reality, erodes trust, and deeply undermines a person's sense of self-worth. This form of abuse not only affects the targeted individual but also ripples outward, impacting children, coworkers, friends, and others, because the power dynamics it establishes are often systemic and far-reaching.

Let me first clarify what I mean by "narcissistic" in this context. Some people display narcissistic traits, others may engage in narcissistic behaviors without having a full personality disorder, and then there are those who meet the criteria for Narcissistic Personality Disorder (NPD). Additionally, some individuals exhibit Machiavellian narcissism—a particularly calculating form characterized by strategic manipulation, cunning exploitation, and the deliberate use of others as tools for personal gain. Individuals with psychopathy or sociopathy (ASPD) may also fall under this category, as they often share many of these same characteristics in their abusive behaviors.

NPD is characterized by an inflated sense of self-importance, a constant need for admiration, a lack of empathy, and a pattern of exploiting others for personal gain. In this section, I'm focusing on abuse carried out by individuals who either meet the clinical criteria for NPD or consistently display these harmful patterns of emotional exploitation, lack of accountability, and persistent disregard for others' boundaries and needs. When we add lack of remorse (characteristic of ASPD), the abuse may feel even worse.

Let's peel back the layers of narcissistic abuse and examine the subtle dynamics, the lasting psychological effects, and how healing can begin.

WHAT DOES NARCISSISTIC ABUSE DO TO YOU?

Narcissistic abuse is a distinctive form of emotional abuse perpetrated by people who demonstrate limited empathy and are primarily motivated by maintaining their inflated self-image and exploiting others for personal benefit. They think, feel, and act as though their harmful behavior is completely justified—usually targeting their partners or those who depend on them. Some narcissistic abusers are particularly calculating—Machiavellian narcissists or sociopaths who strategically plan their manipulation for maximum control. To show how it unfolds and wounds, let's consider Lisa's story.

Lisa got married a few years ago to a previously married man who shows clear NPD symptoms. She hasn't recognized the pattern yet, despite noticing some warning signs. They're likely in what I call the Glamorizing Phase (see my Psychology Today piece: "The Phases of a Narcissistic Relationship")—a deceptively happy time where she still laughs off his manipulative jokes and behaviors. But to others, her happiness is slipping—her reactions aren't as cheerful, and she's starting to act differently, revealing her recent mental struggles.

He's already using all the usual narcissistic abuse tactics: showering her with love mixed with lies that make her doubt herself, treating her like an object, using sex and gifts as transactions, and putting her down often, mentioning her poor upbringing, her flaws, and her lack of resources. In front of others, he belittles her ideas with mean jokes or ignores her requests despite having promised to listen. Lately, she's asked about their finances—he controls everything, even while saying, "All I have is yours." He's also keeping her away from friends, family, and normal activities with excuses like special dinners, his interests, or enticing trips, making her depend on him more and more as time goes by.

She hasn't noticed how he's projecting his own insecurities onto her. At a recent party, a friend disagreed with something he said. Later, when they were alone, he told her, "I'm sorry he doesn't like you. I got upset when he laughed at how you ate." Shocked, Lisa started questioning herself: "Why would he say that if it wasn't true?" That doubt and many others stick with her and debilitate her confidence.

They're still in the early days—no big anger fits or scary threats yet—but signs of trouble are showing up. Recently, she didn't want sex; he offered a foot massage to change her mind. When she said no again, he snapped, "It doesn't matter much—you're not that good in bed anyway." Her reaction? After that, she began having sex with him almost every day, making a strong effort to become a better lover.

What it is: A pattern of emotional manipulation and control by someone who lacks empathy and prioritizes their self-image over your well-being.
What it looks like: Love mixed with lies and blame, subtle put-downs, projection of insecurities, and control, isolation from support systems, conditional affection (transactional), cruel jokes
What starts to happen: Growing self-doubt and confusion, loss of confidence, joy, and identity, increased anxiety, shame, and emotional reactivity, fear of abandonment and overcompensation for love, physical or psychological symptoms (e.g., fatigue, brain fog, dissociation)
What it hides: Power imbalance masked as romance, emotional dependency and trauma bonding, suppressed needs, blurred boundaries, and loss of self-trust
Level of dysfunction: Mild to severe psychological harm, often resulting in C-PTSD symptoms if sustained. Healing is possible but requires reconnection to self and reality, often with support

Narcissistic Abuse

What makes narcissistic abuse particularly devastating is how it systematically dismantles a person's sense of reality and self-worth. Unlike other forms of abuse, narcissistic abuse creates three distinct psychological wounds:

Reality distortion: Lisa is already questioning her own perceptions—*"Did the friend really laugh at how she ate?"* This constant gaslighting makes victims lose trust in their own judgment and memory, creating a dependency on the abuser's version of reality.

Adaptive compliance: Notice how Lisa responded to his cruel bedroom comment by trying harder to please him rather than addressing his cruelty. Narcissistic abuse teaches victims that resistance leads to punishment, so they adapt by becoming hypervigilant about the abuser's needs while abandoning their own.

Trauma bonding: The intermittent reinforcement of love mixed with cruelty creates powerful psychological bonds. Lisa likely feels most connected to her husband during the brief moments he shows affection after being cruel—a cycle that becomes addictive and extremely difficult to break.

If this pattern continues, Lisa will develop the complex trauma symptoms we discussed earlier—such as hypervigilance, emotional numbing, and difficulty trusting others. But she'll also experience something unique to narcissistic abuse: a complete erosion of her sense of self. She may no longer know what she likes, wants, or believes without checking with her husband first.

Depending on how severe her husband's narcissism is and how long the abuse continues, Lisa's recovery may take time. A strong support system could help her recognize the manipulation before it completely takes hold. But if she remains isolated, breaking free becomes exponentially harder. That's why people with NPD work so hard to keep their partners away from others' "bad influence"—meaning those who might see the abuse and encourage them to leave.

One sobering reality is that narcissistic abuse often ends not when the abused wants out, but when the narcissist finds someone new to focus on and discards their current target—in this case, Lisa.

Is psychological projection just another word for gaslighting?

No, they're different mechanisms, though they often overlap in abusive situations.

Projection is a largely unconscious defense mechanism where people attribute their own unwanted feelings, thoughts, or behaviors to others to avoid confronting them. For example, someone who feels envious may accuse others of being jealous of them. While projection can create confusion in relationships, it typically lacks malicious intent. In contrast, **gaslighting involves deliberate manipulation** aimed at making someone question their perception, memory, or sanity. Gaslighters use lies, contradictions, and denials to gain control and maintain power.

For instance, when someone says, *"I've been feeling ignored lately—I'd love for us to spend more time together,"* a gaslighting response might be, *"You're always so dramatic! You're the one ignoring me. Why do you always blame everything on me?"*

They intersect because projection often becomes a tool in gaslighting. A gaslighter projects their own traits onto their victim, then uses those accusations to undermine reality. Picture someone secretly having an affair who begins making baseless infidelity accusations: *"I saw you flirting," "You were practically devouring that guy with your eyes."* Because the accusation carries the gaslighter's guilt, it feels strangely charged. Repeating these projections with feigned certainty pushes the partner to doubt their innocence and defend against something that never happened.

So while projection can be an unconscious coping mechanism, when combined with intent to manipulate, it becomes a powerful gaslighting weapon.

How Do I Know If Gaslighting Has Damaged My Ability to Think Clearly?

It's important to distinguish between true gaslighting and what we might call "pseudo-gaslighting." Some people use the term loosely, thinking simple phrases like *"I never said that"* or *"You're too sensitive"* are gaslighting on their own.

True gaslighting is sophisticated and requires a calculated mindset. The gaslighter deliberately undermines their target's ability to distinguish truth from falsehood, right from wrong, and reality from appearance. They typically know their target's insecurities and fears intimately, systematically exploiting these to create pathological dependency on the gaslighter's version of reality.

For example, imagine someone who knows their partner struggles with memory issues due to past concussions. A Machiavellian gaslighter might move objects around the house, then when their partner asks about it, respond with concerned worry: "Honey, you put that there yesterday. Don't you remember? Maybe we should talk to your doctor about your memory getting worse." They're not just denying reality—they're weaponizing a known vulnerability to make their partner doubt their basic cognitive abilities.

The effect becomes particularly damaging when the person fears the consequences of challenging this narrative. However, facing gaslighting doesn't always make someone a victim. Many hold on to their strength, push back against the manipulation, set clear boundaries, and shield themselves from harm. With awareness of the tactic, being gaslighted could be like getting barked at by a dog—it doesn't mean you're hurt by it.

- Being gaslighted can be like getting barked at by a dog—you may be startled, but it doesn't mean you're wounded
- Some dogs bark to scare you, but if you don't run, they lose their power
- Gaslighting is like a fog—you don't fight it, you step out of it
- You can still trust your compass, even when someone else keeps moving the map
- Not every lie you hear deserves a seat at your table

Resilience in the Face of Manipulation

While online lists of "gaslighting phrases" can help identify concerning patterns, they become problematic when people treat isolated statements as definitive proof of manipulation. True gaslighting requires sustained, calculated effort to distort someone's reality, not just occasional dismissive remarks.

Gaslighting Reality Check. When someone close to you uses dismissive phrases, run a quick mental check:

"Is that phrase repeated whenever I raise a concern?" "Do they dismiss clear evidence—texts, timestamps, witnesses—that contradicts their version of events?" "Do I leave the conversation doubting my own memory or judgment more than before?" "Does the conversation shift from facts to questioning my sanity or perception?" "Afterward, do I feel clearer about what actually happened—or more confused?" "Does their response seem aimed at avoiding accountability or maintaining control?"

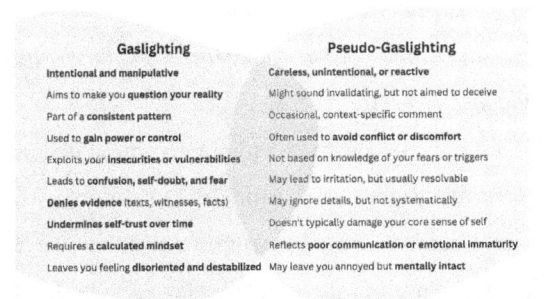

Gaslighting	Pseudo-Gaslighting
Intentional and manipulative	Careless, unintentional, or reactive
Aims to make you **question your reality**	Might sound invalidating, but not aimed to deceive
Part of a **consistent pattern**	Occasional, context-specific comment
Used to **gain power or control**	Often used to **avoid conflict or discomfort**
Exploits your **insecurities or vulnerabilities**	Not based on knowledge of your fears or triggers
Leads to **confusion, self-doubt, and fear**	May lead to irritation, but usually resolvable
Denies evidence (texts, witnesses, facts)	May ignore details, but not systematically
Undermines self-trust over time	Doesn't typically damage your core sense of self
Requires a **calculated mindset**	Reflects poor communication or emotional immaturity
Leaves you feeling **disoriented and destabilized**	May leave you annoyed but **mentally intact**

> If you consistently end up confused and self-doubting while your evidence is brushed aside, you may be experiencing gaslighting, regardless of the specific words used. However, if dismissive phrases occur only occasionally without intent to distort reality or avoid responsibility, it's not gaslighting—just careless communication worth addressing. The table here could help you further.

How do you see through a narcissist who acts loving but is actually toxic?

Have you encountered someone whose negativity is so intense that their mere presence affects others' well-being and the mood of the room? That's probably why some individuals are described as "toxic"—because they have the capacity to poison others' lives, drain us, block our growth, violate our boundaries, and sabotage our efforts to lead a happy and productive life. With narcissists, this toxicity is particularly confusing because it's often masked by periods of genuine-seeming love and charm.

From a psychological perspective, it's more constructive to describe specific problematic dynamics rather than labeling the whole person as toxic. I've encountered this challenge with clients. Initially, they may describe someone as toxic, and I take their word for it. But when I investigate further, I'm often surprised to discover I've made assumptions that don't match their actual behavior.

For example, one of my clients initially described their partner as toxic. I assumed the partner was actively undermining or emotionally damaging in significant ways. Later on, I learned that what the client meant by "toxic" was their partner's neediness disguised as "caring." While neediness is undoubtedly bothersome, understanding the specific patterns—rather than just accepting the "toxic" label—helped me see what interventions would actually help.

Since "toxic" is a subjective construct without an official definition, rather than providing a checklist for diagnosing everyone else, it's more useful to tune in to your own experience. If someone's presence consistently leaves you feeling suffocated, wounded, or drained—even when they're being "loving"—limit your exposure and recognize their negative influence on your mental state. **A toxic person's impact is proportional to how much of their negativity you absorb.**

When you're dealing with a narcissist who can be both kind and harmful, engage with their positive side when it's present—and give yourself permission to step away when their destructive patterns surface. If you're unsure whether you're facing toxic behavior masked as kindness, there are some consistent signs to watch for as a pattern: hypocrisy or double standards, subtle manipulation or shifting narratives, abrupt mood or value inconsistencies, lack of empathy or dismissiveness, chronic negativity or drama creation, refusal to take accountability, or opportunism—kind only when it serves them.

CONFRONT THE PRICE OF CLOSENESS AND BONDING

"The most powerful relationships are those that lift us up, not those that hold us captive."

I once heard someone describe attachment as *"holding a special place in their mind for you."* That simple idea helps us feel like we matter—and allows our nervous system to feel safe. As mammals, attachment is an essential need.

Unfortunately, when we need something and we don't get it, we suffer. Some wounds occur before we even have words to describe them—broken or misattunements that shape our earliest experiences of safety and connection. Much has been written about attachment trauma, particularly when disruptions in the child-caregiver bond happen in the first year of life. For an infant whose survival depends entirely on the caregiver, misattunement can feel terrifying, activating survival circuits very early and shaping how they trust and connect for years to come, in addition to the effects it can have on their nervous system and brain development.

Unlike psychological injuries that happen later in life, attachment wounds alter development at its core, especially when the caregiver who should provide safety becomes a source of fear, rejection, or emotional unpredictability. These early patterns can feel as natural as breathing, even though they carry deep pain. In this section, we'll explore how these early injuries occur, how they differ from other forms of hurt, and why understanding them is so important in the healing journey.

We'll also examine another distressing form of attachment: the trauma bond. This doesn't refer to shared trauma but to a destructive dynamic where one person exerts control while the other becomes emotionally trapped, despite being hurt.

Is Attachment Trauma a Big Deal?

At its core, attachment trauma is an injury to the bond between a baby and the primary caregiver, with the aftermath primarily affecting the maturation of the developing brain and stress-regulation systems. Human babies are born exceptionally dependent—without someone to feed them, keep them warm, and soothe their immature nervous systems, they are biologically at risk. When that intimate connection fails or is disrupted, the baby's system finds it very difficult to develop normal regulation strategies. So, yes, it's a really big deal.

During the first months of life, a child's nervous system is still under construction. Calming an upset baby isn't just about stopping the crying; it is a brain-to-brain attunement that teaches the infant how to shift from distress to calm. If no one reliably steps in, the infant's body remains in a high-stress state—almost constant mild panic that further hinders the development of regulatory mechanisms.

Occasionally the break is literal: the mother is absent after birth, and no substitute caregiver provides consistent comfort—like when the baby spends extended time in an incubator, the mother dies, or leaves the baby to be raised by someone else. In other cases, the caregiver is physically present but too depressed, overwhelmed, or emotionally shut down to bond. But not every separation results in trauma. Some babies prove more resilient or quickly bond with another reliable caregiver.

Most attachment wounds go unaddressed until the person begins struggling seriously in relationships, often manifesting as ongoing difficulties with emotional regulation, identity, and self-worth. This phenomenon is sometimes seen in personality disorders (mainly BPD), where the person never truly learned to feel secure or emotionally stable. They may also experience a sense of "emptiness"—an existential, ongoing dissatisfaction that shapes how they relate both to others and to themselves. This symptom often stems from early caregiving relationships where the child didn't feel mirrored or responded to and actually felt rejected instead. As a result, they may experience an underlying sense of *"I'm not safe"* and *"I don't even know who I am or why I'm here,"* which distorts their ability to form connections and manage stress throughout life.

Attachment wounds can feel like part of every fiber of your being. The absence of bonding is a significant injury. Yet, there is still hope since the nervous system never stops learning and moving toward improvement. It needs repeated experiences of safety, attunement, and choice to begin rewiring. Those experiences may come in therapy, where a steady, responsive relationship recreates what the early bond lacked, but they also arise in everyday life. Each time you share a genuine feeling with a trustworthy friend and are met with kindness, your brain absorbs a corrective experience. Additionally, every time you meet yourself with compassion—reminding yourself that your worth is not measured by one person's failure—you strengthen your own calm center.

Are Attachment Trauma and Developmental Trauma the Same Thing?

We just learned that attachment trauma is tied to the very first bonding experience between a baby and their primary caregiver—typically within the first three years of life, when babies are almost entirely helpless. Developmental trauma, on the other hand, involves a breach of safety and security that doesn't necessarily start in those first few years or stem from attachment failures.

Consider how many children might enjoy reasonably attuned care at first but, at a certain age—four, eight, or twelve—find the environment turning abusive or neglectful (divorce, new parent, change of location/school, etc.). When the child's system can't handle that later stress, developmental delays and trauma symptoms can follow. While attachment trauma often includes developmental impacts, not every case of developmental trauma involves an earlier rupture in the attachment bond. Developmental trauma is no less serious than attachment trauma, but the timing and context differ, so each calls for its own understanding and healing approach.

Is Disorganized Attachment Why My Relationships Are So Chaotic?

If your relationships feel chaotic—swinging between desperate clinging and sudden withdrawal—then, yes, disorganized attachment may be the underlying cause. From birth, infants learn how the social world works—and how to calm their own nervous systems—through daily interactions with their primary caregivers. When a caregiver consistently meets a baby's needs through warm, attuned responses, the child forms a secure attachment and carries that confidence into future relationships. If the caregiver is inconsistent or emotionally distant, the child still bonds, but insecurely. This condition creates two main patterns: a) **anxious/ambivalent** infants protest loudly, cling, and stay hyper-alert, as if saying, *"Don't leave—I can't manage without you,"* or b) **avoidant** infants minimize their displays of need, acting aloof or shutting down affection to avoid the pain of rejection, as if saying, *"I need you, but I hate that I do."*

Disorganized attachment is different. Here, the caregiver is not just inconsistent but also frightening, frightened, or unpredictable—sometimes soothing, sometimes threatening. The child's brain can't settle on either the clinging strategy or the distancing strategy, so it switches chaotically between both. When attempting to connect with the caregiver, a disorganized infant may become paralyzed, approach and then abruptly back away, display a dazed expression, or exhibit other conflicting behaviors. This chaotic internal disorganization doesn't disappear in adulthood—it becomes the template for how you navigate intimate relationships. The same push-pull dynamic that developed as a survival mechanism in childhood now creates the relationship chaos you may be experiencing today.

Factors linked to disorganized attachment include chronic caregiver unpredictability, unresolved trauma or grief in the parent, severe depression, substance abuse, or outright maltreatment. Later in life, this attachment pattern is associated with difficulties in emotional regulation, identity formation, and threat perception. It has been linked to an increased risk of developing certain personality disorders, such as borderline personality disorder. However, understanding these patterns marks the beginning of healing—our early attachment styles are not permanent sentences but rather starting points for interaction and connection.

WHAT ARE THE KEY DIFFERENCES BETWEEN TRAUMA BONDING AND ACTUALLY CARING FOR SOMEONE? IS HEALTHY BONDING POSSIBLE?

When we hear "healthy bonding," we might immediately think about attachment between an infant and a caregiver, but "trauma bonding" has little to do with that. It refers to cycles of abuse interspersed with positive reinforcement that create a powerful emotional tie where the victim feels dependent on or loyal to the abuser. This dynamic occurs most commonly in romantic partnerships or cults but can extend to other relationships, including parent-child dynamics.

Healthy bonding develops between people who come together through mutual trust, affection, or shared interests. They might start as coworkers or friends connecting over common ground. Over time, they learn to respect boundaries, navigate conflicts without fear, and offer support while maintaining individuality. This kind of bond feels safe and encouraging—both people retain their sense of self and freedom to make decisions.

Trauma bonding arises in relationships marked by persistent power imbalance and cycles of hurt, often because one side has power and the other side feels weak and lacks resources. The "trauma" comes from repeated injury, and the "bond" from intermittent moments of care that keep the victim hooked. One person wields control while the other clings to the relationship, hoping for improvement. Brief reconciliations or validation maintain the victim's investment, but the overall pattern revolves around fear, shame, confusion, and the chemicals involved. Hormonal surges, such as oxytocin during affection and dopamine during intermittent rewards, intertwine feelings of threat and comfort, making it feel physiologically and psychologically impossible to leave. Rather than fostering growth, this dynamic gradually erodes self-worth.

For example, consider a woman whose partner alternates between explosive anger and lavish affection. After verbal abuse, he might buy flowers and promise change, only to criticize harshly days later. Despite the harm, she makes excuses, believing he needs her understanding, and feels oddly closer after each reconciliation. She thinks, "No one else understands him like I do," while friends watch her self-esteem deteriorate.

These dynamics often overlap with **"codependency,"** originally describing someone who directs all energy toward helping an addicted partner. In trauma bonding, the "addiction" becomes the ongoing abuse or the struggles of the other, but the pattern remains the same: one person desperately wants to "save" the other, tying their identity to that role while prioritizing the abuser's needs over their own.

What patterns show up in trauma-bonded relationships?

As we discussed earlier, trauma bonding is common among adults, but it may begin in childhood if children rationalize abusive caregiving to preserve essential relationships. That's when the same patterns are carried forward into adult relationships, where they manifest differently across various contexts.

Adult trauma bonds manifest differently across relationship types. In the case of a narcissistic boss, there may be just enough moments of recognition or flattery to outweigh the belittling and harsh criticism. These brief windows of calm reignite hope— *"They see who I really am,"* the person thinks—while keeping them trapped in exploitation. The employee might work unpaid overtime, accept verbal abuse, or compromise their values, all for occasional praise that feels disproportionately meaningful.

In romantic relationships, trauma bonding often involves cycles where intense conflict is followed by passionate reconciliation. The victim learns to crave the relief and intimacy that follows the storm, mistaking this emotional whiplash for deep connection. They might think, *"No one else could understand our love,"* while friends watch the relationship destroy their self-worth.

Cult dynamics represent perhaps the most extreme form of trauma bonding. Followers endure psychological manipulation, financial exploitation, and social isolation, yet remain devoted because the group provides identity and belonging. The leader alternates between harsh punishment and special attention, creating desperate loyalty. Members dismiss obvious exploitation because acknowledging it would mean losing their entire support system and worldview.

The brain plays along by sometimes dissociating or downplaying actual danger. It might compartmentalize memories of the worst incidents while amplifying the significance of positive moments. This survival strategy helps people cope with an impossible situation—if you're facing relentless harm from someone you depend on, a voice in your head might say, *"They're just stressed,"* rather than risk acknowledging your world is unsafe.

Am I Trauma-Bonded? A Quiz. This quiz is not a diagnostic tool but a starting point for reflection.

Answer **Yes, Somehow,** or **No** to each question as honestly as possible.

__ Do you feel emotionally attached to someone who repeatedly hurts, disrespects, or dismisses you?

__ Do you often find yourself defending this person's behavior to others—even when you know it's harmful?

__ Do you feel anxious or guilty when you think about setting boundaries or pulling away?

__ Do you focus more on their potential or their moments of kindness than on their consistent behavior?

__ Do you minimize or rationalize things they've done that would concern you if it happened to someone else?

__ Do you believe that if you just try harder, love better, or stay longer, things will finally improve?

__ Do you feel responsible for their emotional well-being—even when it drains or hurts you?

__ Do you struggle to imagine life without them, even if the relationship is consistently painful?

___ Do you think leaving would mean you've failed or given up on them?

___ Do you doubt your memory, feelings, or judgment after talking to them?

___ Do you feel like you've lost touch with your own needs, values, or identity in the relationship?

___ Do you often ignore your own emotional pain to prioritize the relationship?

___ Do you silence yourself to keep the peace?

___ Do you feel more like a caretaker, fixer, or emotional container than an equal partner?

___ Do you believe love means enduring pain or sacrificing yourself for the other person or your beliefs?

If you answered **Yes** or **Somehow** to many of these questions, you may be caught in a trauma bond. These dynamics often create **emotional confusion,** keep you stuck in cycles of hope and hurt, and leave you unsure of where you end and the other person begins. Recognizing the pattern is the first act of clarity—and a powerful beginning toward healing.

WHY AM I SO ATTACHED TO SOMEONE WHO TREATS ME BADLY?

Let me be clear: trauma bonding is not something anyone chooses. It emerges as a consequence of being in relationships defined by intense emotional swings, where a person clings to the hope of safety and love despite ongoing pain. The core reason this bond forms is because humans are wired to seek attachment—even when the attachment figure is frightening or hurtful. We need to believe in a connection that might protect us, or at least offer moments of solace, in order to survive both the immediate chaos and the terror of complete abandonment.

Many times, the person who develops a trauma bond already carries emotional **vulnerabilities**—but, ironically, also distinct strengths. They may **tend to dissociate, fantasize, self-sacrifice, and people-please,** believing deep down that they don't deserve much. At the same time, they may possess strong religious beliefs, deep faith, a high capacity to tolerate discomfort, and a profound ability to love and forgive. This is often a characteristic of someone who was emotionally neglected and learned early to minimize their needs in hopes of having at least some of them partially met. In these cases, this type of bond becomes a familiar pattern that mirrors their earliest experiences of love and connection.

Trauma Bond and Its Dissolution

Often, leaving the relationship doesn't feel like a real option. They might not have confidence in their ability to manage independently, or they might be influenced by cultural messages that discourage family dissolution, portray divorce as a sign of weakness, or suggest that love is the ultimate power. Instead of facing the painful truth that they're stuck in a harmful situation, they may cling to the idea that it's love, loyalty, or personal values keeping the relationship alive. **This becomes their way of preserving hope, dignity, and meaning while staying in an impossible situation.**

Understanding that this attachment isn't evidence of "real love" but a conditioned survival response can be the first step toward breaking free. The bond feels so real because it is—but it's built on fear and intermittent relief, not genuine care and safety.

> **Turning Toward Yourself Exercise: A First Step in Dissolving a Trauma Bond.** If you suspect you're caught in a trauma bond—or simply feel confused about why it's so difficult to let go—this exercise is a first step toward clarity. It's not about forcing a decision but about turning your attention inward and beginning to reconnect with your own needs, voice, and worth. All you need is a quiet space, paper or a journal, and a pen.
>
> Start by writing down what keeps you emotionally tied to the person who hurts you.
>
> Complete this sentence: *"Even though I've been hurt, I still stay (or keep going back) because..."*

Let yourself be honest. List all the reasons that come to mind—even if they sound illogical or conflicting. Stay grounded by feeling your feet on the floor and your body in contact with your chair. You don't want to become too emotional because you may fall back into your familiar pattern of justifying the person you're trauma-bonded to.

Now, for each reason you listed, write a follow-up sentence beginning with, *"What I need, but haven't been giving myself, is…"*

For example: *"I stay because I feel responsible for their emotions."* → *"What I need, but haven't been giving myself, is permission to not carry someone else's pain."*

"I stay because I'm afraid no one else will love me." → *"What I need, but haven't been giving myself, is the belief that I am already worthy of love—starting with my own."*

Repeat this sentence as many times as possible. Repetition is necessary to rewire your brain.

Now, write one sentence that begins with, *"Today, I choose to protect my own heart by…"*

Examples: *"…not explaining myself again when they twist my words." "….saying no, even if I feel guilty." "…reminding myself I matter, even if they don't see it."* Let this be a small but meaningful act of reclaiming your voice.

Choose a reminder that reconnects you with your truth when doubt creeps in. This could be a quote or phrase (e.g., *"I don't have to earn love by suffering"*), a song that reminds you of your strength, or a small object you carry (stone, ring, photo) that represents your self-worth. Keep it nearby. When the urge to please, explain, or return rises, use this as your anchor.

To finish, close your eyes and say silently or aloud, *"I am not responsible for fixing others. I am responsible for protecting and honoring myself and my needs. I'm a valuable person, and I'll respect myself from now on."* Take three slow, deep breaths. Feel into the part of you that wants peace—not just in this moment, but long-term.

> This exercise can help you shift focus from the abuser to yourself—interrupting the trauma-bonded loop by strengthening internal awareness, self-compassion, and agency.

Choose Yourself and Participate in Healthier Love

"Repair doesn't mean rushing into closeness. It means learning to feel safe enough to stay."

It is widely believed that if an emotional injury came through a relationship, repair has to come through relationships too. That doesn't mean handing your heart to the first kind stranger or forcing yourself to trust before you're ready. It means retraining your nervous system—step by step—to notice when a moment is actually safe and to let that safety register. Most therapeutic approaches rely on the therapeutic alliance to repair relational wounds. Studies indicate that a strong therapeutic relationship is one of the strongest predictors of positive outcomes in therapy, regardless of the specific modality used. Beyond therapy, supportive social connections help your system learn to relax, contribute to resource development, and build resilience. And this support doesn't require deep intimacy, only genuine connection.

This premise isn't just therapeutic theory—there's a biological basis for why relationships can heal. Human brains are wired for connection. That's why early wounds from caregivers or later disappointments never stop shaping emotional and social patterns. Corrective relationships—whether therapeutic, platonic, or romantic—can rewire these patterns by offering safety, validation, and trust, helping to heal shame, insecure attachment, trauma bonds, and many of our unresolved emotional wounds. **Relationships don't automatically resolve our pain, but healing begins when we're willing to risk connection and learn to trust ourselves again.**

In this section, we'll look at the practical side of "rewiring" after abuse, attachment wounds, or other bond failures: how the brain learns to settle when a friend listens, how it updates its old prediction that closeness equals danger, and how you can build new circuitry for connection without ignoring healthy caution.

How do I stop assuming everyone will hurt me like my abuser did?

Traumatic experiences often impair our ability to trust, perpetuating emotional wounds and making us unable to form the healing connections we need. This is especially true for those who never developed basic trust in childhood due to unreliable caregivers.

We may see trust as something that depends entirely on others' actions, but trust is also a decision and a tool that helps us rebuild safety. Trust develops through two connected processes: evaluating reliability based on evidence and deciding to lower our defenses despite inherent risk. Trust combines both emotional and cognitive processes as our brain evaluates who deserves our confidence, making it simultaneously a mental state, an emotional feeling, a lived experience, and an evolving process. **In short, you can decide to trust at any moment.**

Research suggests we're wired for trust as a survival mechanism—we must trust to form bonds with those who care for us, which explains why infants can identify their primary caregiver before recognizing almost anything else. When we establish trust and connection, our bodies release oxytocin—the "bonding hormone"—which naturally calms our stress responses. Fear and trust operate like opposing forces: the more we fear, the less we trust, and the less oxytocin our bodies produce.

However, traumatic experiences often shatter this natural process. People who have been abused typically struggle to trust because their survival-oriented brains keep them on constant alert, scanning for potential threats or anticipating repeated injuries. Such behavior creates an unconscious belief that *"trusting is dangerous,"* which prevents oxytocin production and keeps the person on guard.

The path forward involves practicing trust in small, manageable ways. Like exercising a muscle, choosing to trust—even briefly—can stimulate oxytocin production and help us reconnect. Trust after abuse isn't a single leap; it's a series of gentle, repeated invitations for your body to discover that connection can coexist with safety. With enough lived—or carefully imagined—moments of reliability, your brain begins to conclude, *"Maybe I can let my guard down here."* Eventually that conclusion becomes a habit, and the habit becomes your new baseline for relationships.

> **The Trust Restoration Protocol.** The first step in learning to trust after abuse is to recognize why your system stopped trusting to begin with. Invite into your mind a memory of a recent event where you stopped trusting someone.
>
> As you think about it, tell yourself that when someone you counted on became the source of harm, your brain stayed on guard and the quiet chemistry of attachment dropped out. You didn't choose mistrust; your body chose it to keep you protected. Recognize and honor that protection. You could visualize it as an electromagnetic shield.
>
> Rather than forcing yourself to trust, let's start by lowering the alarm. *"Right now, nothing is attacking me or betraying me."* Fill yourself with that piece of confidence and allow that moment of calm to accumulate. The protective shield will soften just enough for a flicker of safety to slip through.
>
> If you can, tell yourself, *"Removing the mistrust, even if just a little, feels good."*
>
> Next, pick the lowest-risk relationship you can find: a friend, a gentle relative, or perhaps even a pet. Imagine you are spending short, predictable intervals in that presence while paying attention to your body. Can your shoulders drop for a breath? Can your jaw unclench for two? That micro-ease may be oxytocin peeking back in. Repeat these images or bring new ones; the nervous system rewires through many tiny proofs, not one grand gesture.
>
> Now, pick someone whose kindness has never wavered, even if that person lives only in memory or fiction. See yourself sitting beside them, hear their steady voice, and feel a sense of warmth in your chest. Maybe you approach or even allow them

> to hold your hand. Thirty seconds of this visualization can bump oxytocin just enough to remind your brain what safety feels like.
>
> Practice often; test slightly larger steps. Maybe you share one small truth about your day and watch as nobody weaponizes it.
>
> Each success updates the previous negative inner script and replaces it with *"Trust means I am recovering my power."*
>
> There will always be moments of doubt; an old trigger will flare, and you'll pull back. That's normal. Return to the protocol, look for regulation and balance, shorten the exposure, and try again.

Did the person you used to be ever come back after you recovered from narcissistic abuse?

Every relationship—especially a painful one—shapes how you approach future connections. Recovery from narcissistic abuse isn't about reverting to who you were before; it's about becoming someone who can no longer be abused—someone wiser, stronger, and more self-aware.

We're not the same people we were yesterday—and, ideally, not the same people we'll be tomorrow. Growth and change are natural as we adapt to new challenges and learn from our experiences. After abuse, the need to evolve becomes especially clear.

At first, you may long for the uncomplicated trust or openness you once had. But that earlier self often lacked the wisdom and protective instincts you've since gained. Narcissistic abuse inevitably alters how you view yourself, others, and your capacity for trust and willingness to stay open. At your core, you're still the same person—but you react differently when you sense potential manipulation or disregard. When your sense of safety and confidence returns, you often emerge stronger: better at setting boundaries, spotting hidden motives, and protecting yourself from coercion. This isn't just a defensive posture—it reflects a deeper understanding of your own emotions and the complexities of human behavior.

You can reclaim the best parts of who you were before the abuse—kindness, generosity, enthusiasm—but with new awareness. If someone exploited your kindness, you might believe you have to abandon it altogether. But kindness can evolve into discerning compassion: you still care, but now you evaluate people and situations more carefully. You may become more selective about who receives your trust, but that's wisdom, not damage.

However, we need to be realistic: someone who has experienced prolonged abuse will likely be more easily triggered. The sensation of being controlled or manipulated can feel overwhelmingly real, even when the current situation isn't abusive. That's why trauma work is essential. Without processing these experiences, there's a risk of staying hypervigilant or developing victim narratives, always anticipating the next threat.

> **Core Self-Reconnection Exercise.** We remain ourselves at the core, yet we always have the option to grow. Healing means integrating the lesson, not erasing the experience. With that in mind, here's a brief exercise to anchor the shift.
>
> Close your eyes and recall a quality you valued in yourself before the abusive relationship—perhaps trust, humor, or optimism.
>
> Notice how that quality feels now. Has it hardened, faded, or simply become more guarded? Ask yourself, *"How do I want this trait to look going forward?"*
>
> Picture it balanced by the discernment you've gained. Let the quality come alive in your body, then imagine using it in a specific situation.
>
> Breathe in that image for ten seconds, as if you're carrying it into all future relationships.
>
> Repeat this whenever you fear you've "lost" your old self; in truth, you're shaping a more conscious, empowered version—less susceptible to manipulation and more aligned with who you choose to become.

If trauma rewires your brain, what can be repaired, resolved, reprogrammed, or improved?

The encouraging truth about trauma's impact on the brain and body is that many of its effects can be meaningfully addressed through targeted healing approaches. While trauma does create lasting changes in how we process experiences and emotions, neuroscience is clear that our brains maintain the capacity to form new neural pathways and respond differently to old triggers. This neuroplasticity means that while the repair process rarely happens all at once, significant improvement is possible across multiple domains, even if it takes time. All the exercises I include in this book are designed to be used repeatedly for this purpose.

There are many areas we need to work on: emotions, dysregulation, memory, cognition & perception, sense of self, dissociation, and others. I'll guide you through the most important ones next.

Let's start with the memories that have made you feel upset. Traumatic memories are not the villain, as many people believe—their emotional charge is. While these memories might stay with you, their emotional charge—the pain they carry—can be neutralized or diminished to cause less distress and weaken the strong connection to the past. Several modern trauma therapies can help your brain disentangle these memories and process their negative emotions. Many of the exercises in this book can do that too.

> **"A Memory Among Many" Exercise.** When a familiar or disturbing flashback surfaces, practice this:
>
> Pause, sit, and plant your feet on the floor. Then picture the scene on your phone's screen while you breathe slowly out for twice as long as you breathe in.
>
> For example, if you tense up whenever you recall the night your abuser came back home in a rage, let the image become an icon among all the other pictures in your phone. Make it as small as you want. Consider making it in black and white.
>
> At the same time, focus on feeling the chair beneath you, maybe trace the rim of your sock, and keep breathing long breaths until your shoulders soften.
>
> If you can, choose the picture and send it to the Trash. Look how it's sent there and disappears from your Library. Connect with your body and notice the shift.
>
> Each time you do this, the brain files an update: *"Yes, that happened, but right now I'm safe." "I know how to keep myself safe now." "I don't need that reminder anymore,"* and the emotional charge gradually drains away.

Besides memories, we know that trauma affects our system. The **nervous system disruption** that shows up as hypervigilance, constant anxiety, depression, or mood swings can be reprogrammed and brought back to equilibrium. Working on your regulation is like resetting blown breakers that overheated because of strenuous use of electrical power. With the right approaches, you can expand your capacity to handle stress without going into extreme responses or crisis mode.

> **Handling Stress Better Practice.** There are many exercises to help your system regulate. This is just an easy and quick one.
>
> Each time you feel yourself edging into crisis mode, pause and give your body a downshift signal: plant both feet, inhale for a count of 4, exhale for 8, and press your fingertips together until you feel the subtle pulse in each one.
>
> Say you find yourself scanning every doorway in a busy café; do this brief breath-and-press drill until your shoulders drop and your gaze softens.
>
> Repeat whenever the surge appears. Over weeks, these small resets expand your capacity to handle stress without tipping into alarm.

Dissociation—either disengagement or numbness—can and should be addressed and, if necessary, corrected. Knowing that it once served as protection, meaning that several switches got unplugged and certain functions slowed, can motivate you to learn new ways of staying present and engaged, bringing your brain up to speed. Thanks to evolving therapeutic approaches—ranging from immersive virtual reality environments that safely replicate triggers to neurostimulation techniques—the path to reconnecting with yourself is becoming much more effective. Even apps, devices, and brain exercises can assist you with that.

> **Manage Dissociative Tendencies Practice.** Pick one neutral object in front of you—a pen, a light switch—and silently describe it in five sensory details (color, temperature, texture, shape, and weight).
>
> If you feel yourself fading during a tense meeting, slide a finger along the edge of your notebook and name its coolness, its smooth spine, the faint scent of paper, the off-white shade, and the slight bend at the corner.
>
> That simple act of sensory naming pulls scattered awareness into the here-and-now and helps reprogram the tendency to disconnect when uncomfortable or scared.

> Practice for thirty seconds whenever you notice fog settling in; each repetition teaches the brain that staying present is safe, steadily shortening the distance between you and your surroundings.

One tricky part about rewiring our brain is how trauma shapes **personality and perception.** Changing how you see yourself and the world takes time, especially if trauma occurred early in life. But I've witnessed countless "aha moments" where people suddenly see their situations differently, opening doors to new ways of seeing, or when people stop identifying themselves with the limitations imposed by past interactions. Growing a strong sense of self repairs many of the psychological sequelae that trauma may have left.

> **Self-Separation Practice.** A simple way to loosen that tint is to step outside your story for a moment each day.
>
> Select one limiting thought, such as *"I consistently ruin relationships," "People are untrustworthy,"* or *"I'm too damaged to succeed."*
>
> Write it down, then rewrite it in the third person, as if observing someone else: *"He believes he always ruins relationships."*
>
> Now add an opposing observation: *"Yet three friends asked his advice this week, and he listened with patience."*
>
> Read the two sentences aloud. Observing the belief from a different perspective and supporting it with evidence often leads to a realization that the belief may not be entirely accurate.
>
> Now rewrite in first person and allow yourself to connect with the changes it promotes in your system.
>
> Do the same exercise with a different belief each day. Over time, these brief reality checks carve out space for a sturdier sense of self, and the old trauma-shaped identity begins to fade.

Can all the alterations of traumatization completely disappear? Perhaps not every single change will vanish completely, but the injury can be resolved—much like a house repaired or even rebuilt after a storm. While the structure may still carry some signs of past damage, it can become just as sturdy and secure as before. When we work through your fears, your system can reverse many of the changes, leaving behind markers of what you've overcome. Over time, the power of most symptoms will fade, becoming part of your story rather than the force that drives your life.

Can someone be exposed to terrible things over and over and not be affected?

As I've explained throughout, much depends on how the individual interprets and responds to the experience. The event itself matters—but so do meaning-making, internal resources, context, and the presence or absence of support. For instance, we might all agree that certain situations—like handling venomous snakes—are potentially life-threatening. Yet there are people who keep snakes as pets or work with them daily, feeling completely at ease because they've gradually learned to manage their fear (and the snake). Trauma unfolds not just from what happened but from the person's perception of danger and their sense of lack of control.

People maintain resilience when facing threats through several key factors. Professional conditioning plays a significant role—first responders, war journalists, and doctors develop mental frameworks that make danger seem "just part of the job." Through repeated exposure and specialized training, they become partially desensitized, viewing threatening situations as manageable challenges. Some individuals also seem naturally fear-resistant, whether through temperament or learned behavior—their brains simply don't activate the typical "danger" signals that lead to traumatic responses.

Cultural and spiritual frameworks also shape threat perception. Many people draw strength from beliefs in fate, divine purpose, or cosmic meaning, transforming threatening experiences into something purposeful. Think of those raised hearing that *"suffering builds character"* or that *"today's hardship leads to tomorrow's reward."* Growing up with teachings that struggles are tests of strength or pathways to blessing creates an entirely different relationship with fear and pain.

That sense of meaning isn't just comforting; it actually changes how the brain processes stress. Many trauma-recovery programs encourage spiritual practices—prayer, meditation, and communal worship—because faith can be physiologically healing. The secret is not in what you believe but in believing. These practices help regulate emotions and create a sense of safety, offering both a cognitive reframe *("this ordeal has purpose")*, a community buffer *("I'm not alone")*, and a biological reset that calms the alarm system.

These varied mindsets—professional conditioning, natural temperament, and cultural or spiritual frameworks—become resources that help keep stress responses in check, often preventing traumatic symptoms even in objectively difficult circumstances. So, yes, there are many ways that people go through horrible experiences without becoming traumatized.

WHAT MAKES SOMEONE SECURELY ATTACHED DIFFERENT FROM EVERYONE ELSE?

I remember traveling with a friend who wanted to visit someone she hadn't seen since that person had a child over two years earlier. My friend brought three different gifts for the child and one for the mother—all beautifully wrapped in colorful paper. The mother opened her gift right away, showed it to her child, hugged my friend, and encouraged her child to open theirs. But during our entire visit, the child stayed right next to the mother, occasionally glancing at the gifts but never approaching them. As you might imagine, that's the behavior of a child who doesn't feel safe enough to separate—even briefly—from their primary attachment figure. These children often lack curiosity, motivation, and sometimes even physical energy.

Someone who lacks the trust and confidence that they will be protected tends to cling to those who might offer safety as a way to ensure they won't be abandoned. Others go the opposite direction—rejecting help altogether because they've learned that the only way to survive is through self-reliance: *"The only person I can count on is myself."*

In both cases—hallmarks of insecure attachment—the capacity to explore the world becomes limited. The clingy child (anxious attachment) avoids venturing out because doing so might risk losing proximity to the person they depend on. The avoidant child, on the other hand, stays close to home emotionally by detaching from others and over-relying on internal problem-solving, often limiting their options because fewer choices feel safer and more manageable.

Only the securely attached child feels free to explore, because they carry an internalized belief: *"If I need the other person, they'll be there for me."* That opens the door to try new things, take risks, make mistakes, and learn—because they "know" they'll be supported. I use quotation marks around "know" because attachment isn't based on signed contracts; it's a "felt sense" of confidence built through experience—one that isn't always objectively accurate. Some people are naturally more trusting and may believe they can count on others even when evidence suggests otherwise. This underscores that what matters most is the capacity for trust—and, as I've said before, trust can be a choice. Even if someone doesn't grow up with a secure attachment, they can later decide to trust and begin to experience the benefits of secure relationships.

I know couples where one partner has a securely attached style, even though their spouse is not particularly dependable. That secure partner isn't naïve; they simply operate from a default belief, *"People will probably come through."* If evidence builds that their partner can't truly be counted on, they feel disappointed—sometimes deeply—but they don't live in constant anxiety, waiting for the other shoe to drop. They enjoy real peace and emotional freedom—at least until reality proves otherwise. That may be a very smart choice, don't you think?

Secure attachment also fuels resilience. If a securely attached person is betrayed, the pain still cuts deep—but they tend to recover far more quickly than someone who has always expected abandonment. Their inner template says, *"Support exists elsewhere, and I'm worthy of it,"* so they rebound with acceptance and forward movement, rather than getting trapped in rumination or self-doubt.

So how do you build secure attachment if you didn't have it as a child? A powerful starting point is learning how to do **repair work** in your relationships—especially when there's been a rupture. Here is an exercise.

> **A Relational Repair Practice: Repairing the Rupture.** Try this practice to rebuild trust and connection after emotional tension, miscommunication, or disconnection. This is not something you do once. It's a constant practice that

could become habitual in your relationships. You do need, however, a willing partner open to mutual repair.

Any time you have an argument or an uncomfortable and tense interaction with someone, try to follow these steps. Before approaching the other person, take a few minutes to work on your nervous system. Breathe deeply, stretch, or walk. If you're activated or defensive, repair won't land well. You're not aiming to be perfectly calm but grounded enough to listen and express with care. Your social engagement mechanism should be on, which means that your system is not activated to fight or flee. Once you feel more balanced, ask yourself, *"Am I ready to listen without interrupting or defending?" "Can I stay with this process even if it feels uncomfortable?"*

When you feel ready, gently name the disconnection. This might sound like, *"I've been thinking about what happened between us." "I feel there's been a distance, and I'd like to understand it better." "Something felt off, and I care enough about us to look at it."*

Focus on **curiosity, not blame.** Accusations ignite defenses that prevent repair from succeeding.

Begin your conversation by taking ownership of your own contributions to the disconnection—even small ones. Use *"I" language: "I noticed I got defensive." "I think I shut down when I felt criticized." "I didn't know how to express how much that moment hurt me, and I withdrew." "I know I was aggressive and didn't consider your feelings."* These statements set the tone for openness rather than defensiveness.

Invite the other person's perspective with receptiveness: *"How did you experience that moment?" "Was there something I missed or didn't see?" "Did anything I said or did land differently than I intended?"* Be willing to really hear their experience—even if it's difficult.

Repair isn't only about what went wrong—it's about what matters. Bring in the connection you want to rebuild. *"I love how easy things usually feel between us." "I care about you, and I don't want this tension to keep growing." "You're important to me, and I'd like to repair this."* This gesture reaffirms safety and goodwill.

Together, name one small action each of you can take to help the relationship feel safer or more connected again. Keep it simple and doable. Examples include: *"Let's agree to pause next time we feel overwhelmed and check in after." "I will tell you more clearly when something's bothering me." "Can we make space for a no-devices conversation once a week?"* Small steps matter more than grand gestures.

Repair isn't one conversation. It's a process of showing up differently over time. Leave the door open for follow-up. You might say, *"Let's check in again in a couple of days to see how this feels."*

Many people, especially those with insecure or avoidant attachment styles, fear that once a rupture happens, the relationship is permanently broken. This practice helps replace that fear with a new reality: safe bonds can bend, stretch, and even crack—but they can also be repaired.

How can I tell if I'm addicted to this person or actually love them?

What may be unfair about assigning the label "trauma-bonded" to some people is that it can lead them to question the sincerity of their own feelings—almost as if their love were a lie or a naïve mistake. In my experience, there's a striking pattern: people who find themselves trauma-bonded often have exceptionally generous hearts. They feel compassion easily, value self-sacrifice, and look for the good in others. This warmth is not a flaw; it simply signifies their tendency to view the world through a hopeful, rose-tinted perspective.

Ironically, those very qualities can attract partners who crave constant emotional support—narcissists, individuals with borderline traits, or others whose wounds limit their ability to give back. Trauma bonds often thrive on an addictive roller-coaster dynamic—you endure cycles of hurt because you keep waiting for the "good moments" to repeat. Any small sign of kindness or remorse feels like validation. Many believe the connection they share with the abuser is uniquely intense—something that couldn't be found elsewhere. The "addiction" feeling comes from this intermittent reinforcement pattern—your brain craves the unpredictable rewards, creating obsessive thoughts, compulsive checking of their messages, or physical anxiety when they're unavailable. And the chemicals do their job, causing you to crave the ups after the downs.

The key difference between healthy love and "love addiction" lies in how the relationship affects your overall well-being and sense of self. Healthy love feels secure and enhancing; addictive attachment feels desperate and depleting. To break unhealthy cycles, you need to learn to assess your current relationship objectively. Start by noticing when you're predicting harm without evidence—catch thoughts like *"they'll definitely betray me"* and ask yourself what proof you actually have. Also notice when you're making excuses for hurtful behavior or waiting for someone to change back into who you thought they were. Remember: your past experiences say nothing about what this person will do.

> **The Love vs. Attachment Inventory.** The first step in distinguishing genuine love from a trauma bond is to direct that same compassion toward yourself. Ask yourself with complete openness to hear the truth: *"Does this relationship honor my needs as much as I honor theirs?"* *"When I give, do I feel nourished or drained?"* Seeing yourself with kindness helps you sense whether the bond is built on mutual care—or on your willingness to overlook hurt because your heart is so open.
>
> Next, ask whether there's a pattern of recurring abuse—emotional, physical, or subtler forms like constant belittling. If negativity cycles through the relationship, you may be dealing with more than a rough patch.
>
> Consider, too, what you believe love is. Some people confuse dependency or the craving for attention with love. Authentic love usually feels safe and uplifting overall, even amid conflict. It's marked by mutual respect, trust, acceptance, and a genuine desire for each other's growth. A bond rooted in fear, relentless self-sacrifice, or ongoing suffering is not love but an emotional entanglement formed to cope with deeper pain or insecurity.
>
> Answer **Yes**, **Sometimes**, or **No** to each of the following:
>
> __ Do you feel more anxious than at peace in the relationship?
>
> __ Do you often find yourself trying to "fix" the other person or the relationship, even at the cost of your own well-being?

___ Do you excuse or minimize hurtful behavior because of brief moments of kindness or remorse?

___ Do you believe this relationship is uniquely special—even if it frequently makes you feel small, unsafe, or emotionally drained?

___ Do you struggle to imagine life without this person—not because of joy but because of fear, emotional dependency, or breaking the expectations of your commitment?

___ Do you often think that your love can heal them, change them, or make it all worth it?

___ Do you feel responsible for their emotions or actions—especially their anger, jealousy, or insecurity?

___ Have you stayed in the relationship despite knowing, deep down, that it's hurting you?

If you answered **Yes** or **Sometimes** to several of these, it may be time to gently ask yourself, *"Am I sacrificing my emotional safety for hope?" "Is my care for them overshadowing care for myself?" "Do I feel loved... or just needed?"*

How does a trauma bond finally come to an end?

A trauma bond typically ends when a person reaches a tipping point—realizing that if they don't break free, their well-being and sanity will be at serious risk. It's important to remember that the problem isn't the trauma bond itself, but the imbalance that the bond enables and sustains.

The breaking point often begins with a firm determination to let go of a harmful relationship—the decision to prioritize one's safety and peace above all else. Once that inner shift takes place, a crucial reality check tends to follow: seeing the relationship for what it truly is, rather than what you wish it could be, or what you still feel obligated to offer despite your own unmet needs. People stuck in trauma bonds often carry a magical belief that unconditional love can redeem relentless mistreatment or that fulfilling their duty matters more than protecting their well-being. Letting go of that illusion can be painful, but it's a necessary step toward recovering. You may need to speak with a spiritual counselor or someone you trust to help validate your decision to move on.

Humility also plays a major role in dissolving a trauma bond. That doesn't mean being meek or accepting blame. It means acknowledging that—even with the best intentions—you may have been misled, manipulated, or taken advantage of, and that you may have been too idealistic or naive. This process can be incredibly hard for someone who prides themselves on being caring, loyal, and persistent in the face of challenges. When you've poured your heart and soul into a relationship, it can feel like defeat to walk away. Yet recognizing that there was abuse—or that the other person never truly respected your emotional reality—can open the door to genuine freedom.

From there, the work turns inward: redefining certain values you once took pride in. Kindness is a beautiful quality, but when it becomes a justification for tolerating harm, it undermines your well-being. Realizing that a "good" trait can evolve into a self-destructive pattern or enable someone else's dysfunction is one of the hardest, yet most liberating, insights. This process leads to rediscovering who you are outside the relationship. People in trauma bonds often forget what it's like to be an individual—with personal needs, boundaries, and interests. Turning inward and remembering those aspects of yourself—whether through therapy, creative pursuits, or reconnecting with understanding, supportive friends—helps you rebuild an identity that isn't entangled in someone else's chaos or quest.

All of these elements—determination, reality-checking, humility, self-acceptance, redefinition, and rediscovery—gradually liberate you from the unhealthy bond. A moment comes when the pain and confusion of staying outweigh the fear of leaving. That's when the bond truly begins to crack. No one casually walks away from a person they once deeply cared for, especially when so much time, love, or energy has been invested. But eventually, the choice can become clear: dissolve the bond or live in misery. Choosing yourself—however shaky or late it may feel—is what ultimately breaks the bond. And that choice is where freedom begins.

Chapter Six

THE DEEPEST WOUNDS

HOW TO UNDERSTAND THE IMPACT OF UNAVOIDABLE CIRCUMSTANCES

"The pain that we cannot control may be the one that could teach us the strength we never knew we had."

Have you ever felt completely powerless as pain crashed into your life through no fault of your own? That moment when life shifts from predictable to unrecognizable—when a phone call, a diagnosis, or a single event shatters everything you thought you knew about safety.

Some pain is simply beyond your control, arriving uninvited through natural disasters, accidents, sudden loss, or growing up with parents who couldn't offer the love you needed. These experiences don't just hurt—they can fundamentally alter how your nervous system perceives the world, leaving invisible wounds at different levels of depth that continue influencing your thoughts, relationships, and sense of self—sometimes for years, sometimes for generations—until you intervene proactively.

In this chapter, we will continue to explore the hidden mechanics of traumatization that we began discussing in Chapter Three—how your brain's protective responses, while life-saving in the moment, can become outdated patterns that no longer serve you. We'll uncover why some people seem to bounce back while others remain spiraling down.

Importantly, I'll clarify what childhood trauma really means and when childhood experiences truly constitute trauma versus other forms of emotional wounding.

Finally, we'll examine how to bring past and present into dialogue, reclaim your sense of agency, and discover that while emotional pain may be unavoidable, remaining trapped by trauma is not. Your story doesn't end with what happened to you; it begins with how you choose to relate to it. The deepest wounds require the most precise understanding—knowing whether you're carrying active trauma or resolved scars changes everything about your path forward.

Recognize the Realities of Trauma Beyond the Event

"Safety isn't a fortress you live in—it's a resting place you learn to return to."

Many people assume that "traumatization" simply means "experiencing trauma," but these terms actually refer to two distinct aspects of traumatic experiences.

Trauma is an active injury. In contrast, traumatization is a particular process: **the physiological and psychological activation of the nervous system's extreme survival responses that remain heightened long after the threat has passed, during the time when the brain assumes danger still exists.**

In what follows, I'll help you understand how traumatization works and some of its manifestations—as well as the important role we each can play in its resolution.

Do trauma and traumatization mean different things?

Yes—and understanding this distinction may save you many headaches.

Trauma is the active, unresolved injury that **carries the alterations** of multiple parts of your system when survival responses remain "on" long after a threat has passed. **Traumatization** is the ongoing internal process that **generates those alterations** while it's still unclear whether you'll overcome a perceived threat. During this phase, your system works overtime trying different strategies to restore safety—diverting vital resources from healthy functions toward emergency responses.

Think of traumatization like being a ship caught in stormy waters: your nervous system works to keep you afloat but hasn't decided to abandon the ship. The storm may have passed, but you're still clinging to the rail, bracing yourself, convinced you could still drown.

The key difference is that traumatization is the active struggle phase where your brain still has hope and keeps trying different survival strategies. Trauma is what remains when most attempts have failed and your system's default way of operating has shifted.

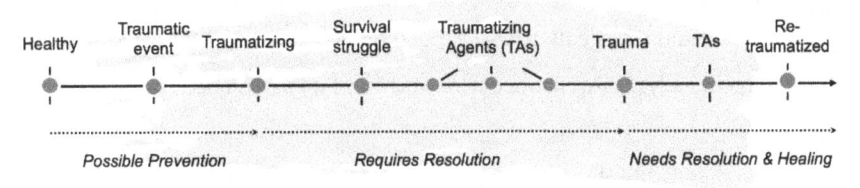

Healthy	Traumatic event	Traumatizing	Survival struggle	Traumatizing Agents (TAs)	Trauma	TAs	Re-traumatized
Possible Prevention			Requires Resolution			Needs Resolution & Healing	

Traumatization Progression

Recognizing you're in a traumatization process means your system is still actively trying to resolve the original fear, and you can still work on giving it a rest by finding a solution: reconnecting with your present situation and recognizing you are alive and safe. The storm has passed.

Many people wonder if they're truly traumatized or just struggling with difficult emotions. Understanding that your system is actually working diligently to keep you safe, rather than to damage you, can motivate you to maintain hope for recovery.

WHAT ARE FLASHBACKS DOING TO MY BRAIN AND MENTAL HEALTH?

"Flashback" is one of the most popular trauma symptoms and has become a loaded term people use to explain how bad their situation is. We've come to view them almost as enemies—perhaps similar to how we fear hallucinations or psychosis.

The reality of flashbacks is less scary. Flashbacks are just an element of the brain's sophisticated warning system in action. They signal caution through images or sensations that are specifically encoded to help us recognize and anticipate potential threats. Much like nightmares, flashbacks (unlike hallucinations) don't come with "instructions" for how to respond or demands to act in hazardous ways. Yes, they typically carry the same intense emotions we felt during the original experience, which makes them intrusive and bothersome, but not dangerous.

A flashback on its own has minimal impact on our overall health. It's usually short-lived and, in many cases, simply serves to bring something to our attention for an instant. Flashbacks only become problematic when the warning signals continue to intensify over time.

Why might they escalate? You've probably guessed it: either because the brain assumes we're ignoring an important message and turns up the volume, because we remain fearful and repeatedly reinforce the traumatic memory internally, or because the threat genuinely persists in our environment and we haven't been able to neutralize it.

It's true that flashbacks may pull us back into the past as a way to protect us from future risk. Still, experiencing them doesn't mean we lose the capacity to reassess the present, especially if we are not in danger. During a flashback, the brain briefly reactivates some of the circuits that fired during the original threat, especially those responsible for strong emotional and sensory memories. We might see, hear, or feel traces of what happened before, as though the danger is unfolding again, but an instant later we can assess whether we're experiencing a trauma symptom or facing genuine present danger.

Take, for instance, someone who was assaulted at gunpoint. In the beginning, they might see the attacker's face everywhere they go—fleeting mental images, flashes of recog-

nition. *If, over time, they regain a sense of confidence—perhaps through practical steps like carrying pepper spray, moving to a safer area, or simply feeling more in control by taking self-defense classes—these disturbing images tend to appear less frequently or with less intensity. While upsetting, they usually begin to fade as the brain and body settle back into more regulated functioning.*

But if the person remains convinced that the danger never really ended—or worse, internalizes the belief that they are cursed or an easy target—the nervous system stays locked in fear and hypervigilance. They might begin obsessively searching for people who resemble the attacker, scanning for threats everywhere, and bracing for another assault. In that state, each flashback—of the face, the gun, and the place—becomes more vivid, more terrifying, and more difficult to recover from. The brain, interpreting this ongoing fear as evidence of persistent threat, ramps up its emergency responses. Flashbacks shift from being a signal to becoming a loop—exhausting the system and making daily life progressively harder.

Flashbacks, then, are a perfect example of how our system tries to protect us—even if it overreacts for a while after the threat has passed—and how we can make this protection worse by misusing the power of our mind. Not surprisingly, the brain also has mechanisms to evaluate what memories need to be reinforced, maintained for a while, or faded, which is how flashbacks naturally begin to fade over time. But we need to give the brain the right instructions.

Dual-Screen Exercise to Reduce Flashbacks. You can use this simple exercise to reduce the strength and intensity of a flashback.

When a flashback brings a disturbing sensation or when intrusive memories feel overwhelming, picture two mental screens side by side in your mind.

On the right screen, visualize a vivid, colorful safe place. Choose somewhere that feels genuinely peaceful to you—a calm beach, cozy room, favorite park, etc. Add rich sensory details: warm sunlight on your skin, the sound of gentle waves or rustling leaves, soft textures like sand or comfortable cushions, and pleasant scents like ocean air or fresh flowers. Take a long breath, making the inhalation longer. Feel your body come alive.

> **On the left screen,** place the disturbing scene, then gradually shrink the image until it becomes small. Drain the color from it, making it grayscale. Push the screen away from you until the image appears distant and blurry. Take a long exhalation and release any tension.
>
> **Focus and strengthen:** Deliberately shift your attention to the right screen. Let the safe place image grow brighter and more vivid. Allow the left screen to continue fading until it's barely noticeable.
>
> Breathe slowly, feeling your body in the present and allowing yourself to experience the calmness and peace of the safe place image. Practice regularly to strengthen this technique over time.

I DON'T THINK I'VE EVER FELT TRULY SAFE—WHAT AM I MISSING?

If we are discussing trauma resolution, we have to talk about safety. I'm struck by how frequently people express, *"I never feel safe."* What's revealing is that when I gently probe deeper, most people struggle to describe what safety would actually look or feel like in their lived experience. Such an observation raises a crucial question: are some traumatized individuals postponing their healing while waiting for an elusive feeling of complete safety to arrive first?

Safety isn't an objective condition or permanent state—it's primarily a subjective mental experience felt when our mind successfully reassures our body that we aren't in danger. If we mistakenly equate trauma healing with achieving a risk-free existence, we've established an unattainable prerequisite. When in our complex world is danger ever really absent?

Consider the risks we navigate constantly: a momentary loss of balance could result in serious injury; microscopic pathogens invisibly surround us; those closest to us might abandon us or cause emotional harm without warning. Meanwhile, our nervous system operates as a sophisticated threat-detection mechanism, continuously scanning for potential dangers—silently assessing our surroundings—and is so committed to our protection that it readily identifies potential threats even in relatively secure environments. Is that person's voice tone indicating anger? Did their expression shift? Is it safe to speak up? To rest? Should I voice my needs? Every step of our journey carries risks.

My grandmother used to say, *"If you look for it, you'll find it."* This vigilant monitoring fits her wisdom perfectly. If you look for danger, you'll find it.

Feeling safe, then, is not a steady state but a fluctuating experience—something that comes in waves, moments, and pockets—and these pockets look different for each person. For some, safety manifests as warmth, ease, and connection. For others, it's about feeling accepted or respected. Some associate safety with financial security or physical health, while others experience it as the freedom to express feelings without fear of judgment or rejection. There are as many ways to feel safe as there are dangers to fear.

So, when someone aspires to feel safe to resolve traumatization, they need to either be specific about what kind of safety they're cultivating—such as ending emotional abuse in their relationship, recovering physical health, or achieving housing stability—or reconsider whether their hoped-for safety is realistic and attainable.

INTERNAL
Self-regulation techniques
Deep breathing
Grounding exercises
Internal reassurance (self-talk)
Mindfulness or meditation
Soothing touch or textures (self-applied)
Personal rituals
Humor or play
Creative expression (art, music, writing)
Feeling understood
Holding onto meaning or purpose
Spiritual or religious faith
Having control over choices
Routine and predictability
Information and learning
Imagination and positive visualizations

EXTERNAL
Physical distance
Locked doors
Familiar environments
Trusted relationships
Financial stability
Cultural or community belonging
Access to information
Carrying protective tools (pepper spray)
Quiet or low-stimulation environments
Soft lighting
Calming music
Therapy or support groups
Medical or mental health support
Physical presence of a safe person
Pets or emotional support animals
Nature or outdoor spaces

Internal and External Sources of Safety

Think of safety as a mental frame. You can't always control the picture, but you can adjust the frame. How you interpret words, sensations, interactions, or risks determines how your system responds. The same moment can feel overwhelming or manageable depending on the meaning and attention you give it.

What we can realistically cultivate is not permanent safety, but rather more tolerance for uncertainty and stressful situations, along with acceptance that we cannot control our fate. To nurture this experience of safety, we need internal resources like trust, hope, tolerance, and faith—and perhaps most importantly, compassion and a joyful determination to improve our well-being.

> **Mapping Moments of Felt Safety Exercise.** This practice can help you identify what safety feels like for you in real-life terms—so you can recognize it, nurture it, and return to it more easily by activating neurons that will start reprogramming your brain.
>
> **Support through music:** If you feel comfortable, do this exercise wearing headphones and listening to instrumental music: soft piano, gentle strings or acoustic guitar, ambient soundscapes, nature-infused tracks (ocean waves, forest sounds with soft harmonics), or music tied to personal meaning (a song that always brings you a sense of warmth or familiarity). You can also pick a bilateral stimulation sound playlist. Music can help open emotional access points while offering gentle regulation.
>
> **Recall a safe moment:** Think back to a time—however brief—when you felt safe. It doesn't have to be recent or perfect. It might be sitting next to someone you trust, lying in bed with a book, laughing with a friend, having a predictable routine, or hearing reassuring words. If nothing comes to mind, imagine a scenario where you'd ideally feel safe (wrapped in a soft blanket, in nature, or with a pet). Once you choose it, make it vivid in your mind with as many details as you can include.
>
> **Notice body sensations:** How does it feel in your body to bring up those images? Do you feel warmth? Stillness? Softness in the chest? A quiet mind? Lack of judgment? Does it feel like silence, support, privacy, or familiarity? Don't worry if it feels vague—just be curious.
>
> **Identify safety elements:** From the image you picked, find 2–3 elements that seem to support your feeling of safety. These could be being around people who don't demand anything from you, having control over your time, knowing you

can leave a situation if you need to, or whatever speaks to what you're looking for to increase your feelings of being safe.

Take action: Choose one element from your list and think of a small way to bring it into your life this week. For example, if familiarity made you feel safe, revisit a comforting place or object; if supportive presence helped, schedule time with a person who feels easy to be around; if quiet helped, protect a few minutes of silence in your day.

Set your intention: Write down your intention as a sentence: *"This week, I'll set aside five minutes each evening to enjoy a warm cup of tea in solitude."*

Close with affirmation: Close your eyes for a moment and say, *"Yes, there is danger, but I can feel safe and connect to a sense of protection if I put my mind to it. And that's enough."*

Take a slow breath and let the images and sensations of that safe moment settle into your body. You're not chasing safety—you're reconnecting with the parts of you that already know what it feels like.

How does unresolved trauma affect your life?

Many people with unresolved trauma maintain highly functional lives while carrying the burden of a dysregulated system. Externally, things seem fine, but internally, they carry a weight that makes life feel increasingly miserable. As some of my clients have commented, they *"mask very well the symptoms most of the time until masking them becomes as dreadful as the dysregulation itself."*

This internal struggle may manifest as being extremely emotional, perpetually worried and anxious, emotionally numb and disengaged, struggling with unexplained physical or medical issues, experiencing constant ruptures in social relationships, or displaying what appear to be personality traits that actually reflect ongoing survival responses.

Let me clarify an important distinction: unresolved trauma differs from unresolved psychological pain. Some people carry emotional wounds from specific situations, yet their system never lost equilibrium—they were disturbed but can still distinguish one painful experience from another. *For example, someone might feel hurt because their partner shows no affection, yet they can still believe they're worthy of love and remain hopeful about possibilities. While they experience emotional pain, their suffering isn't survival-focused distress where past and present become experientially confused.*

Serious cases of unresolved trauma involve individuals whose condition continues to deteriorate: their nervous system remains dysregulated, they present new or worse symptoms, and their brain constantly seeks danger while their mind stays defeated, seeing no escape from misery. This may be particularly disconcerting for those who "inherited" the dysregulation and feel lost about what to do.

I remember a client who came to me saying, "I've been anxious my whole life, but I don't know why. I had a normal childhood, but I wake up every night terrified that something terrible will happen. I mentally review all the ways I might die during the night." She had no idea that her mother's untreated trauma had shaped her nervous system from birth. Imagine trying to get restorative sleep in that state.

Paradoxically, some people can overcome significant childhood trauma through life circumstances that implicitly restore safety—finding secure relationships, achieving professional success, or creating stable environments. Their systems may gradually reset as these positive experiences accumulate. However, if someone's narrative consistently blames trauma whenever something goes wrong or they suffer from "aggregated trauma" (an accumulation of injuries I introduced in my first book), this mindset can prevent resolution.

How can you tell if someone is traumatized?

You can recognize traumatized individuals by their disproportionate reactions to everyday situations. Their behaviors may appear out of coherence, puzzling, and difficult for themselves or others to manage. They might alternate between periods of restlessness and complete shutdown, depending on which part of their nervous system is dominant.

Restless individuals may be irritable, dismissive, hypervigilant, or intolerant of minor irritations such as loud noises, a perceived lie, or certain people. They might avoid responsibilities, have trouble sleeping, or struggle to focus.

Disengaged individuals might appear aloof, disconnected, or emotionally absent. They often avoid interactions and become increasingly isolated, neglecting their appearance or hygiene. They may also experience crying spells, nightmares, excessive napping, or prolonged sleep.

There are individuals dominated by a combination of both—a kind of fight-or-flight-on-hold state—marked by an extra level of caution, as if constantly anticipating that something tragic is about to happen. This state leads to rigidity, emotional guardedness, difficulty experiencing pleasure, and a tendency to suppress joy or connection before it can cause harm. They may appear controlled or composed on the outside, but their system is bracing internally, unable to fully relax or engage.

Even so, we must be cautious about seeing a few signs and automatically labeling someone as traumatized. Indicators that persist, become entrenched, and regularly disrupt daily life may require deeper assessment rather than isolated expressions of emotionality, temperament, or even adaptation.

Imagine someone who startles loudly every time someone else is driving but shows few other symptoms. That startle response might—or might not—indicate trauma. Some people are naturally fidgety or hyperalert by temperament. But if someone can't sleep after driving, screams during dreams involving car crashes, cries, feels deeply disoriented, or lashes out when another driver brakes suddenly or misses a light by a few seconds, and displays ongoing signs of distress or dysfunction related to driving, it's reasonable to suspect they may be carrying unresolved fear around accidents.

WHAT IS THE PHOBIA OF INNER EXPERIENCE? AND IS IT ASSOCIATED WITH CHILDHOOD TRAUMA?

A phobia of inner experience is an intense, irrational fear of one's own emotions, thoughts, sensations, or memories. People with this condition worry they'll lose control, feel overwhelmed, or be unable to tolerate what they find inside. This creates constant, automatic avoidance of inner states—not just discomfort, but a fear so strong it becomes debilitating.

Unlike external phobias, this involves fearing your own internal world. This fear can lead to patterns of suppression, distraction, dissociation, or compulsive external focus to avoid going inward.

While this internal avoidance was historically labeled "resistance" in therapy, we now understand it differently. Many people aren't resisting intentionally—they genuinely cannot tolerate the intensity of their inner experiences. This intolerance often originates early in life, when emotions were overwhelming, invalidated, or never safely processed. When the nervous system learns that certain feelings (like fear, shame, or grief) are dangerous or unbearable, it develops automatic protective responses to avoid them entirely.

For instance, someone might avoid acknowledging grief after a significant loss, instead immersing themselves in work or other distractions. When sadness begins to surface, they might experience physical symptoms—like a racing heart or tight chest—which they interpret as dangerous. This fear reinforces the avoidance, prompting them to suppress both the emotion and its physical sensations.

This phobia can also serve as a protective strategy: rather than rejecting the entire self, the fear isolates specific parts—those that might harbor anger toward parents or authority figures or impulses that feel intolerable. The person develops an irrational fear of experiencing these aspects of themselves. In very severe cases, this reinforced fragmentation can lead to significant psychological disorders, including certain personality disorders and Dissociative Identity Disorder (DID), where the inability to tolerate certain parts of the self leads to compartmentalizing them into separate identities.

This experience exists on a spectrum—most people have some discomfort with certain emotions, while extreme cases involve disorders like DID.

Cultural and family dynamics significantly influence these patterns. In many cultures, certain emotions are discouraged based on gender, social status, or values. Children raised in environments where emotions are dismissed or punished *("Stop crying, or I'll give you a reason to cry")* learn early that inner experiences are dangerous, setting the stage for severe avoidance patterns in adulthood.

Become an Expert in Trauma Responses

(Beyond Fight or Flight)

"Some scars don't form on the surface. They become part of the way we breathe, think, and dream."

After experiencing traumatic circumstances, many people feel like strangers in their own bodies—disconnected, on edge, or numb in ways that seem to have no clear explanation. You might find yourself jumping at sounds that never bothered you before or feeling emotionally flat when you want to care. These aren't character flaws or signs of weakness; they're your nervous system's attempts to keep you safe in a world that once felt dangerous.

The relationship between trauma and the body is more nuanced than popular phrases like *"the body keeps the score"* might suggest. While trauma doesn't literally hide in your muscles like some mysterious entity, it does leave real, measurable changes in how your brain and nervous system function. Understanding these changes—and recognizing that you have more influence over them than you have been told—can be the first step toward feeling at home in your body again.

Is hypervigilance a common experience for everyone? How can one cope with it when it occurs?

Everyone has moments of heightened alertness—your body tenses up at a sudden noise, a tight deadline, or walking alone at night—but hypervigilance is something more pathological than that because it becomes a chronic state beyond ordinary caution or anxiety. In this state, the brain stays in continuous, exaggerated scanning for danger, as though constant surveillance were the only way to stay safe. This assumption often results from prior experiences where the person felt overwhelmed and couldn't establish control or confidence in their safety. Essentially, hypervigilance and dysregulation coexist as trauma symptoms, with hypervigilance being one manifestation of dysregulation—a perpetual high alert inside the larger problem of poor overall regulation.

Let me share a vital characteristic of hypervigilance that is crucial to keep in mind if we want to be mentally healthy: **hypervigilance consumes a significant portion of the brain's energy budget,** which is not only substantial but also detrimental to overall well-being.

Let me use a "vacation budget" as an example of how the brain's energy allocation works. Imagine you have $1,000 to spend during a week-long trip to a beautiful city. You need to distribute this money among lodging, food, entertainment, and gifts. You learn your favorite actor is performing that week, so you spend $300 on a ticket. This forces you to downgrade your hotel choice to accommodate the reduced $700 budget. Then, on day three, you lose your phone and must spend $200 on a replacement. Now you have only $500 left, which means you have to limit your meals to once a day and forget about buying gifts. By day five, you're offered a $50 restaurant voucher in the town center. While most people would accept this chance to stretch their budget, some might decline for emotional rather than logical reasons—perhaps pride, shame, or food preferences.

Survival Mode (+/- 60%)
- Hypervigilance
- Impulsivity
- High emotionality

Everything else (25%)
- Creativity
- Learning
- Introspection
- etc.

Adaptation (+/- 5%)

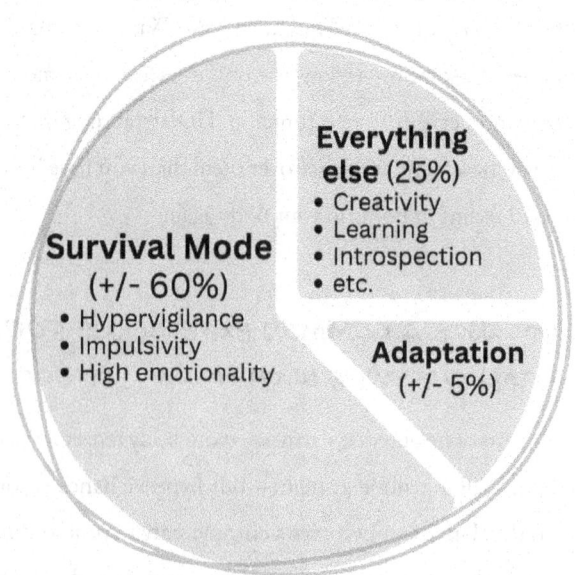

Brain Energy Budget Allocation on Survival Mode

This scenario mirrors how our brain manages its limited energy budget. When the brain dedicates substantial energy to hypervigilance (like spending $300 on the ticket), this depletes energy available for other functions. If unexpected demands arise (like the phone loss), the brain must adjust again, often by cutting back on certain functions (like introspection). Just as you might skip meals, your brain might reduce energy to areas where reasoning happens, causing weaker executive function or even dissociation.

Regarding the voucher, a healthy brain typically favors energy-efficient solutions—it would accept the voucher to conserve resources. This mirrors how positive or neutral thoughts require less energy than the negative, worry-driven ones tied to hypervigilance, which burn extra fuel by constantly anticipating worst-case scenarios. Yet many people struggling with hypervigilance essentially "reject" these more efficient mental options, much like someone might decline the voucher due to pride or emotional reasons rather than logical ones.

So, is hypervigilance a common experience for everyone? No—it's not typical in healthy individuals. What helps in the moment? Try the following exercise.

> **The Hypervigilance Reset Practice.** Just follow this quick grounding technique to redirect excessive threat scanning.
>
> When you notice hypervigilance taking over, recognize and name it with a reflection like this, *"Am I getting too focused on finding danger? Oh! That's my hypervigilance guessing wrong."*
>
> Redirect your attention with intention: *"Let me help it by coming back to the present, exhaling longer, and giving my brain a safety cue (touching something cool, wrapping a light blanket around my shoulders, playing a favorite calming song, and using a mantra like "Right now, I'm safe!")."*
>
> Hypervigilance can decrease when your brain learns that instead of staying in scanning mode, you can choose to reconnect with the present and reinforce safety. The more consistently you practice, the more your brain will thank you—and eventually, it will learn to make this your default habit.

What is a trauma response, and what are some examples?

The term "trauma response" has become part of our regular vocabulary, often used incorrectly. Most people use it to describe reactions we have to something scary or painful, but it generally refers to the body's built-in reactions when we feel threatened or to learned reactions that resurface when a new situation resembles a dangerous situation we went through.

A common misunderstanding is thinking that all natural reactions to threat are "trauma responses" or that any sympathetic nervous system activation is "fight-or-flight," whether it's an everyday stressor or a true crisis. Our nervous system operates on a spectrum, using only as much energy as necessary for each situation. What we call trauma responses are specifically the intense protective reactions that activate when our system perceives genuine threats to survival.

I call them "immediate" or "pre-programmed" when they are automatic and essentially the same for everyone and "conditioned" when they differ according to what we unconsciously learned during past threats.

Pre-programmed trauma responses—our automatic survival reactions—appear the moment we detect danger. These responses don't equal trauma in themselves; once the threat passes, the system usually returns to baseline. We can recognize three main mechanisms that typically follow a sequence as they attempt to protect us:

- **Paralyzation (or freeze)** involves muscle rigidity and breath-holding. It may be a brief hesitation while we orient and decide what to do or a response to shock and terror that takes us by surprise. It is largely preventive and activates both branches of the ANS—the sympathetic and the parasympathetic—at the same time. *Example: You see a car speeding directly toward you in a crosswalk. Your body instantly locks—muscles rigid, breath suspended, heart racing—caught between the impulse to run and the overwhelming shock of the moment, unable to move in any direction. An instant later, your reflexes may propel your body out of the car's way.* The freeze often feels like "shock," but it's built-in efficiency—tightening core muscles protects vital organs, and holding breath stiffens the torso for impact.

- **Mobilization (or fight-or-flight)** includes tensed muscles, clenched fists, feelings of anger or rage, aggressive posturing, rapid heartbeat, shallow breathing, an urge to run, and restless movements. It reflects full sympathetic nervous system activation. *For example, when a stranger's dog charges, you either sprint toward a gate (flight) or raise your arms and shout to scare it off (fight).*

- **Immobilization (often called freeze, though freeze more accurately describes the initial paralyzation response instead of the numbing that comes after mobilization)** includes two types of immobility—tonic and collapse. It begins with tension and then a loss of muscle tone, diminished breathing, cold limbs, dissociation from surroundings, disconnection from the body, extreme fatigue, and sometimes feeling faint or actually fainting. These signs show the parasympathetic system—specifically the dorsal vagus—trying to dampen the sympathetic overload and conserve energy when success seems unlikely. *Example: After a sudden physical assault, a person may go completely slack—muscles losing all tension, legs giving out, potentially crumpling to the ground while feeling far away from their body and emotionally numb. If they perceive the threat as inescapable, they may even faint.*

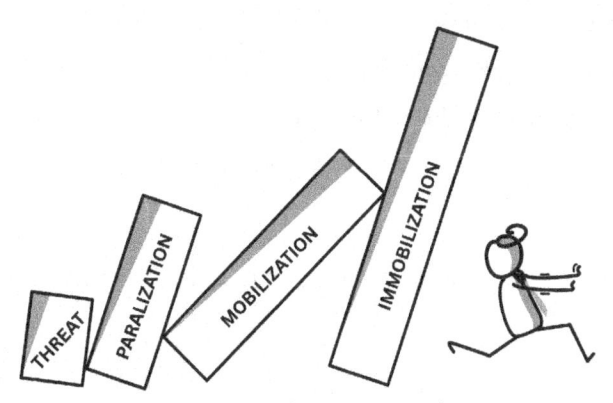

Pre-programmed Responses to Threat

Conditioned trauma responses are learned protective reactions that become unconsciously triggered when current situations resemble past dangers, varying from person to person based on their unique traumatic experiences. They can include a war veteran dropping to the ground at the sound of fireworks, a person who experienced emotional abuse becoming disconnected when someone screams, someone who survived a car accident braking at every corner when riding in vehicles or even feeling unsafe as a pedestrian near traffic, or someone who experienced physical violence wanting to escape in crowded spaces.

These reactions feel automatic because, at one point, the nervous system "chose" them as the safest strategy. Some authors say the person is "stuck" in a trauma response, but it's often more accurate to see it as the system's learned wisdom when danger seemed unending—a way the body adapted to stay alive. Once real safety becomes the norm, that same wisdom can be gently retrained so the old alarm no longer fires.

Imagine a person who learned that shouting louder than their abusive partner decreased the likelihood of receiving a hit. After leaving the relationship, they may still raise their voice in conflicts. If shouting later jeopardizes their job, they might shift to walking away (flight) rather than immobilization because their system is conditioned to favor action.

Viewing these responses as adaptations, not malfunctions, helps us meet them with understanding. When the reactions become overpowering and out of voluntary control, they signal dysregulation: the system is still operating as if survival were continuously at stake. In such cases, the responses are no longer random—they become predictable signs that the nervous system has shifted its operation. The reactions themselves have become trauma symptoms because the system continues looping on unnecessary protections.

Is the way you respond to trauma your choice?

When facing a situation that feels threatening, our capacity to choose or make decisions operates on a spectrum shaped by powerful neurobiological mechanisms. While we theoretically retain the ability to make conscious choices even in extreme circumstances, intense fear can temporarily overwhelm our awareness that choices exist by depleting the cognitive resources needed for decision-making. The very perception of having options becomes clouded when our survival systems are fully activated, as our cognitive functions don't receive enough energy—it gets diverted to fear and basic self-preservation.

However, understanding how the brain works reveals strategies we can use to regain some control. When faced with threatening situations, our brain operates through two distinct pathways: an **automatic survival circuit** that activates instantly and a **reflective system** that engages more slowly but enables conscious decision-making.

REFLECTIVE: slow, conscious, serial (only one process), analytical

AUTOMATIC RESPONSE: fast, unconscious, able to think in parallel

Brain Processing Systems

The automatic system triggers immediate physiological responses—flooding our body with stress hormones and preparing us for survival—before we're even consciously aware of the threat. This initial response isn't a choice; it's an evolutionary mechanism designed to keep us alive. It's fast and can process multiple tasks simultaneously, but it doesn't make the best decisions for our long-term well-being.

The reflective system can step in, adding a layer of agency. This system allows us to evaluate the situation, consider multiple options, and make conscious choices about our response. It engages higher brain functions to assess the actual level of danger, recall previous experiences, and draw upon learned strategies. Unlike the automatic circuit, which operates in a binary "danger or safety" mode, the reflective system can recognize nuance, context, and proportionality. It's slower but produces better results. Many people who struggle to resolve trauma rarely learn to activate this reflective system.

> **The Pause-and-Prepare Method.** Practice this exercise to strengthen your reflective response under threat.
>
> First, build up the habit throughout your day by practicing taking one deliberate deep breath before responding to any mild stressor (a text that annoys you, someone cutting in line, a work interruption). Create a micro-pause between the

> jolt of threat and your next move. Say internally, *"Pause... breathe... now choose."* That split-second gap may be enough for the reflective brain to come online.
>
> Second, take advantage of the brain's anticipatory wiring. Rehearse safe responses in advance—whether through mental imagery, brief grounding drills, or real-life practice. "Pre-load" alternatives. For example, imagine that your supervisor approaches with a harsh tone. Instead of immediately defending yourself or shutting down, you:
>
> 1. Take one deep breath (micro-pause).
>
> 2. Access your pre-loaded response: *"I can listen without taking this personally."*
>
> 3. Respond from choice rather than panic: *"Let me make sure I understand what you need."*
>
> When real threats appear, your rehearsed options become easily accessible, allowing your reflective brain to engage instead of defaulting to survival panic.

Through training, we develop new neural pathways that allow us to stay calm and make conscious choices even in challenging situations. This doesn't mean we can simply "choose" not to react to threats—that would be like trying to choose not to blink when something flies toward your eye. Instead, we can develop the ability to notice our responses sooner and gradually introduce more conscious choices into our response sequence. While the initial automatic response may be beyond our control, we can influence what happens next.

What Does It Mean When People Say They Dissociate?

Dissociation is a broad term, and different psychological theories define it in varying ways—making it difficult to generalize its meaning. In its broadest sense, dissociation is a separation or disconnection among parts of experience that are normally integrated—memory, identity, sensory perception, or emotion. This discontinuity is not always pathological; it can be a natural protective strategy. At other times, however, it becomes disruptive or harmful. I include it here because, for many people, disconnection is the symptom that lingers longest after a traumatic event—making emotions feel dull, awareness unreliable, or the sense of self fragmented.

We can think of dissociation as one of our brain's natural functions, similar to sensing, thinking, or remembering. In essence, it's an adaptive and protective mechanism that helps us manage when we're overwhelmed—whether by too much stimulation, intense emotions, or situations we're not ready to handle, including mental exhaustion and pain. To understand dissociation clearly, we need to look at it from several angles: a) as a normal function versus a pathological response, b) by the severity of the disconnection, c) whether it's serving us (adaptive) or causing problems (maladaptive), and d) how it manifests—either as compartmentalization or as disengagement.

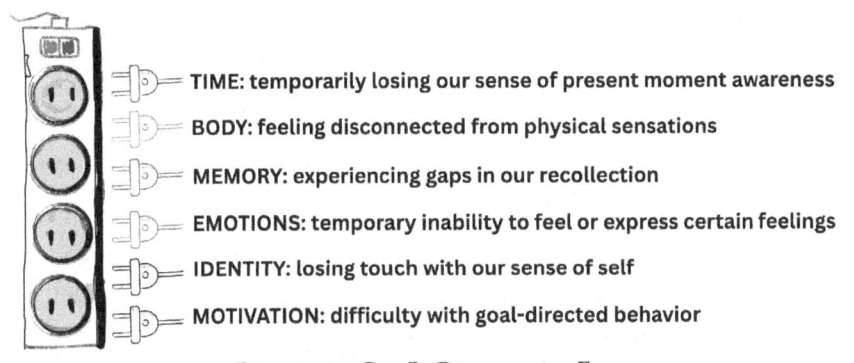

TIME: temporarily losing our sense of present moment awareness
BODY: feeling disconnected from physical sensations
MEMORY: experiencing gaps in our recollection
EMOTIONS: temporary inability to feel or express certain feelings
IDENTITY: losing touch with our sense of self
MOTIVATION: difficulty with goal-directed behavior

Dissociation Can Be Disconnection From

A Normal, Adaptive Process: Dissociation can be as ordinary as zoning out while reading and suddenly realizing you have no idea what you've just read. It can also be "highway hypnosis," where you arrive but don't recall the drive. Daydreaming and "flow" states are further examples: you might be so immersed in a task that you lose track of time or forget you're hungry or worn out. In these instances, dissociation helps your brain filter out less important information so you can manage whatever is most urgent or intriguing at the moment.

From a survival standpoint, when faced with overwhelming or painful experiences—especially in childhood—temporarily "shutting down" certain sensations, memories, or emotions can help a person cope or maintain the relationships they depend on. At this adaptive end of the spectrum, dissociation offers short-term relief or a mental break. It's intended to be brief, just like other extreme reactions. Dissociation can appear during mobilization, but it is most severe (and possibly damaging) when it emerges in the immobilization phase, where the system shuts down to conserve energy and the disconnection becomes part of the brain wiring. When the shutdown state is recruited again and again, the brain learns to reach for it faster, turning an adaptive "time-out" into a habitual disconnection.

Dissociation becomes harmful or problematic when it solidifies into a lasting, habitual pattern—one the person no longer controls or benefits from. This situation usually happens under prolonged stress or repeated threat, whether the danger is real, perceived, or constantly replayed in fearful thoughts. *Picture a child who learns to block out the pain of an abusive household. They might keep dissociating long after the danger has passed until it becomes a default.*

Unfortunately, modern factors can perpetuate dissociative patterns. Social media can exacerbate the situation by suggesting that every distraction is dissociation and a "trauma response," which increases feelings of shame and the urge to withdraw. Over time, this fear-based cycle may lead to amnesia, emotional numbness, identity confusion, or feeling detached from reality.

In more severe cases, individuals may experience profound memory gaps, lose touch with their sense of self and awareness, or switch between different self-states without conscious control—phenomena sometimes described in dissociative identity conditions. They might forget major parts of their personal history or struggle to control their own actions because this disrupts or slows down some cognitive functions.

CAN I BE TRAUMATIZED TOO EVEN IF I AM THE ONE WHO CAUSED SOMETHING BAD TO SOMEONE?

It's not difficult to imagine that causing harm to someone else could evoke intense emotional distress and create an emotional wound connected to guilt and shame, but does it create the sense of threat that survival circuits require? In certain cases, a person who harms another might fear the consequences—being seen as a bad person, facing legal repercussions, or even fearing divine punishment. Their survival mechanisms can be triggered by this fear, regardless of its source or whether others consider it valid. However, the path from fear to traumatization isn't straightforward.

This question is a bit like asking, "Can I become deaf from yelling at someone?" Theoretically possible under extremely rare circumstances, but practically speaking, your voice would give out long before you could damage your hearing—so the odds are virtually zero.

Several factors influence this likelihood: Was it a single incident, or have you harmed multiple people? How close are you to the person you injured, and does your future depend on that relationship? Is your resilience already worn thin by earlier stress? Have previous threats left your system hypersensitive to danger? Have you lived in fear for a long time? Or does the harm you caused leave you so ashamed and fearful of the consequences—so overwhelmed and hopeless—that you see no way forward?

Trauma becomes most likely when the harmful act creates overwhelming helplessness and moral distress—when you feel both responsible for the damage and powerless to repair it. In most cases, people do not develop lasting trauma symptoms from isolated incidents of causing harm.

DETECT THE VARIED IMPACT OF A

TRAUMATIC CHILDHOOD

"Some childhoods leave clear cracks. Others leave quiet imprints. Many fill us with unexpected lessons. All invariably shape who we become in ways we're still learning to understand."

If you've ever wondered whether your childhood experiences "count" as genuine hardship, you're not alone. The term "childhood trauma" has become so widely applied to everything hurtful that happens to children that we all wonder if we suffer from it. This leaves many people confused about their own history and unsure how to make sense of their struggles.

Here's what I've observed repeatedly in my practice: people who endured truly devastating childhoods often don't recognize their experiences as particularly harmful, while others feel deeply affected by difficulties that, while real and painful, may not have fundamentally altered their development. This isn't coincidence—it's how our minds protect us and make meaning of our experiences and how easily we can be influenced by media narratives. When a child depends entirely on harmful caregivers, their brain develops powerful defenses to survive. They might idealize abusive parents *("My mom was strict, but she loved me")*, forget painful memories, or normalize devastating experiences *("Every family has problems")*. The alternative—seeing reality clearly—could have been psychologically unbearable for a child with no choices.

Meanwhile, those who had challenging but not devastating childhoods sometimes identify strongly with descriptions of severe hardship they encounter online or in therapy. This pattern often reflects a genuine attempt to understand real emotional pain, even when their experiences fall into a different category entirely.

The truth is that childhood difficulties exist on a vast spectrum. A brief separation from a caregiver who returns quickly creates a very different impact than years of chronic abuse. Parental conflict that eventually resolves affects development differently than violence that is never addressed or explained. Yet our current conversations about childhood often treat all difficulties as equally significant regardless of duration and type, which serves no one well.

Understanding your own childhood requires recognizing that children are both remarkably resilient and uniquely vulnerable. The depth, duration, and timing of difficult experiences—combined with protective factors like supportive adults, natural temperament, and available resources—all determine how childhood struggles affect adult life.

Doesn't everyone, or at least the large majority of people, have some form of childhood trauma?

Many people assume "childhood trauma" describes any painful childhood experience. Under that definition, most people would qualify, right? However, childhood trauma refers to something much more severe: circumstances that made **the entire childhood feel threatening and unsafe.**

Childhood trauma results from severe, overwhelming threats that persist throughout the formative years. These circumstances force a child's developing system to struggle for survival on a constant basis, ultimately interfering with normal emotional, social, and cognitive growth.

Not every hardship—like a parent's occasional drinking or a sibling's illness—crosses that line into childhood trauma unless the child feels unsafe or abandoned consistently across at least their first 12 years of life. Children are neurologically plastic and highly adaptable. While they have fewer cognitive tools than adults to contextualize and process difficult events, they also experience and express fear differently, often with fewer resources to manage it effectively but also with some advantages. Their fears tend to be more immediate and concrete (monsters, the dark), less abstract (they don't fear financial ruin or societal judgment), and more dependent on developmental stage: separation anxiety in toddlers, fears of the dark or imaginary creatures in preschoolers, social rejection concerns emerging in school-age children, and identity and future-related anxieties becoming prominent in adolescents.

Until about age seven, children view the world through an egocentric lens, focusing on their own needs. They might notice family arguments but won't feel scared unless they fear losing the parental bond they rely on or believe they're unloved. For them, it may be more frightening to see Mom frustrated because they didn't eat lunch than to see Mom angry or sad for not having money to pay the rent. Only when their own safety feels jeopardized does fear activate their survival circuits. This happens when they see a caregiver as dangerous (through violence or aggression) or when they fear abandonment (through illness or loss).

Many kids face tough times—poverty, family stress, neglect—yet thrive if they feel basically safe within their world's limits. The idea that children are fragile often overstates their vulnerability; most are resilient, bouncing back like the old saying, *"Kids are made of rubber."* What I think has happened is that our imprecise language has led us to conflate unresolved emotional wounds with genuine trauma. This confusion risks planting shame or anxiety in young adults who may not have felt threatened as kids but accept the narrative of childhood trauma. When we talk about it, let's be precise, considering age, severity, and the child's own sense of danger to avoid mislabeling painful wounds as lasting survival injuries. Let me offer you a quiz that could help you assess your childhood experiences.

Did I Experience Childhood Trauma? A Quick Assessment. Here is a self-assessment to explore early life experiences and their lasting impact.

Please rate each line with the number that you feel is most accurate. Start by reflecting on these questions: How persistent were these experiences? Did they begin when I was very young or highly dependent and last until I became older? Was there an absence of supportive adults to buffer or protect me? Do I notice recurring patterns in adult life that echo these early experiences?

Now rate the following:

For each item, rate how true it was for you growing up (before age 18):

0 = Not at all | 1 = Occasionally | 2 = Frequently | 3 = Constantly | 4 = Always

_____ My home environment was objectively dangerous, and I felt at risk.

_____ I was on high alert, expecting something bad to happen.

_____ I worried about my safety and the safety of others I loved.

_____ I experienced situations where I felt helpless, trapped, or unable to escape.

_____ I was physically harmed, neglected, or had to hide injuries.

_____ I experienced sexual boundary violations or coercion.

_____ I was regularly belittled, humiliated, or made to feel worthless.

_____ Fear and intimidation were used to control my behavior.

_____ Basic needs (food, shelter, medical care) were unmet.

_____ I lived in a home with domestic violence, substance abuse, or untreated mental illness.

_____ I witnessed repeated violence in my home.

____ I was isolated from friends or adults who could support me.

____ I had to earn love by meeting others' needs or performing well.

____ I took on adult responsibilities as a child (e.g., caring for siblings or parents, cooking, working).

____ Caregivers were unpredictable—sometimes loving, sometimes absent or cruel.

____ I felt responsible for managing others' emotions or problems.

Scoring Guide:

0–10: Likely no significant trauma, but reflect on isolated pain points.

11–25: Possible cumulative emotional wounding; pay attention to relational or emotional struggles.

25-35: It'd be good to assess for emotional dysregulation.

36–40+: Strong likelihood of chronic developmental trauma; healing may require support and deliberate attention.

Important: This quiz isn't a diagnosis—it's a mirror. It's here to help you see what you may have been carrying and why healing deserves compassion, not shame.

How much will a 3-year-old remember about bad things that happen to them?

We don't recall most experiences from before age three or four because the brain structures that form detailed autobiographical memories (mainly the hippocampus and parts of the prefrontal cortex) are still under construction.

Language also plays a huge role. Children only begin to form narratives *("I did this, then that happened")* around ages two to three, and this skill is crucial for labeling and organizing events into something the mind can recall later. If a child hasn't quite established a strong sense of self—that continuous *"I"* who experiences life—it becomes harder for them to bookmark events.

However, kids can still store certain moments if their brain flags them as critical—especially when accompanied by a strong emotional charge. Let me share a personal story:

When I was three, I was playing with my brother and banged my leg on a table corner. I started rubbing where it hurt. One of the workers nearby came over and offered to rub it and make it feel better. Something in me just said no—my whole body instinctively recoiled. I don't remember much from when I was that little, but I can still picture his face, especially his eyes. Something about the way he looked at me felt wrong, even though I couldn't have explained why at the time. My brain's built-in danger detector (called neuroception) was picking up on something threatening. I probably just went back to playing, but I remember that as soon as I saw my mom, I told her, "That man wanted to rub my leg." My parents looked into it and found out the guy had been drinking on the job.

This experience illustrates an important principle about early memory formation. The episode wasn't traumatic because I was able to trust that internal warning and avoid potential harm. Even without adult-level language or conceptual thinking, the fear I felt anchored that moment in my memory.

Experiences that activate our protective systems—like detecting danger—get stored through different pathways, which is why threatening or highly emotional events from early childhood can sometimes be remembered clearly even when most other memories from that age are lost.

WHAT ARE THE SUBTLE SIGNS OF CHILDHOOD TRAUMA THAT PEOPLE MISS?

It's much easier to spot the big, obvious traumatic events—like a kid witnessing a car crash—than it is to pick up on the persistent, low-level stressors that accumulate over years, like constant parental cruelty or unpredictable violent episodes. It's even harder to know what's really going on behind closed doors at home. These ongoing difficulties can disrupt a child's nervous system and development just as significantly as dramatic events, but they're often overlooked because they develop gradually. I'll share the story of Mikey and Pam to illustrate how this works in real life.

Mikey's Story

Mikey grew up with parents struggling with addiction who rarely cared for him in any meaningful way but had episodes of aggression and demands that included sending him to get the drugs. By the time he was 10, he was scrounging for food, struggling to find clothes on his own, and even working odd jobs for money. For Mikey, the parental neglect and abuse meant:

Physical underdevelopment: *He's notably shorter and thinner than his siblings or age-matched peers. If his outward appearance reflects stunted growth, it's possible his organs and internal systems (immune system, metabolism, digestion, and of course brain and neural connections) are also underdeveloped.*

Motor skills delays: *With minimal adult interaction and no children to play with, Mikey missed out on opportunities to refine fine motor tasks like drawing, writing, or using utensils and gross motor play like running and climbing.*

Emotional and social signs: *Low self-esteem is common in neglected children who feel invisible and scared. Mikey comes across as depressed or fatigued to those who observe him closely. Meanwhile, he's great at hustling and negotiating, which some adults admire as "street smarts," thanks to his ability to hide the truth—that he had no choice but to parent and protect himself.*

These signs went unnoticed because teachers, neighbors, and other adults in Mikey's environment assumed he was just "naturally small" or "quiet and independent," not realizing his lack of growth or withdrawn demeanor signaled emotional and physical malnourishment. They may also have overlooked that he barely read or studied, chalking it up to laziness or limited capabilities instead of understanding he never had stable support, motivation, guidance, or stimulation.

Pam's Story

Pam, the same age as Mikey, grew up with highly religious, cruel, and sadistic parents. She wasn't physically neglected—she had good shelter, food, clothes, education, social support, etc.—but she was tormented by constant emotional and sometimes physical punishment. For Pam, the abuse throughout her childhood manifested as:

Perpetual stress and somatic symptoms: *Living with strict, fear-inducing parents triggered nausea or "inexplicable" fevers. The adults around her saw her as "sickly," missing that her body was responding to unrelenting stress.*

Hyper-achievement with low self-esteem: *Pam did really well at school, probably to earn her parents' fleeting approval, but inside, she carried a sense of unworthiness because deep down, no matter what she did, they were never satisfied. Teachers saw "the star student," unaware she was terrified of failing, constantly criticized and mocked, and perpetually scared of being punished at home.*

Anxiety vs. depression: *Compared to Mikey's more depressive demeanor, Pam appeared highly anxious—restless, constantly worried, but also angry, with sudden explosive outbursts, and highly critical of others. Outsiders mistook her stress for "just normal teenage nerves," ignoring the emotional torment behind it. From the outside, Pam looked well cared for, which made others (including her parents) fail to suspect that her "intelligent daughter" act was a shield for deep-seated fear, shame, anger, contempt, and dissatisfaction.*

Individual responses vary widely. I could give you many other examples of similar situations where the children turned out differently. Many abused and punished kids like Pam lose motivation and do poorly at school; some neglected kids like Mikey become responsible adults with successful careers.

Regardless of their survival strategies, most children from these environments struggle emotionally as adults. Some develop severe physical issues, and many have difficulties maintaining solid relationships. Each person develops their own way to adapt to their living conditions, which creates specific but often unnoticed signs of the difficulties they encountered while growing up in circumstances that were adverse to healthy development.

WHAT RED FLAGS SUGGEST A CHILD IS TRAUMATIZED?

If a child regularly explodes or completely shuts down over relatively small challenges, it may indicate either traumatization or trauma. Let's examine the different scenarios.

Extreme, out-of-proportion emotional responses. Think of every child as having an emotional dial from -10 to 10 that indicates how they can handle emotional highs (anger, frustration) and emotional lows (sadness, disappointment) without feeling desperation. If a child regularly explodes (screaming, threatening, or becoming violent) or completely shuts down (withdrawal, numbness) over relatively small disappointments, showing very low tolerance for normal frustrations, it may indicate that their nervous system either never learned to regulate or has lost its balance. *For instance, a six-year-old who says they want to die just because their toy broke suggests their frustrations are overwhelming.*

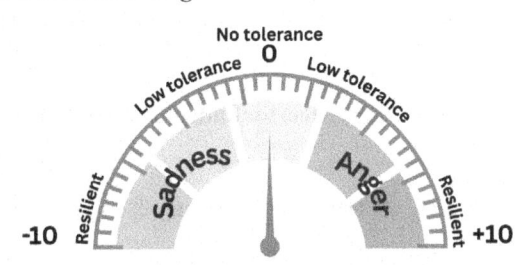

Emotional Tolerance Gauge

Out-of-place fear or panic. Look for situations where the child's fear is way more intense than the real risk. *A three-year-old going "ballistic" upon seeing their mother get a massage—behaving as though it's a life-or-death threat—signals their alarm system is in overdrive.*

Shutting down or "going blank." Some traumatized children withdraw socially, barely engage with peers, and seem chronically "somewhere else." *A nine-year-old who stares vacantly during group activities and doesn't respond when classmates invite them to play, despite having normal hearing and cognitive abilities.*

Learning and developmental delays. Constant fear can stall normal development, causing kids to lag behind age-appropriate milestones. *A seven-year-old who still can't tie their shoes or follow two-step instructions, despite having no diagnosed developmental issues, because their cognitive resources are consumed by monitoring for threats.*

Bizarre or incongruent behavior. Children may act in ways that don't align with what's happening around them. *A child who laughs inappropriately when reprimanded or shows no emotional reaction to winning a competition they worked hard for.*

Still, always assess whether the child is experiencing ongoing adversity versus a single traumatic event (which would show different symptoms), and consider whether behaviors reflect individual temperament, learned behavior, or family patterns rather than trauma manifestations.

Why do so many childhood trauma victims take so long to process their trauma?

First, we need to distinguish between "childhood trauma victims" and people who experienced difficult childhoods. Childhood victimization involves actual harm from someone's actions or inactions. Not everyone who carries trauma has been victimized, and this distinction matters for understanding the processing journey.

Children don't interpret adverse events as threatening when they're happening—they're like sponges, absorbing whatever their environment presents and treating it as "normal." Without concepts of "right or wrong parenting," they may not realize for years that what they experienced was harming them. They may feel hurt, but they can handle passing emotions.

This normalization is particularly strong because children form intense bonds with their caregivers. During early years, parents are perceived as godlike figures. When a caregiver responds with contempt, rejection, or unpredictable anger, the child's developing brain interprets this as evidence of their own unworthiness rather than the adult's limitations.

Many people don't recognize the need to process childhood experiences until adulthood, when they notice chronic anxiety, overreactivity, or trust problems and wonder, *"Why am I so sensitive and needy?"* or when they read something exaggerated that portrays adversity during childhood as childhood trauma. Only then do they start making connections to their childhood experiences and either recognize them accurately or over-identify with some.

When protective defenses finally drop in adulthood, old emotions may flood in at once. This is when many seek help, but they often misunderstand what "processing" involves. Many assume it means revisiting painful memories in detail, when it's actually about resolving the emotional states—fear, shame, distrust—that continue driving today's reactions.

Processing involves integrating fragmented pieces: understanding why experiences still hurt and reconnecting dissociated parts. The complexity of identifying what actually needs healing, combined with years of protective avoidance, explains why childhood trauma processing often takes so long to begin.

HEAL FROM TRAUMA USING YOUR OWN WISDOM

"The gift of being human: our system holds strength, our mind holds wisdom, and healing is already part of the plan."

The journey through trauma recovery isn't linear—it's filled with unexpected questions that arise as you process and heal. This section addresses the common yet deeply personal inquiries that emerge when you're ready to move beyond simply understanding trauma to actively rebuilding and reclaiming your life. Whether you're questioning why healing feels frightening, wondering if growth is possible after suffering, or struggling with memories that seem both too present and too fragmented, these concerns represent the natural evolution of trauma work. As you explore these topics, remember that ambivalence about healing is normal, forgetting isn't the same as healing, and moving forward doesn't require having all the answers.

Is post-traumatic growth a common experience for individuals after a traumatic event, even if it is not immediately apparent?

Post-traumatic growth (PTG) is considered a common experience following traumatization, though it's not universal, rarely emerges immediately, and is less straightforward than we might hope. Research suggests that approximately 50–60% of "trauma survivors" report some form of positive transformation or growth, often appearing months or years after the traumatic experience. However, it's difficult to assess how it's happening, since it usually coexists with ongoing distress rather than replacing it entirely. The process follows a nonlinear path, with individuals oscillating between struggles and moments of meaningful insight before sustainable growth emerges.

After a traumatic event, the body's first priority is to address the physiological changes caused by the perceived threat—this may take a couple of months if the person has adequate support and their reactions are properly managed—similar to the time a fracture takes to resolve. During what we often call "processing," people begin to assess how the traumatic event affected not just their past, but also the present and future. If they're able to derive positive meaning—such as *"I'm a fighter"* or *"I have a new perspective on life"*—then post-traumatic growth has a chance to emerge. As post-traumatic symptoms naturally diminish for many people with resources, they may then develop new skills, strengthen relationships, or find new purpose—all facets of PTG.

By the way, this growth process also applies to emotional wounds, even when the growth isn't immediately recognized. Most individuals have the reflective capacity to learn from adversity, leading to gradual changes in how they view themselves, their relationships, or their goals. In a way, we could say that our everyday adaptive capabilities exist on the same continuum as PTG—with routine resilience handling life's regular challenges on one end and the profound transformations of PTG addressing life-shattering experiences on the other. Both draw from our inherent capacity to find meaning and adapt.

For individuals with complex trauma syndromes, PTG frequently happens as the healing process unfolds and the person better understands themselves while integrating emotions, reactions, and meaning. In short, many people do experience meaningful growth over time, even if they don't initially recognize these positive changes or struggle with ongoing symptoms. If our system's tendency is to learn from our experiences in order to be better prepared, growth is the natural outcome.

WHY AM I SCARED TO HEAL MY TRAUMA?

Many people find themselves reluctant to let go of familiar strategies, even when they no longer serve their best interests. Just think that they started using them very early in life, and many times, they helped them overcome challenges. *Consider someone who became a master at manipulating neglectful parents to get something out of them—it may be hard for them to believe they'll get what they need without manipulating.*

Beyond the attachment to familiar strategies, resolving trauma begins with recovering a sense of safety, but full healing demands much more. It requires identifying and reconstructing fear, learning emotional regulation skills, developing realistic and objective thinking patterns, recognizing defenses and triggers, managing relationships without reactivity, strengthening their sense of self, and cultivating inner resources and hope.

One common obstacle is **fear of failure**—the worry that you'll invest time and effort only to discover you can't be helped. If past attempts at change ended in disappointment, you may carry a deep-seated belief such as *"No matter what I do, I'll never get better."* Remember that defeat is intrinsic to why people get traumatized. The belief that you're beyond help can become a self-fulfilling prophecy, preventing you from even attempting recovery.

Similarly, fear of change itself can trigger anxiety. What's familiar—even when painful—feels safer than the unknown for many. Because trauma is fueled by fear, it's natural to cling to the patterns and strategies you've relied on, worried you'll be less capable without them.

Hesitation can also be tied to identity. If trauma led you to develop, say, a quick temper or a perpetual victim role, and they have become part of your identity and how others relate to you, letting them go can feel like losing a piece of who you are. In truth, healing from trauma doesn't erase your most significant traits; it simply gives you the freedom to choose how you'll respond instead of being run by harmful reactions.

There's also the possibility of getting some rewards from your suffering. Some people receive tangible benefits—attention, leniency, even financial support—because of their trauma symptoms or narrative. The prospect of losing those advantages can feel risky, no matter how miserable the symptoms are.

This dynamic can create unexpected conflicts. *I once worked with a client who was pursuing a lawsuit against her abuser. We were prepared to help her process her flashbacks and intense emotions when she realized something troubling. If those reactions faded through therapy, she might end up forgiving him—and she felt it wasn't the right time given that the legal case was still underway.*

> **Identifying Your Recovery Roadblocks.** It's very helpful to begin your healing journey by acknowledging that you're afraid of it and naming the reasons why. This exercise helps identify the specific fears and obstacles that may be preventing you from moving forward with trauma recovery.
>
> Start by asking yourself these questions. Take time to honestly reflect on and answer them. Write down your responses or simply sit with each question and notice what comes up for you.
>
> "What am I afraid might happen if I start healing?"
> "What parts of my current coping strategies am I reluctant to give up?"
> "What would I lose if trauma no longer defined parts of my identity?"
> "Who might I become without these protective patterns, and will I feel safe?"
> "What previous attempts at healing have disappointed me, and why?"
> "Am I afraid of the emotions that might surface if I allow myself to feel?"
> "Do I believe I truly deserve to heal and live differently?"
>
> Simply naming these fears can remove some major obstacles to healing. Once you start—slowly—learning to manage them and build a few small successes in calming your system, your confidence will grow and your motivation will rise. Moving beyond fear means leaving survival mode and stepping into a space where you can truly live and enjoy your life.

How Do You Forget A Trauma That's Haunting You?

A common misconception around trauma resolution is that you need to forget your traumatic memories in order to heal. What's important is not forgetting what happened but processing and releasing the negative emotions connected to those haunting memories.

Traumatic memories persist because they are imprinted on your brain as significant, serving as reminders and warnings of past dangers in an attempt to protect you from similar risks in the future. Once you feel safer, they will lose their purpose and, consequently, their power.

The fastest way to reduce the disturbance they bring is to process them. By processing these memories—rather than trying to forget them—you can reduce their emotional impact. They will be integrated into your full story and lose their distressing potential.

Your brain won't forget if it considers that you still need those warnings to stay safe. The brain tends to let go of memories it deems irrelevant. Some people try to forget by using strategies like denial or compartmentalization. Some techniques involve overexposing the system to fear, aiming to desensitize it. However, these approaches often require numbing your senses or your awareness. Not ideal!

Disconnection often creates worse mental health consequences than simply remembering and working through disturbing memories. At least by remembering, you may feel motivated to do something about your lack of safety, whereas if you compartmentalize, you may stay in a state of defeat or numbness that puts you at higher risk of developing other disturbing symptoms.

> **Safety-Anchored Memory Integration.** Before attempting to process traumatic memories, ensure you're physically safe and have basic self-regulation skills to manage distress.
>
> Please identify something that represents safety for you—your **safety cue**. It could be the image of a wall, the name of a protector, the sound of an alarm, or whatever you can come up with that brings a sense of protection to your system. Bring it to your mind and allow your system to identify it internally as real.
>
> Allow your system to feel that protection and to run through it.
>
> Then, gradually approach a traumatic memory in small doses rather than avoiding it completely or taking chances of drowning in it. Once you feel some of the disturbance (emotion connected to the memory), allow yourself to feel the

> emotion until it becomes too much. In that moment, go back to your safety cue and stay with it until the disturbance feels tolerable.
>
> When you're ready, return to the memory, connect with the emotion, and tolerate it for as long as you can before returning to your safety cue. Repeat this gentle oscillation between memory and safety as many times as feels manageable.
>
> After returning to your safety cue, speak to yourself as you would to a friend experiencing the same thing, with understanding rather than judgment. Consider how your experience has shaped your values, strengths, or perspective on life.
>
> Repeat this sequence once or twice a week. Each round helps your nervous system pair the old memory with present-moment safety, gradually downgrading its threat level. If distress spikes or you feel overwhelmed, stop, get grounded, and seek support—processing works best when safety is real, not forced.
>
> Remember: the goal isn't to forget; it's to remember differently—without the hijack of fear, shame, or helplessness.

WHY DO I FEEL I AM UNDESERVING OF COMFORT FOR MY TRAUMATIC EXPERIENCES?

A key effect of traumatization is the way it distorts how you see yourself and your place in the world. Rather than simply internalizing blame, the mind can adopt a view of reality that doesn't match what's objectively true. If you grew up feeling powerless or held responsible for events beyond your control—especially in childhood—you may have learned to interpret every setback as *"I'm unworthy"* or *"It's my fault."* Over time, this view can rewire your brain circuits—strengthening neural pathways between threat detection and self-blame while weakening connections to self-compassion—so that whenever emotional pain surfaces, the reflexive conclusion is *"I don't deserve comfort."*

Imagine a child who was scolded for crying after being bullied and told to "toughen up" because "other kids have it worse." As an adult, that same person might survive a car accident yet refuse help, thinking, "I'm fine—other people were injured more than me; I don't deserve support." The old message—*"My hurt isn't valid"*—automatically overrides the present reality that comfort is both available and warranted.

This altered perceptual framework becomes so convincing that even reassurance from others cannot override it. You continue to perceive yourself as responsible for harm you received or unworthy of care you're offered. From the outside, it looks like self-blame; from inside this altered perception, it feels like reality. You may also believe you must handle your pain alone or that seeking comfort would burden others.

This same dynamic plays out in countless situations. *Picture someone who, after surgery, waves off a friend's offer to bring meals, saying, "Save it for someone who really needs help."* That reflex springs from the same distorted perception that took root when danger first threatened their sense of security.

Resolving trauma means challenging the belief that you're undeserving—a belief often rooted in deep shame. Trauma-focused therapies don't just rely on thinking differently—they help your body and emotions stop reacting as you were forced to. Through safe, supportive experiences, you can challenge the *"I'm not enough"* story and begin to feel the right to reach out, even if it feels unfamiliar at first. Self-compassion can dissolve shame's grip, and with time and practice, you can embrace yourself.

> **Self-Compassion Exercise.** This exercise may help you dissolve that idea of not deserving comfort.
>
> Place a hand on your heart, breathe deeply, and notice any warmth or resistance. Notice the physical sensation of your hand's warmth and gentle pressure. This is already an act of self-comfort your brain may resist.
>
> If you can, stand before a mirror, look into your eyes, and softly say, *"You are enough, and you deserve care."*
>
> As thoughts arise *("I don't deserve this" or "This is stupid"),* simply notice them without judgment. These are the old perceptions speaking.
>
> Softly say to yourself, *"Just like everyone else, I deserve comfort when I hurt."* Repeat it several times until it begins to feel more natural.
>
> Notice any sensations in your body. Breathe slowly while maintaining the hand contact for 1-2 minutes, keeping eye contact with yourself, even if it feels uncomfortable or foreign.

> Practice this daily for a week. Initially, it may feel mechanical or false—that's the old perception fighting to maintain itself. Over time, your nervous system can learn that comfort is both available and permissible.
>
> This process isn't about "positive thinking" but about retraining your body to accept care, beginning with your own touch and recognition. The hand that provides comfort serves as physical evidence against the belief that you do not deserve soothing. Allow it, and then, at the right time, enjoy it! Touch produces oxytocin, even if it's your own touch.

Should I forgive my parents for causing my complex trauma?

Forgiving parents who created fear, pain, and instability during your childhood isn't required for healing, since resolving trauma is an internal journey, not an external commitment. Start by reflecting on what you're considering forgiving—were their actions intentional harm, or did their limitations, sense of responsibility, and dysfunction create an environment that felt threatening to you?

When parents are still in your life, timing matters. If they still can't offer safety, forgiving too soon might lead you to continue exposing yourself to threatening situations. This is particularly important for those whose nervous systems require sustained calm to rewire. Consider whether your forgiveness might unconsciously signal to yourself that their behavior was acceptable, potentially lowering your guard.

Parent-child dynamics add complexity that doesn't exist in other relationships. When parents recognize the harm they caused and are genuinely willing to repair the relationship, it can open a path to reconciliation—and to resolution for you. However, many parents defend their actions or minimize the impact, making forgiveness feel like betraying your own experience.

While releasing chronic resentment can reduce your stress load from a clinical perspective, this only works when paired with firm boundaries that keep you safe. Unlike forgiving someone from your past, forgiving parents often involves ongoing relationship decisions that affect your current well-being.

Remember: Their growth and accountability are their responsibility, not yours. Forgiveness, if it happens, should support your safety and well-being—not compromise it for the sake of family peace or imposed values.

> **Boundary and Forgiveness Process.** Here's a simple exercise to clarify both forgiveness and boundaries.
>
> Name the hurt. On paper or in your mind, finish this sentence in one line, as if you were talking to your parents (or whoever caused you continuous distress):
>
> *"When you _____, I felt _____."* Keep it factual and focused on a single traumatic event each time you write.
>
> Name the need: *"To feel safe now, I need _____."* This might be *"less contact,"* *"no yelling,"* or simply *"space to heal without pressure."*
>
> Set the boundary. Add one concrete action that protects that need:
>
> *"I will speak by phone, not in person"* or *"I'll leave the room if voices rise."*
>
> Release the emotional charge. Breathe out slowly, and silently say, *"I keep the lesson; I release the poison."* Imagine the resentment leaving your body on the exhale.
>
> Close with choice. Decide: *"Does forgiving internally serve me now, or do I still need distance first?"* Write a one-line intention: *"For now, I choose _____,"* and date it. You can revise it anytime.
>
> Repeat the exercise for each hurt as it arises, tackling one grievance at a time. This deliberate pacing keeps the work manageable and fair to your system. Each cycle names the pain, secures a boundary, and allows your nervous system to settle—so that forgiveness, if and when it comes, is an informed choice, never an obligation.

CAN TRAUMATIC MEMORIES BE SIMPLY FORGOTTEN INSTEAD OF REPRESSED?

Our understanding of how the brain handles traumatic memories continues to evolve, revealing a more complex process than simple repression.

Most of the time, parts of traumatic experiences don't get fully recorded in the first place. During traumatic events, intense stress affects how memories are recorded. When our brain focuses on survival, it prioritizes tracking threats over creating complete memories. *Think of "tunnel vision" like a camera—the lens narrows to focus intensely on perceived danger while everything else becomes blurry.* Missing details doesn't mean they were repressed; they were never fully captured.

Traumatic memories (as painful ones) also get processed differently than ordinary ones. Normal memories integrate various elements (sight, sound, emotion) into a coherent story, but traumatization fragments these elements, storing them separately and encoding them with unbalanced strength, so the association between pieces is weakened or poorly contextualized. This creates a warning system that keeps the most survival-relevant pieces readily accessible and those with intense emotions fresher, explaining why certain sounds, smells, or feelings can trigger intense responses years later.

Meanwhile, other pieces of the experience might seem "lost"—either blurred during the event or deemed less relevant for survival. Our brains rarely "forget" completely; they prioritize and consolidate information.

When details no longer seem useful or were never properly encoded, the specific circumstances fade, and essential emotional information gets blended with similar experiences. This is why sometimes entire years feel missing from memory.

Understanding this process helps explain why traumatized people often have fragmented rather than completely absent memories—it's not repression but the natural result of how our brains prioritize relevant information.

As discussed previously about forgetting haunting memories, the goal isn't to erase these fragments but to process them so they lose their emotional charge and integrate into your broader life story.

Memory Gap Acceptance Ritual. Here's an exercise you could practice if you are struggling with gaps in your memories.

Place two objects in front of you—perhaps stones or small items. One represents *"what you remember,"* the other *"what seems missing,"* and acknowledges the gap.

> Place your hands on both objects and say, *"My brain recorded what it needed for my survival. Some pieces were captured clearly; others weren't fully recorded."*
>
> Hold the "missing memories" object, acknowledge any frustration or anxiety it creates, let yourself feel it in your body, then place it slightly farther away while saying, *"I don't need complete memories to heal or feel safe."* Notice how your body responds.
>
> Place your hand on your heart and say, *"My body carried me through then, and it carries wisdom now. The gaps in my story don't diminish my experience or my healing."* Breathe deeply and let go of any tension.
>
> Place both objects in a small container and say, *"My story is whole even with its missing pieces. What matters most is how I care for myself today."*
>
> This exercise helps shift focus from what's missing to what's present—your capacity to heal regardless of memory completeness. It physically represents the process of accepting memory gaps as a normal neurobiological response rather than a personal failing or obstacle to recovery. Remember, your nervous system's priority was survival, not documentation. The incompleteness of the memories doesn't make your experience any less real or valid.

Understanding how deep your wounds truly go—and how your remarkable brain adapted to protect you—is the first step toward reclaiming your life from fragments of the past.

EPILOGUE

WHERE MY JOURNEY MEETS YOURS

To close this book, I want to share something more personal—a response I once wrote to the question *"Has anyone healed from complex post-traumatic stress disorder?"* It resonated widely, gathering thousands of views and reactions. It might be the right way to end this journey.

What follows is a personal account of how my own healing unfolded. I don't often speak publicly about my story, but I've come to see that openness has power. If my experience can offer hope, clarity, or validation to even one reader, then sharing is worth it.

Has anyone healed from complex post-traumatic stress disorder?

I was exposed to prolonged stress early in life, together with a series of emotional wounds and unresolved issues in my system—even though I didn't fully meet the criteria for C-PTSD at that time. I did some work to heal, but I wasn't fully recovered when I faced more intense and intermittent traumatic circumstances over many years—emotional abuse and several tragedies, including kidnapping, significant losses, and serious medical problems. Eventually, my system reached a state of allostatic overload—the point where it can no longer make small internal adjustments to maintain balance. Life lost its luster, and my system lost its equilibrium. That breakdown brought all my previously overlooked symptoms into sharper focus, and I became seriously ill—both physically and emotionally.

Everything in me felt painful. It took tremendous effort to reverse the damage caused by all those years of invisible traumatization. At one point, I met every single criterion for C-PTSD—and more. I had so many symptoms that dysfunction felt like my first name.

That's also why I have such a personal connection to this subject. I know what it feels like to live with emotional pain, go through adversity and traumatic situations, and live with not only trauma but a full-blown trauma disorder—how the symptoms affect you, how distorted perception can become, how easily you get triggered, and how the pain keeps compounding. And I also know what it takes to heal and what it feels like to finally reach the point where you feel yourself again.

During my journey, I learned that healing from trauma may be slightly different from resolving it. Resolution focuses on the unprocessed fears, beliefs, and emotional charges that remain, activating the survival circuits. Healing, on the other hand, involves repairing the broader disruptions caused by living in a dysregulated system. Healing trauma is more than resolving a memory or changing a belief. It required restoring the complex system I inhabit—brain, mind, and nervous system—that had been knocked out of balance. Since trauma affects our entire being, effective healing usually calls for a combination of top-down (mind-to-body) and bottom-up (body-to-mind) methods.

Of course, I still have some lingering symptoms, but now I can recognize them for what they are. Overall, self-awareness has been my greatest ally on this healing journey.

Now, several years later, I can truly say I'm free from trauma. I am also very skillful at recognizing my emotional pain and resolving it before it persists or evolves into something I really don't want to carry. My nervous system has regained its balance. My brain feels like it's functioning at its best—it can stay present for long hours. My sense of self is strong and grounded. I experience a sense of comfort within myself. My observing-self is well developed and always ready to let me know when my ego wants to take over. My current view of the past is coherent and objective, and I'm able to fully engage with both the people in my life and life itself.

Triggers still show up, but I notice them sooner and respond far differently than before. I ask myself, *"Am I having a trauma response?" "Is someone genuinely causing me harm, or does the situation just hurt because I'm still learning about my sensitivities, my expectations, and my own humanity?"*

I take responsibility for my reactions. I've learned to express my emotions effectively, so they're no longer as intense as they once were. I have rewritten most of the loaded scripts that were making my interactions difficult.

I have also understood how my background taught me to live intensely and what it means to react intensely among people who didn't learn the way I did.

Nowadays, I enjoy being more open and more trusting. I no longer live with shame. I've learned how to set boundaries, and I advocate for myself when others try to cross them. I also know how to accept help and truly appreciate the support people offer. I take all these small changes as enormous achievements, even if they may not sound like much to others. I celebrate them, I honor myself, and I pamper everyone, including me.

I'm aware of my weaknesses and how I need to take care of myself. In the past, I used to pretend I was invincible. Now I recognize both my limits and my strengths, and I keep learning and growing with each new day—whether from my family, my clients, nature, or even brief interactions with strangers or authorities.

I'm no longer surviving on autopilot. I'm fully engaged, fulfilled, and full of hope, compassion, and joy.

If you're still on your way, know that healing is possible. Please, come walk with me.

I came to realize that life is a long journey with many layovers. Some are pleasant—those quiet moments in comfortable places where everything flows smoothly. Others are unpredictable delays that test my patience. Trauma and deep wounds felt like being stranded at a closed airport in the middle of the night, with no clear information about when I might move forward.

But here's what I've learned: first, that even bad experiences are better than no experiences at all. We are here to dare and learn. Even the most difficult layovers teach us something essential about navigating the journey. They force us to find resources we didn't know we had, to ask for help from strangers that can become friends, and to discover patience we thought was beyond us. They show us that we're more capable than we imagined and that connection can emerge in the most unlikely places.

Secondly, that the final destination isn't some perfect place where pain doesn't exist. Home is what we carry with us—the accumulated wisdom from every layover, every delay, every unexpected route change. This deep knowing assures us that we can manage whatever challenges arise next, as we have already overcome so much.

Home is that inner place that gives us what we've always needed—the sense that anything is possible, but now held safely within the understanding and boundaries we've worked so hard to develop.

Welcome home!. You have been waiting for yourself to arrive.

Life offers endless possibilties.

Home!

Exercises List

CHAPTER ONE

    1. Sensory Visualization: The Luminous Orb Practice — 22

    2. Mental Spaciousness: The Expanding Room Technique — 24

    3. The Observer Reframe Technique — 31

    4. Sympathetic Downshift Practice — 44

    5. Taking In the Good Exercise — 50

    6. Graduated Vulnerability Practice — 53

    7. Essential Awarefulness Practice — 57

    8. Emotional Resource Integration — 59

CHAPTER TWO

    1. Deconstructing an Emotion — 63

    2. Tolerating Pain Practice — 90

3. Perspective Shift Check — 93

4. The "Am I Carrying Emotional Pain?" Quiz — 99

5. Uncoupling Emotions Practice — 103

6. Becoming Familiar With Your Emotions Exercise.

    - Quick Instruction (Raw Affect)— 106

    - Quick Instruction (interpretation) — 107

    - Quick Instruction (regulating) — 108

7. ARCO: Exercise to Diminish Reactivity — 109

CHAPTER THREE

1. The Fear Mapping & Safety Anchoring Protocol — 130

2. Breath Equilibrium Practice — 134

3. An Anti-Defeatist Daily Practice — 136

4. Assessing Real Victimization: The B-P-I-D Framework — 139

5. The Victim Alternative Inquiry — 140

6. Intention, Reframe, Action, and Affirmation (IRAA) — 141

7. Identity Reclamation Practice — 146

8. Fear Interruption Protocol — 149

CHAPTER FOUR

1. Return to Sender Exercise — 172

2. Mirror of Strengths Exercise — 175

3. Training the "Observing-Self" to Defuse Insecurity Exercise — 179

4. Building Your Inner-Belonging Circle — 186

5. What Drives Your Impulse to Give? A Quiz — 192

6. Releasing the Weight of the Wound Exercise — 202

7. Maintenance Through the COMPASS Practice — 206

8. Taking Up Space Exercise — 208

9. Engage in a Dialogue with Shame Exercise — 211

10. From Guilt to Growth: The Five-Step Accountability Practice — 212

CHAPTER FIVE

1. A Self-Reflection Quiz: Am I Experiencing Emotional Abuse? — 221

2. The Shame Reframe Practice — 228

3. Gaslighting Reality Check — 235

4. Am I Trauma Bonded? A Quiz — 243

5. A First Step in Dissolving the Trauma Bond — 245

6. The Trust Restoration Protocol — 249

7. Core Self-Reconnection Exercise — 251

8. "A Memory among Many" Exercise — 252

9. Handling Stress Better Practice — 253

10. Manage Dissociative Tendencies Practice — 253

11. Self-Separation Practice — 254

12. A Relational Repair Practice: Repairing the Rupture — 257

13. The Love vs. Attachment Inventory — 260

CHAPTER SIX

1. Dual-Screen Exercise to Reduce Flashbacks — 267

2. Mapping Moments of Felt Safety Exercise — 270

3. The Hypervigilance Reset Practice — 277

4. The Pause-and-Prepare Method — 281

5. Did I Experience Childhood Trauma? A Quick Assessment — 288

6. Identifying Your Recovery Roadblocks — 298

7. Safety-Anchored Memory Integration — 299

8. Self-Compassion Exercise — 301

9. Boundary & Forgiveness Process — 303

10. Memory Gap Acceptance Ritual — 304

QUESTIONS LIST

CHAPTER ONE. WOUNDS

- Is there a real difference between brain and mind? — 19

- My therapist told me I lack mental space. What are they talking about? — 23

- What does it mean to be mentally ill? Does having a diagnosis like PTSD count as being "insane"? — 25

- So, adapting and surviving. Are they actually different things? — 27

- Why do we sometimes perceive reality to be so dark? — 29

- What counts as an emotional wound? — 33

- What makes trauma different from other emotional wounds? — 35

- How do you know where emotional hurt ends and trauma begins? — 36

- What's all the buzz around the "nervous system" about? — 37

- I hear the term "overwhelmed" a lot. Is it always connected with trauma, and what are its consequences? — 39

- What does it mean to be hyperactivated? Is it the same as broken, dysregulated, or stuck in survival mode? — 40

- What does dysregulation really mean for someone that wants to heal from trauma? — 45

- What screams "mentally healthy"? — 48

- Why are so many people afraid of being vulnerable? — 51

- What's the main reason we could believe in healing from suffering if most people spend most of their lives struggling with psychological pain? — 53

- How does mindfulness work in healing everything? Is it really the cure-all? — 55

- How do you heal an emotional wound? — 58

CHAPTER TWO. EMOTIONS

- What's actually happening when we get emotional—is something controlling it? — 70

- What are emotions supposed to be doing for us? Are they helpful in any way? — 73

- What's the purpose of having emotions that make us feel so bad? — 74

- Some emotions feel way more important than others—is that true? — 76

- So apparently everything I learned about emotions is outdated. What's the real story? — 80

- Should we just let emotions play out or try to manage them? — 84

- Do we experience emotions one by one, or do we experience several at the same time? — 85

- Why do emotions make us suffer so much? — 87

- Is emotional pain just in our heads? — 89

- Does emotional pain change someone mentally? — 91

- Why are therapists always asking "Where do you feel it in your body? Are we supposed to feel something? — 93

- How can you tell if someone is hurting emotionally? — 96

- Why can someone be attracted to emotional pain? — 101

- Why every time I feel sad, I also feel angry? — 102

- Is my brain actually in control of my feelings? — 105

- How can we change an emotion? — 108

CHAPTER THREE. TRAUMA

- Why must we all deal with trauma on this planet? — 113

- What, in your own words, is the definition of trauma? — 115

- What does it actually mean when people say you're in "survival mode"? — 116

- So is everything trauma now, or are there actual rules? — 117

- If some argue that trauma is not the event, how do we define what is and isn't trauma? — 119

- What does traumatization do to a person? — 120

- Why do some people stay traumatized much longer than others? — 121
- Does trauma make someone less resilient? — 123
- Does trauma always have to involve fear, or are there other manifestations that don't involve fear/dread per se? — 126
- What are the big fears that can really damage someone? — 128
- How does trauma disrupt our internal balance, and why does this matter for emotional pain and overall mental health? — 132
- Why do some people seem wired to expect failure, and what's fueling that self-defeating trap? — 134
- What qualifies as victim mentality? Is it trauma related? — 137
- What turns a bad experience into actual trauma? — 143
- Is it bad to center your life around your trauma? — 145
- Am I actually healing, or am I just getting used to feeling broken? — 147
- How do you cope with fear and not panic? — 148
- Will trauma always be part of my life? — 150
- How does someone resolve emotional trauma? — 151

CHAPTER FOUR. DISCONNECTION

- What makes some hurts turn into wounds while others don't? — 155
- What factors make emotional pain stick around? — 157
- What are the worst things that can break someone's heart? — 160

- What situations bring out everyone's worst insecurities? — 168
- What's the real relationship between ego and feeling insecure? — 176
- What happens when your feelings were ignored as a child? — 181
- When does neglect cross the line into trauma territory? — 184
- Why am I so terrified of people leaving me? — 185
- What problems do emotionally neglected kids have when they grow up? — 188
- Why do I push people away even when I want them close? — 189
- Is it normal to feel disconnected from yourself after emotional neglect? — 190
- How do you tell if you're genuinely nice or just desperate for approval? — 190
- What happens to a child's brain when they're emotionally hurt? — 194
- Can someone go through a terrible childhood and turn out totally fine? — 197
- Can you tell if you have developmental trauma, or is it invisible to you? — 198
- What's the point of forgiving someone who isn't even sorry about hurting me? — 201
- What would you put in an emotional first aid kit? — 203
- What do you do when you realize you were emotionally neglected? — 207
- What do you do when guilt and shame won't leave you alone? — 210

CHAPTER FIVE. UNLOVE

- What type of abuse can be psychologically damaging? — 217

- Is it an exaggeration to say emotional abuse traumatized me? — 219

- Do people who verbally abuse you actually mean the horrible things they say? Or just connected to their anger and trauma? — 223

- What's it called when people get pleasure from hurting others? What are the possible causes of this behavior? — 224

- How does abuse show up in someone's behavior? — 225

- I have C-PTSD from childhood sexual trauma, which resurfaced as an adult. I'm feeling a lot of shame. What do you feel shame about? — 227

- What does narcissistic abuse do to you? — 231

- Is psychological projection just another word for gaslighting? — 233

- How do I know if gaslighting has damaged my ability to think clearly? — 234

- How do you see through someone who acts loving but is actually toxic? — 236

- Is attachment trauma a big deal? — 238

- Are attachment trauma and developmental trauma the same thing? — 239

- Is disorganized attachment why my relationships are so chaotic? — 240

- What are the key differences between trauma bonding and actually caring for someone? Is healthy bonding possible? — 241

- What patterns show up in trauma bonded relationships? — 242

- Why am I so attached to someone who treats me badly? — 244

- How do I stop assuming everyone will hurt me like my abuser did? — 248

- Did the person you used to be ever come back after you recovered from narcissistic abuse? — 250

- If trauma rewires your brain, what can be repaired, resolved, reprogrammed, or improved? — 251

- Can someone be exposed to terrible things over and over and not be affected? — 255

- What makes someone securely attached different from everyone else? — 256

- How can I tell if I'm addicted to this person or actually love them? — 259

- How does a trauma bond finally come to an end? — 261

CHAPTER SIX. THE DEEPEST WOUNDS

- Do trauma and traumatization mean different things? — 265

- What are flashbacks doing to my brain and mental health? — 266

- I don't think I've ever felt truly safe—what am I missing? — 268

- How does unresolved trauma affect your life? — 271

- How can you tell if someone is traumatized? — 272

- What is the phobia of inner experience? And why is it associated with childhood trauma? — 273

- Is hypervigilance a common experience for everyone? How can one cope with it when it occurs? — 275

- What is a trauma response, and what are some examples? — 278

QUESTIONS LIST

- Is the way you respond to trauma your choice? — 280

- What does it mean when people say they dissociate? — 282

- Can I be traumatized too even if I am the one who caused something bad to someone? — 284

- Doesn't everyone, or at least the large majority of people, have some form of childhood trauma? — 287

- How much will a 3-year-old remember about bad things that happen to them? — 289

- What are the subtle signs of childhood trauma that people miss? — 290

- What red flags suggest a child is traumatized? — 292

- Why do so many childhood trauma victims take so long to process their trauma? — 294

- Is post-traumatic growth a common experience for individuals after a traumatic event, even if it is not immediately apparent? — 295

- Why am I scared to heal my trauma? — 297

- How do you forget a trauma that's haunting you? — 298

- Why do I feel undeserving of comfort for my traumatic experiences? — 300

- Should I forgive my parents for causing my complex trauma? — 302

- Can traumatic memories be simply forgotten instead of repressed? — 303